I PAINTED FOR PHARAOH

Anton Mifsud
Marta Farrugia

2010

Order this book online at www.trafford.com
or email orders@trafford.com

Most Trafford titles are also available at major online book retailers.

Printed in the United States of America.

ISBN: 978-1-4269-4719-3 (sc)
ISBN: 978-1-4269-4720-9 (hc)
ISBN: 978-1-4269-4721-6 (e)

Library of Congress Control Number: 2010916666

Trafford rev. 11/21/2010

 www.trafford.com

North America & international
toll-free: 1 888 232 4444 (USA & Canada)
phone: 250 383 6864 ♦ fax: 812 355 4082

TABLE OF CONTENTS

LIST OF ILLUSTRATIONS

Figure 14. No vessels from the Levant were allowed entry into Malta's Grand Harbour (left); these were obliged to undergo quarantine in the Marsamxett harbour (right) at the Lazaretto on Manoel island (below). The Lazaretto site is arrowed. 67

Figure 15. There is an *ankh* but no armbands on the statuette (above), whereas there is no *ankh* in the engraving published by Sonnini (below), and armbands have been added on to both seated deities. 75

Figure 16. The cripple (above) and the alabaster 'Romulus and Remus with the she-wolf' (below) were also found in Gozo.89

Figure 17. Lord Francis Wallace Grenfell. 101

Figure 18. Ancient Egyptian / Egyptianising artefacts discovered on Malta, (three of the above, arrowed), and on Gozo (below), before the time of Lord Grenfell. 102

Figure 19. Deir el Medina is situated to the extreme right in the drawing, and the Valley of the Queens to the extreme left. The sanctuary of Ptah and Meretseger lies on the small hill in between [arrowed]. 109

Figure 20. Lepsius's *Notizbuch* with drawings of the statuette, 1842. 114

Figure 21. Lepsius's *Notizbuch* with more details of the statuette. 115

Figure 22. The palettes used by the scribe and painter in ancient Egypt. 125

Figure 23. The Skylight stele would have been positioned in the niche of the pyramidal structure above the chapel. 132

Figure 24. The southern wall of the second chamber. This is the first photograph of Neferabet's tomb; it was taken by Ernesto Schiaparelli in 1908. 141

Figure 25. The workman Penchenabu presents a single deity, the ram, symbolic of Amen-Re. 145

Figure 26. The statue of Meretseger, the 'Goddess of the Peak'. 147

Figure 27. The Stele of Wab dedicated to Meretseger. 149

11

PART ONE -

A STRANGE CARVING

A phantom artefact

The chevalier swung his head around towards me in a gentle arc; he nodded his head slightly and focussed his eyes directly into mine. "Please follow me downstairs, doctor, and I'll show you something that you've never seen before."

Before receiving my silent consent, he was already enhancing the invitation, pointing out to me that "very few people today have been granted the privilege of even *knowing* about its very existence!"

A few seconds earlier I had reassured him that his infant grandson, the youngest descendant of his clan, was not suffering from anything serious. The chevalier was disproportionately relieved to hear this piece of good news, and a pleasant surprise was in store for me as a reward.

After handing the infant back to the young mother, his only son's wife, he led me down the stairway of his extensive mansion to the equally massive floor below. He crossed the grandiose hallway in between the various pieces of recently polished antique furniture, most of which were immaculately upholstered in shades of crimson and dark green. The chevalier then opened a heavy wooden door that led into what evidently was his personal study and invited me to pass through.

I walked right beside him across the room to a *gradenza*, one of the four dark brown antique chests of drawers that were spread out evenly about the room. The layout of the chamber we had entered was more like an antique furniture shop than a study, but there was one massive wall unit that was crammed with paper documents and old volumes. A dehumidifier in the furthermost corner suddenly sparked into activity as it sensed our approach and started humming a monotonous but reassuring tone. The chevalier opened one of the two small drawers at the top of the *gradenza* and went for something that was evidently bulky and also seemed to be moderately heavy. It was wrapped up in a white cloth which he started to unfold with the greatest care and attention.

Out of its soft linen wrappings a white limestone statuette gradually emerged before our eyes, and once it was fully unwrapped, the chevalier placed it rather precariously near one corner of the *gradenza*.

"What on earth is that?" I asked myself. I had never seen anything like it before in my life.

"What do you think?" asked the chevalier. His face beamed with a smile that combined contentment, satisfaction, and earnest anxiety as he awaited my response to his revelation.

Somewhat spellbound by the unusual object that was being presented to me, I cautiously approached the statuette and scanned it from all its angles. I consciously forced myself to stay back and refrain from palpating its surface.

I distinctly recall being struck by the unusual composition of the artefact before me. There was the figure of a male with a Cleopatra type of hairstyle. He was holding a small table in front of him with three smaller figures. Two were human, and the middle entity was a snake.

"It looks like it's ancient Egyptian!" was my first comment, but I immediately added that it was way out of my line of interest and that I did not feel at all competent to remark upon it. I was at the time more engrossed in the Phoenicians in Malta, and that was Iron Age. The artefact I was being presented with to remark upon had probably derived from Late Bronze Age Egypt.

"It is ancient Egyptian, correct, but it was found in Malta, or rather in the sister island of Gozo, sometime early in the eighteenth century AD!"

What was an ancient Egyptian statuette doing on the tiniest of islands in the very centre of the Mediterranean, more than a thousand miles away from Egypt?

Figure 1. The phantom artefact unveiled by the chevalier.

I looked at the statuette one more time and analysed it with greater intensity. The larger figure at the back wore a vertically striped wig and a pleated tunic. He was standing behind a pedestal – this was basically a small platform with a single central support. Two smaller figures each sat on a chair upon this platform and were separated from one another by what appeared to be the head and neck of a rearing snake.

Despite the fact that it had been carved a few millennia before the present time, most of the engraved hieroglyphs were still clearly visible all over its surfaces. A slanting fissure was evident upon the head of the larger figure, but this had been immaculately repaired, and all that remained was a linear surface mark.

I speculated upon the options. One conjecture in my mind led to another, and it seemed like I might ponder forever without coming to any conclusion. Finally the chevalier volunteered that the artefact had once formed part of a small funerary monument in Thebes. Naturally I nodded in agreement, but I was not particularly interested in Egyptology at the time, and when I left the home of the chevalier I must have voluntarily attempted to shut the statuette off from entering the memory compartment of my cerebral cortex. But it must have found a niche there somewhere, for it resurfaced several years later in the form of déjà vu.

Archaeology

In the meantime, my time-frame in Maltese archaeology gradually extended backward to the pre-Phoenician period. I started to nurture a particular interest in the preceding Bronze Age, and eventually in the prehistoric period in general. The Old Stone Age in Malta provided the theme of my first publication in archaeology, *Dossier Malta: Evidence for the Magdalenian.*[1]

It was in 2001 that I first visited Egypt, and henceforth Egyptology sprung to the fore within me. Three years later, I was there again for two separate archaeological visits, and 2005 saw me go beyond the Nile Valley with a group into the western desert, which we explored over three weeks right up to its confines with Libya and the Sudan.

The question as to whether there were any possible links between ancient Egypt and Malta occupied my mind for a while. At one point in time, my research focussed on one particular Egyptian artefact that, together with a few other items, had entered the reserve collection of the National Museum of Malta and had not been seen for several decades. The last time it had featured in the museum's catalogue of archaeological artefacts was in 1931.

Though I felt convinced that I must have seen this artefact displayed sometime before, I just could not recall the instance.[2]

One thing led to another, until this query of mine on the missing archaeological artefacts led to an article. On 16 June 2002, *The Sunday Times of Malta* carried a feature by Natalino Fenech, the interviewing reporter, entitled "Missing Archaeological Artefacts Linking Malta with the Ancient World". There was an Egyptian statuette in the group and it was assigned its traditional context, namely that it had been discovered at an archaeological site in Gozo way back in 1713. In this article mention was also made of the fact that in the 1960s the curator at the time, David Trump, was the first not to include the statuette within the catalogue of archaeological artefacts in the National Museum of Archaeology.

There was no apparent response to this feature, yet without my being aware of it, the matter was immediately taken up by an American Egyptologist.[3] The article had actually triggered an investigation within the precincts of the museum establishment, a modicum of research involving an international set of scholars, and ultimately the presentation of their findings.

21

An Egyptian statuette exhibited

A year later, in November 2003, the artefact resurfaced as the star item in an exhibition put up by Heritage Malta and displayed at the Museum of Archaeology of Malta. Attending the exhibition were two local British residents, Helen and Peter Foster, and they inquired as to whether there was a local Egyptology Society on the island. And after being told that there was none, the Fosters advertised their intent to start one through a letter that appeared in one of the local newspapers. The response to their letter was very encouraging, and a local Egyptology Society has since been fully functional with Helen Foster as President.

The meetings heightened my archaeological interest in Egyptology. The other members urged me on until two of our number, the present authors, embarked upon a number of research projects. The Society has also been recognised amongst similar Egyptology societies that are spread out around the globe.

On 18 July 2002, a scholar from Forest Hills in New York contacted the reporter Natalino Fenech for further information on his article of 16 June through an overseas telephone call. The Egyptologist was Ms. Alicia Meza. She had come across the article on the Internet and decided to investigate the matter further. Whilst in Malta, she was allowed to examine, photograph, and work on the Egyptian statuette. The outcome of her research was an article in *The Journal of the American Research Center in Egypt*[4] the following year. This write-up formed the basis of the exhibition of the statuette at the National Museum of Archaeology in Valletta.

And so it was that in the later months of 2003, the statuette with the so-called triad of gods eventually emerged into the public eye after a century in hiding in the reserve collection vaults of the Malta Museum of Archaeology.

The name Alicia Meza started to ring a bell, and I thought I would check this out in my journals. As it turned out, Alicia had been on the same excavation campaign with me, precisely in the same trench that I had been allocated during the 1996 season. The archaeological site in question was that at Tas-Silg on the south-eastern part of Malta. I remembered vaguely that we had met and talked briefly on site and at some associated function, but since that time we had lost track of one another. Alicia had subsequently obtained her Masters in Egyptology from the University of Toronto.

Heritage Malta had not merely adopted the content but also most of the conclusions that were drawn by Meza in her *JARCE* article. The most significant of these was that the Egyptian statuette had not been discovered on the Maltese islands in 1713, but that it had actually derived from Thebes and had reached Malta via Cairo in the later decades of the eighteenth century.

The name of the owner of the statuette had been known for some time. The artefact had been examined by a number of scholars since its discovery, and in the early twentieth century a consensus had already been reached that the statuette belonged to Neferabet[5], one of the tomb workmen in the Valley of the Kings. His home was close by in the workmen's village that was known at the time as the *Set-Ma'at*, the Place of Truth, and today's Deir el-Medina[6].

It was purely by chance that I was alerted to the exhibition, and that was through a little three-year-old girl named Catriona. I knew precisely when she was born, for that was just one day before my granddaughter Zea.

It was on a Tuesday, 28 October 2003 – I even kept the newspaper cutting – that Catriona was included on my morning list of home visits for a minor complaint. The parents had just moved house and were then living in Zebbug on mainland Malta.

Their new residence was fitted out with most of the contemporary amenities. They made me feel quite at home.

There was a newspaper opened out on the marble table in the kitchen annex – it was *The Malta Independent*. Whilst the mother was ritually preparing a double espresso for me, I sat awhile browsing through the paper until I was arrested by the image on page 17.

There on the top right hand corner was a photograph that looked all too familiar. It was the very same statuette that I had been instrumental in reporting as missing the year previously. There was a half-page article provided by Heritage Malta under the title "Shedding new light on the Egyptian statue of Neferabet"7. Right there in front of me was a modern photograph of the Egyptian statuette that I had been seeking out to have a proper look at over the previous four years.

I had no option but to read on there and then. *The Malta Independent* announced the inaugural talk that was delivered just before the start of the exhibition the previous evening. Alicia Meza had spoken about the results of her research that she conducted upon this particular statuette along with a few other Egyptologists.

According to the announcement on the newspaper, the statuette had last been exhibited to the general public precisely a century earlier, in 1903, after which time it was placed in the reserve collection. This, it was further stated, was one of the reasons why it had been believed at one time that the statuette had disappeared from the Museum of Archaeology in Valletta.

It was being exhibited until 4 December, and so I had five weeks at my disposal. But I was certainly not going to wait that long. In fact, a sudden surge of impatience got the better of me. I decided that once I was done with the more urgent of my home visits, I should just go to the museum, spend an hour at the exhibition, and plan the strategy for a full documentation of the statuette while it was on display.

I thanked Catriona's parents most heartily for bringing the article to my attention and also for the excellently prepared espresso. I then left straight towards my flat in order to get my recently acquired Minolta, a DiMAGE S414. A four-megapixel digital camera in 2003 was still something to brag about.

There were another three ill children who needed early attention, and I saw to these first. Within seventy-five minutes I was ready to go. I shot off to the Auberge de Provence in Valletta where the Museum of Archaeology was situated and arrived there whilst it was still another two hours before closing time.

The exhibition was being presented in the side hall of the Museum of Archaeology in Valletta, immediately to the left of the main ticket office on the ground floor. Right in the centre of the hall, the statuette itself was mounted on a stand reaching up to eye level. It was neatly enclosed all around in a square transparent Perspex case.

The original glass case of the nineteenth century had been in the form of an elongated cupola. Its substitution by this one with flat, smooth and transparent surfaces was a godsend, for it permitted extraordinary photography at very close range.

The statuette itself was displayed under immaculate illumination with all its hieroglyphs clearly visible for all to see.

The experience of beholding it was nothing compared to that of the golden mask of Tutankhamen two years earlier – that was simply stunning. This time around it was more of a satisfaction that I had finally seen the artefact despite everything to the contrary. It had suddenly and unexpectedly fallen into my lap, so to speak, and I had five weeks to exploit it to the maximum. My agenda for the next few weeks would be an exceptionally exciting one.

Photography of the statuette inside the exhibition hall was fortunately allowed, and I decided to make the most of it. My priority was documentation, and this was readily achievable through my *Minolta* with its macro-photography function and high-resolution digital imaging. The close-ups that I took of the statuette together with the photographs of the several information panels that were spread about the hall facilitated the research routine later on in the day.

These information panels gave a resume of the contributors to the exhibition, the panel of experts that was involved, and the basic information on relevant matters in Egyptology. One of the panels had the genealogy of Neferabet's clan and his own multiple offspring.

Large boards showed the blown-up transliterated hieroglyphs that were engraved upon the statuette. There were also larger-than-size photographs of the statuette from its front, back and the two sides.

The interpretation of the hieroglyphs was being exhibited in three formats on either side of the panel, respectively as hieroglyphs, a transliteration, and a translation into English. It was thus possible to make comparisons with relative ease and get an immediate idea of what the hieroglyphs were saying, and also where each inscription was located on the surfaces of the statuette.

The translation of the hieroglyphs was given in text. Those on the proper right side of the pedestal spoke of '*a royal offering of Amun-Re, king of the gods, giving everything good and pure for the ka of Neferabu*'.

Those on the proper left translated into '*a royal offering of Great Mut, giving life, soundness, and health for the ka of his father Neferrenpet, justified*'.

AM

Figure 2. Neferabet's statuette on exhibition in 2003 at the Museum of Archaeology in Valletta, Malta

On the base of the statuette, from left to right, the text ran as follows. *'A royal offering of Ma'at, daughter of Re, lady of the sky, mistress of all the gods [and all the gods] of the Delta and the Nile Valley (?), giving life, soundness, and health for the ka of the servant in the place of Ma'at, Neferabu, justified, perfect in peace. A royal offering of Re-Horakhti, the great god, king of the Ennead, giving my mouth sound and that (I) come to the pure place, for his ka'.*

Two vertical lines of hieroglyphs on the front face of the pilaster mentioned respectively *'Re-Horakhti, the great god, king of the Ennead'* and *'Ma'at, daughter of Re, lady of the sky, mistress of all the gods'*.

The left and right proper sides of the pilaster made remembrance respectively of *'his beloved brother 'Anhotep, justified, perfect in peace with the gods'* and *'his son, who has caused his name to live, Neferrenpet, justified'*.

The long vertical line of hieroglyphs on the back pillar repeated *'a royal offering of Amun-Re, king of the gods and Great Mut, lady of Isheru, giving everything good and pure for the ka of Neferabu.'*

Neferabet was thus being mentioned three times and his deceased close family relatives once. On the pedestal, Neferabet was being paired with his father Neferrenpet, 'justified'. On the pilaster, his son Neferrenpet, 'justified' was being paired with his brother 'Anhotep, 'justified'. On the back pillar was the main dedication; Neferabet was invoking *'Amun-Re, king of the gods and Great Mut, lady of Isheru'*.

As could readily be deduced from the hieroglyphs, the statuette had been dedicated by Neferabet at a time when three of his family had already passed away. These were his brother 'Anhotep and his father and son, both named Neferrenpet.

The statuette was not the only item on display. At a distance of approximately two metres in front of the

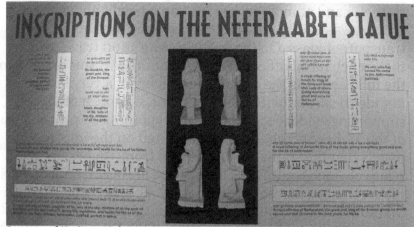

AM

Figure 3. The information panel with the four views of the
statuette in the centre; these are flanked by the
transliteration of the hieroglyphs and their translation.
Detail below.

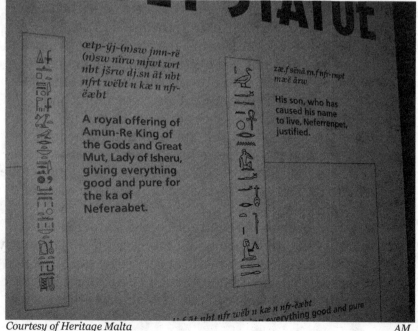

*ætp-ÿj-(n)sw jmn-rë
(n)sw nîrw mjwt wrt
nbt jšrw dj.sn ãt nbt
nfrt wëbt n kæ n nfr-
ëæbt*

A royal offering of
Amun-Re King of
the Gods and Great
Mut, Lady of Isheru,
giving everything
good and pure for
the ka of
Neferaabet.

*zæ.f sënä m.f nfr-mpt
mæë ãrw*

His son, who has
caused his name
to live, Neferrenpet,
justified.

AM

29

statuette and at more or less the same height above the ground was another display case covered in shiny, transparent glass. On the inside was an 1800 travelogue by the French naval officer Charles Sonnini; this was opened to the folio showing the author's engraving of a very similar, if not identical, statuette. This depiction was presented as supporting evidence for the newly hypothesised provenance of the Maltese statuette. It was asserted on the information panels that the statuette had derived from Thebes in relatively modern times. This statement was extremely interesting, for it went contrary to what I had believed until that time. This engraving by Sonnini was also presented at the exhibition as the first depiction of the Egyptian statuette in question.

The engraving showed the statuette at an angle of approximately 45 degrees from its proper left side. Charles Sonnini had apparently produced this engraving in 1778, twenty years before the book's publication. At the time, he was a twenty-six-year-old officer in the French navy, and he had visited Cairo in the company of a certain French 'diplomat', the baron Monsieur Françoise de Tott.[8]

There was a small placard next to the engraving, and this stated that Sonnini and his travelling companion de Tott had first seen the statuette in Cairo in the hands of an Italian monk of the Propaganda Fide.[9] The monk had allegedly declared to them that although he had not excavated the artefact himself, the information he had received was that the statuette had derived from the Thebaid area. Furthermore, the monk had then donated the statuette to de Tott, and the trail of the statuette was lost there in Cairo.[10]

I went back to the centrepiece, the statuette in its transparent case, and I scanned it intensely. It was tediously familiar. Observing the statuette at very close range created an intense déjà vu experience, though I could not place it at that point in time. I had seen two very similar artefacts in

Figure 4. The engraving of the statuette first published by Charles Sonnini in 1798.

Egypt, one preserved in the Cairo Museum and the other in Luxor. Both of these consisted of a dedicatee presenting a triad of gods, and I had photographs of both somewhere that I would later compare with the one in Malta.[11]

The statuette had been carved out of white limestone. Despite its very great age, the freshness of its surface gave me the distinct impression that it had only been recently carved.

The sculpted group of figures comprised a dedicatee, or a devotee, with a fine double wig of curled and braided hair.[12] He was wearing a light pleated Egyptian linen skirt that extended from his upper abdomen to the mid-calf.

The devotee's right shoulder was engraved with a seated figure of a hawk-headed god with a solar disc and uraeus on his head and an ankh in his hand; the left shoulder of the dedicatee was similarly engraved with a goddess with a feather on her head and an ankh sign in her hand.

This figure of the devotee was standing behind the pedestal, a small platform[13] upon which rested three proportionately smaller figures, a triad of Egyptian gods. For the sake of precision, it should be stated that two of the deities in the triad were seated upon a throne with a back support, and this throne rested upon the pedestal.[14] The third deity was situated between the feet of the other two on the front of the throne.

On the pedestal towards the proper right of the statuette was a sitting falcon-headed deity wearing an archaic tri-partite wig and a knee-length kilt. A female figure was sitting on the proper left; she was wearing a similar tri-partite wig and a tight, long sheet dress that extended from the breasts down to the ankles. These figures were separated by a rearing cobra surmounted by a round disc.

The two principal deities both had small orifices at the very tops of their heads and were respectively identified

AM

Figure 5. The dedicatee with the triad of deities in front of
him

with Re-Horakhti and Ma'at. The central cobra with the solar disc was proposed as the goddess of Lower Egypt, Wadjet.[15]

In a nutshell, Heritage Malta was promoting the hypothesis that the Egyptian statuette on display was one and the same with that first described by Sonnini in 1798[16], and also that it had been discovered in the Thebaid region in Upper Egypt shortly before this time. Furthermore it had reached the hands of a priest in Cairo, who gave it to Sonnini's companion, the baron de Tott. However, no explanation was given to account for the statuette reaching Malta after this time.

It seemed to me at the time that these conclusions hinged upon a number of controversial statements that were crucial to their main argument.

Firstly, Heritage Malta was assuming that the exhibited statuette was one and the same with the one that had allegedly been seen by Sonnini in 1778 and subsequently published by him in 1798. This assumption of theirs had in turn led them to assume that the hieroglyphs on Sonnini's engraving had been immaculately copied from the original and that they were identical to the ones on the exhibited statuette. In its turn, this process of serial assumptions had eventually led to a translation of the hieroglyphs in Sonnini's engraving rather than those on the statuette. In fact, on several of the surfaces of the statuette the hieroglyphs were impossible to read or were missing altogether; in these instances those of Sonnini had been automatically adopted for transliteration and translation on the information panels.

The entire exercise that resulted in this exhibition had equated similarity with identity. Although the two representations of the statuette were very similar, this did not make them identical. For instance, there are at least two similar statuettes from Thebes that are very much alike but are definitely not identical.[17](Fig. 6)

Courtesy of the Museum of Ancient Egyptian Art in Luxor   *AM*

Courtesy of Museum of Egyptian Antiquities, Cairo   *FC*

Figure 6. Similar but not identical triads of gods offered by officials in the service of the pharaoh.

The conclusion reached by Heritage Malta that the statuette on exhibition was an import into Malta in modern times automatically nullified the assertion of the curator Dr Annetto A. Caruana in 1882 that it had been discovered in the sister island of Gozo in 1713. Dr Caruana's context was described as unfounded, "without any evidence."[18]

From a purely personal point of view, I felt that there was yet another message that was being subliminally transmitted. This was clearly that the article of 16 June 2002 in *The Sunday Times of Malta* about the *missing* Egyptian triad was unfounded. The Egyptian statuette was right there, fully researched, no longer missing and on exhibition to the general public!

One of the information panels in the exhibition hall said it all. Entitled "Shedding New Light on the Egyptian Statue of Neferabet", the fifth paragraph ran thus: "Due to [the statuette] not having been on display since [1903], assumptions were made that the statue had actually disappeared from the museum, while in fact research was being conducted that was to yield the rewarding results about the statue's owner, his social status and his family."

A good number of various interdisciplinary scholars had become involved in this project from all over the world – from New York, Cairo, and London. The person who had translated the hieroglyphs on the Maltese statuette was a professional archaeologist and Egyptologist. Although they would not have been directly involved in the finer details, these international scholars were adding their weight of authority to the authenticity of the undertaking and the exhibition.

Amongst the foreign Egyptologists who were quoted as having participated in the exercise were the supreme head of Egyptian antiquities, Zahi Hawass; James P. Allen from the Department of Egyptian Art in the Metropolitan Museum of Art in New York; and Morris Bierbrier, previously an Assistant Keeper in the Department of Egyptian Antiquities at the British Museum.

A decision to research the statuette further

There was a great deal of material that I needed to digest before I could start thinking about researching the statuette further. There was Sonnini's publication that I desired to scrutinize fully, and there was also Morris Bierbrier's publication that was quoted in the exhibition. This too required a thorough perusal.

I also needed to compare the photographs I had taken of the statuette with the engraving published by Sonnini. Furthermore, there would be other tasks that would certainly crop up along the way. I did not know it then, but I was not the only person who was keenly interested in studying the statuette further.

Independently, my co-author Marta visited the exhibition a few days later, and she also took very good photographs. She too had been made aware of it through the newspapers. Soon after joining the ranks of the budding Egyptology Society of Malta, we both nurtured a gut feeling that we would be researching the statuette further in the not-too-distant future.

Déjà vu

Just a few weeks after the exhibition was over, I received an e-mail from a very good friend of mine, who narrated to me his earlier experience with an Egyptian statuette in Malta. "That is extremely interesting," I thought as I read on with a mounting curiosity. He had been in a private home in the late 1980s when he had been shown an artefact that he vividly recollected was practically identical to the one that had been on exhibition.

There was more to read, but I stopped in my tracks at this point of the e-mail and tried to force myself into resolving my déjà vu – I searched inside the recesses of my brain for a similar episode that I might have gone through myself but had since forgotten.

When nothing came up, I resumed reading rather half-heartedly – until the name of the chevalier was mentioned. All of a sudden it all came back to me, and everything fell into place. In a flash I recalled the episode when I had seen the statuette before at very close range. The rapid transition of the déjà vu sensation into vivid recollection allowed me that rare experience of the classical chill all the way down my spine as the rest of me went numb.

Why had it taken me so long to recall the incident with the chevalier? In an attempt to answer this, I calculated that it must have been around twenty years earlier that I had visited the chevalier's grandson and was shown the statuette, and that was also a time when my interest in Egyptology was practically non-existent. Curiously enough, the various photographs and the Egyptian statuette itself had never at any time triggered my memory cells into action. Although the vague recollection of having seen it before persisted throughout, I had concentrated more upon its absence than the nature of the artefact itself. The crucial clue was the chevalier.

As I stared rather blankly at the e-mail before me, a number of possible scenarios presented themselves. Had the chevalier merely shown me a *copy* of the original statuette? Was it possible in any way that there had been *two* original statuettes? But if neither of these two options was the case, then who owned the original statuette, the museum or the chevalier?

There was another query, and this was of a rather pressing nature. Was it already too late to have another look at the ghost statuette? The chevalier had since passed away, and his mansion had been sold for three quarters of a million Malta liri. His sole heir was his son, who had set up an antique shop for a while. When I managed to contact him a few days later, he declared that he knew nothing at all about the statuette. My contacts in the local antique-dealing trade were all questioned and shown a photograph of the statuette, but nothing ever came up.

The chevalier's statuette had seemingly disappeared into thin air, and the one at the Museum of Archaeology in Valletta had returned to its former hiding place in the museum store-rooms once the exhibition period was over. Neither of the two artefacts was available for study at that time.

But there was at least some documentary evidence available, and that consisted of the wide range of photographs that we had taken of the statuette on exhibition. There was sufficient material available for another Egyptological project, so Marta and I set ourselves up to investigate and trace the context of this remarkable ancient Egyptian artefact.

We had already been working in liaison in researching themes that were related to ancient Egypt.[19] When it came to researching the Egyptian statuette, we thought that, instead of an article in a journal, it deserved the format of a small volume that illustrated the statuette in a more detailed manner.

We knew very little about the statuette at the time. According to its first published mention in Malta, it had been discovered in 1713. Its context was not specifically identified, but it was described as having been lifted from an abandoned archaeological site on Gozo, the smaller sister island of Malta.[20]

Problems were immediately apparent. The ancient Egyptians might never have reached the Maltese archipelago. So what was an ancient Egyptian statuette doing at an archaeological site in the sister-island of Malta? Yet the very fact of its having been found in Gozo was in question. Heritage Malta was proposing that it had been discovered in the later eighteenth century in Thebes.

However, we felt unconvinced by this new hypothesis whilst there were still a number of apparent anomalies in our minds that required to be addressed.

Searching for the earlier literature

There were a number of documents and artefacts that just had to be seen if we were to make any conclusions about the Egyptian statuette of Malta. We started with the literature.

The need for further information on the statuette's earlier history lured me to the archives of the University of Malta at Tal-Qroqq with the prospect of finding some early photographs and other documentation of the artefact in question.

The staff members there were extremely helpful and generous towards me. They made all the literary material that was requested readily available in no time at all, and they even allowed me to scan some of the archived material there under their supervision. Some of these documents were old publications that merited respect and special attention during handling.

There was a 1799 edition of Sonnini's book at the *Melitensia* section of the Library and this was available for perusal. The pages that were relevant to the engraving of the statuette were particularly useful, and there was also a great deal of relevant information that referred to the sojourns of Sonnini and his friend in Malta and in Cairo[21].

I thoroughly exploited the *Melitensia* section for old photographs of the statuette and the relevant nineteenth century literature. Within a short space of time, it was already becoming apparent that there were a few definite inaccuracies evident in the exhibition content.

For instance, although the information panels at the Valletta Museum had clearly stated that there had not been any photographs of the statuette before those published by the Maltese prehistorian, Sir Themistocles Zammit, in 1931,

40

I managed to find several photographs that were taken before this date by half a century.

In fact, I came across two photographs of this same Egyptian statuette in the work of the chief librarian at the time, Dr. Antonio Annetto Caruana. The title of this work was *The Phoenician Antiquities of the Maltese Islands* (1882).[22]

Oddly enough, although the text was identical in the two available copies there, both with the same date and publisher, the series of photographs that were inserted as illustrations was not identical in the two volumes. This was fortunate for me, for I ended up with two views of the statuette instead of one. Besides a full frontal view, there was even an original 'side view' photograph that permitted even more extensive research and investigation. These photographs were both dated to or before 1882.[23]

There was yet another volume that had a photograph predating that of 1931. This had been authored by the Reverend W. K. Bedford, one of the main officials connected with the Maltese archives towards the end of the nineteenth century. This photograph of the statuette was available in direct frontal view, together with a similar description of its context as having been found in Gozo in 1713.

There were several editions of Bedford's publication, and the frontal photograph of the statuette was included every time. So in reality there had been at least *six* occasions of the publication of the statuette by photography before the one by Zammit in 1931. Had Heritage Malta completely missed out on these six photographic documentations of the statuette?

Could it have been the case that during the process of organising the exhibition in 2003, the foreign scholars who had participated were not intimately connected with all the circumstances of the discovery and of the artefact itself? They would therefore have been obliged to rely mainly on their Maltese counterparts for their information and data. Should this information have been faulty for some reason or

41

other, then the conclusions reached would likewise have been flawed.

Certain crucial data had clearly been unavailable to the local museum authorities, and these related particularly to the presence of references to the statuette's provenance between Sonnini in 1798 and Caruana in 1882. If there had been none at all, as the exhibition panels stated, then Caruana's reliability would have been less probable.

However, as already mentioned above, Caruana had not been the first Maltese to declare the statuette's provenance. At least three other sources had been completely missed out by the exhibition's panel of contributors, and these had all predated Caruana.

Furthermore, Heritage Malta had constantly assumed that the limestone statuette on display and the Sonnini engraving were one and the same thing. Should this assumption prove unfounded, the interpretative process undertaken and the conclusions reached by these foreign scholars would be totally erroneous.

A similar episode can be cited that demonstrates the manner in which foreign scholars received incorrect information about Egyptian artefacts in Malta. Four ancient Egyptian artefacts known as the Bighi funerary steles were discovered on Malta in 1829.

They had been found by British military personnel beneath the foundations of a villa of the Knights of St John that was being pulled down for the erection of a naval hospital.

When the foreign scholar Albert Mayr was researching them in Malta at the turn of the twentieth century, these were reported to him incorrectly as having been discovered *in the sea* rather than *on land*.[24] Other scholars kept on repeating his error, and several decades later his co-national, the renowned Egyptologist Günther Hölbl published similarly erroneous statements[25].

The end result is that there is now a tendency for this 'underwater' context of the Bighi steles to be accepted despite its gross inaccuracy.

Disappearance of the statuette

As Marta and I analysed the various themes that we felt uncomfortable about in what was being proposed by Heritage Malta, we came upon a blatant anomaly.

The information panels at the exhibition were quoting from Bierbrier's book where he stated that the Maltese statuette had disappeared from public view for a while. Heritage Malta was making a statement to the effect that it was during this time of its apparent disappearance that active research had been going on upon the statuette and that this study then led to the exhibition.

Morris Bierbrier's publication of 1982, *The Tomb Builders of the Pharaohs*, was not available in Malta but I was extremely fortunate to find a copy in a Cairo bookshop just before the start of a three-week long expedition into the Western Desert. I had all the time in the world to peruse it.

When Morris Bierbrier included the statuette in his publication of 1982, he suggested for the first time that the statuette had not been found in Gozo but in Thebes; he was citing Sonnini as his source.

However he must have encountered some difficulty when he assumed that Sonnini was correct in assigning the context of the statuette to Thebes; he could not explain the fact that the statuette, allegedly donated to the Maltese by the baron de Tott, was never seen by anyone between 1778 and 1842. He was therefore obliged to declare that it disappeared from view between 1778 and the middle of the nineteenth century in order to reconcile Sonnini's assertions. In his words, the statuette had 'disappeared from view' between the time that Sonnini saw it in Cairo and the 'middle of the nineteenth century [when] it re-appeared somewhat more damaged in Malta'.[26]

It was unambiguously evident that what Morris Bierbrier had stated about the statuette's disappearance was not that it had vanished during the late *twentieth* century (whilst the research on it in Malta was allegedly going on), but more than a century earlier, that is, between 1778 and the mid-*nineteenth* century.

So what had become of the statuette between 1903 and 2003, the time period when, according to Heritage Malta, the statuette had not been on public display? [27] Had the research on it lasted an entire century?

When we researched the whereabouts of the statuette during this period of time, a few surprises came up.

In 1901 the statuette was examined by the German scholar, Albert Mayr, as part of the repertoire of archaeological artefacts on Malta that he was studying[28].

Then an Austrian Egyptologist from Munich, Professor F. W. von Bissing, had a go at it in 1907 and gave a translation of its hieroglyphs in summary form[29].

The statuette was then being displayed on a stand inside a cupola and placed next to the statue of Hercules and other classical artefacts. (Fig. 7)

The archaeological collection during this time was housed in the Xara Palace that then served as the Museum of Antiquities[30]. A catalogue of the antiquities that were preserved there was published in 1919 by the Director of Museums at the time, Sir Themistocles Zammit.

The statuette was certainly still around during the first two decades of the twentieth century.

But then we hit against a blank wall. We were initially unable to account for an apparent anomaly for the third decade. Between 1921 and 1924 the renowned British Egyptologist Margaret Murray was excavating on Malta at a number of prehistoric sites, and she published these digs and findings in three volumes between 1923 and 1934.

Figure 7. At the turn of the twentieth century the statuette was exhibited under a cupola next to the statue of Hercules at the Xara Palace in Valletta.

Then in 1928 Murray published an article in *Ancient Egypt* where she described ancient Egyptian artefacts that were discovered in Malta[31]. But the Egyptian statuette in question was not included in her list! Had the statuette disappeared during the 1920's?

The solution came up soon enough as we were tracing the movements of the archaeological artefacts during this period of time. Whilst Murray was excavating in Malta the antiquities at the Archaeological Museum were being transferred to another site.

In 1922 the archaeological artefacts started being moved from the Xara Palace to the Auberge d'Italie in Merchants Street in Valletta. During this stage of their relocation most if not all of the pieces would have been packed away safely for transfer until such time as their placing inside the new museum was assigned.

At the very same time a new Director of Museums was being installed in the person of Sir Themistocles Zammit. This post was linked to that of Rector of the University of Malta, and Zammit spent most of his time in the education department and in travel overseas. He would therefore have been for the most part unavailable at the museum.

To make the possibility of Margaret Murray even less likely to see the statuette in question on display at the new museum, this ancient Egyptian artefact was assigned a location amidst the *Punic* and *Roman* remains in one of the exhibition halls abutting on Corridor C on the ground floor. If Murray ever visited the Museum at the Auberge d'Italie she would have concentrated her attention on the prehistoric artefacts that were more in line with her field of interest in archaeology. These were then housed in separate exhibition halls, those abutting on Corridor B. As a prehistorian she would most likely not have bothered with the classical artefacts in the rooms housing the Punic and Roman remains and she would have missed the statuette altogether.

46

When the catalogue of the antiquities in the Museum at the Auberge d'Italie was published by Zammit in 1931[32], the statuette was included among the artefacts on display at the Museum. There was also a frontal photograph of it that provided us with a valuable point of reference for comparative purposes.

There was a Danish Egyptologist a Dr Erik Iversen who studied the statuette in Malta and then handed his hand-notes of the hieroglyphs to the British Egyptologist Rosalind Moss. She furnished a translation of the hieroglyphs, and we noted that her identification of the female deity on the throne was Mut rather than Ma'at.

Moss was also able to analyse the photographs that were made available to her by the director of the museum at the time, the Chevalier Hannibal Scicluna, and an article in the *Journal of Egyptian Archaeology* followed in 1949[33]. Four photographs of the statuette from its four sides served as illustrations.

Another interesting observation in her article was that Moss totally ignored Sonnini's find-spot for the Maltese statuette and she assigned its context to the Maltese islands in 1713[34].

There was yet another relocation of the Maltese antiquities. The archaeological collection reached its present station at the Auberge de Provence in 1955. The catalogue of the antiquities that were housed there was published in 1959 by the British archaeologist David Trump. He was Curator of the Museum at the time[35]. For the first time in the twentieth century, the statuette was not included amongst the archaeological artefacts in the Malta Museum of Archaeology.

The final thread we followed was to Sir Themistocles Zammit's son. From a very tender age Charles used to follow his father around the Museum of Archaeology and the various archaeological sites of Malta. He is seen quite frequently as the human scale for the photographic documentation of the prehistoric megalithic monuments on the islands.

Eventually Captain Charles Zammit officially assumed the duties of Curator of the Museum of Archaeology, and was later promoted to Director until his retirement in 1971. His continuous exposure to the museum of archaeology over six decades of the twentieth century made him an ideal source for further information on the statuette.

I had interviewed Captain Zammit on several occasions and had also tapped his long experience at the Museum for my publications in 1997 and 1999[36].

On the 8th of August 2005 I visited him and his wife at Msida in Malta. I presented him with a copy of my 1999 publication towards which he had significantly contributed.

I also took along with me a few photographs of the statuette in question and showed them to him. Despite his being well advanced in years, Charles recognised the artefact immediately and gave me a few relevant details[37].

He remembered it vividly amongst the archaeological specimens at the Museum. He confirmed that it had originally been displayed on its stand under a cupola but, interestingly, after the Second World War it was kept in a niche in the Director's office at least until his retirement in 1971.[38]

The statuette was subsequently transferred to the reserve collection of the Museum of Archaeology and it then re-surfaced in the public eye for the exhibition in November 2003.

The Egyptian statuette had actually been around the museum for the first seven decades of the twentieth century! It had not disappeared at all until at least 1971. However we were unable to account for its whereabouts after this time, that is, until it re-appeared on public display in 2003.

Figure 8. Four views of the statuette published
by Rosalind Moss in 1949.

Sonnini and the statuette

The Museum curators and directors of the late twentieth century were being given all the credit for the exhibition. According to the *Sunday Times* article, it had been an earlier Director of Museums, Dottor Tancred Gouder, who discovered the first description of the statuette in the travelogue of Charles Sonnini. Dottor Gouder had then passed on his discovery and research to the museums department, and it was thus to his memory that the exhibition was being dedicated.

It had been a major breakthrough for Dottor Gouder to have come across a late 18th century[39] volume with an engraving of an artefact that was similar to one held in the Maltese Museum of Archaeology. With Gouder's discovery of the engraving and Sonnini's text indicating that the specimen had been discovered in the Thebaid, the fate of the statuette seemed to be sealed.

Yet the attribution of the Egyptian statuette to Neferabet goes a long way back in time, before Meza's and Gouder's research studies of the statuette. In fact, although Morris Bierbrier also includes the engraving by Sonnini in his 1982 publication and makes the analogy with Neferabet, he does not acknowledge Dottor Tancred Gouder for the identification or the discovery of the Maltese statuette's similarity to Neferabet. In fact, in his bibliography Bierbrier included Rosalind Moss's article in *The Journal of Egyptian Archaeology*, where she had already made the attribution of the statuette to Neferabet in 1949.[40]

It started to seem likely at that point that the attribution of the statuette to Neferabet was not a clear-cut issue. It had apparently been assumed that the statuette was identical to Sonnini's engraving, and therefore it is most probable that the translation of the hieroglyphs had actually been carried out on those in Sonnini's engraving rather than from the statuette itself. This had to be verified.

Figure 9. The French naval engineer Charles Sonnini.

Analysing the details on the information panels

Despite its shortcomings, the exhibition was truly a remarkable feat on the part of Heritage Malta. The material and equipment for the exhibition were created in such a short period of time. It was a well-organised and coordinated effort all around.

Our preliminary research had already acquainted us with most of the information that appeared on the exhibition boards, such as that Neferabet lived along with the other craftsman in the village of the workmen at Deir el-Medina.

The information panels in the exhibition hall also presented a number of details about the person represented on the Egyptian statuette, his craft, and also his residential details in the present-day town of Deir el-Medina. Marta and I scanned these superbly executed A1-sized boards in our search for more information about the life of Neferabet. As we did so, it seemed that there might have been an element of inaccuracy and extrapolation on certain matters.

For instance, there was a statement on one of the information panels that, apart from the tombs of the kings and queens of Egypt, these workmen were also responsible for the works on the tombs of the nobles in their vicinity. This assertion did not seem to be strictly correct, and a reference to the relevant literature confirmed our impressions. It was not within the workmen's normal course of duties to decorate the tombs of the nobles. However if a pharaoh lived long enough, and his tomb was almost complete, the workmen were usually allowed to take this other form of employment on a temporary basis.

We were not in agreement with what was being described on another panel regarding the accommodation for the craftsman at the village of Deir el Medina, then known as the Place of Truth.

It was being reported by Heritage Malta there were 'seventy residences[41] that lay within the enclosed compound, whereas another fifty lay outside it, and provided the accommodation for these tomb workmen for the Egyptian elite'.

This last statement was incorrect. The accommodation quarters that lay outside the village compound were not designated for the workmen but for their servants or slaves. The government allocated these slaves to see to the various needs of the village workmen. Yet these servants were confined outside the walls of the enclosed village at the Place of Truth and had no access to it. Security there was very tight indeed. It was hard to get in and equally tough to get out.

Since the Place of Truth was situated far away from any water source, these slaves were required to work on a daily basis, carrying water containers from the Nile to the village. Some of these servants were not slaves in the normal sense of the word, but rather professional fishermen who would have been designated by the authorities to provide fish rations for the royal craftsmen. Some others were professional potters who were designated to see to the ceramic needs of the villagers.

We next proceeded to consider the biographical details on Neferabet as presented at the exhibition. It was being stated on the information panels that Neferabet 'hailed from a family of craftsmen, yet his precise specialisation is apparently unknown'. Yet Neferabet's precise occupation was in fact known. According to the British Egyptologist John Romer, he was a painter of the royal tombs and coffins[42].

There was a problem with the family tree. This started off with the grandfather of our Neferabet; his name was printed as Tenhaynu. The parents of Neferabet followed, and these were Neferrenpet and Mahi. Neferabet came next; he was rendered as 'Neferabu', married to Ta-Isis, daughter of Amenmose. Their children were then listed as the fourth generation, respectively as Nedjemger,

Neferrenpet, Ramose, Meriunu, Henuttu, Mahi, Tenthaynu, Hotepy, Mutemopet, Istnofret, Henut-Iunet and Roruti.

For some reason, the brothers and sisters of Neferabet were not included in this family tree. That was one lacuna that Marta and I could fill in during our ongoing research. We also hoped to be able to identify the occupations and achievements, if any, of the various members of the family.

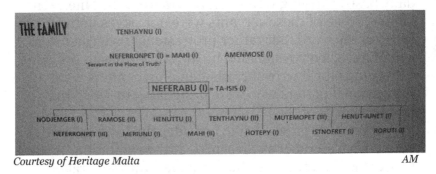

Figure 10. Neferabet's family tree exhibited.

Problems with the new context for the statuette

Apart from the inaccuracies in fine details already hinted at, the story was an attractive one, and initially it seemed to be making a lot of sense. But it soon began to crumble the moment that it was subjected to scrutiny.

Starting with the dates, Sonnini was describing his Cairo episode as having occurred in 1778; according to his version of the events, the statuette must have been found some time before this date in Thebes, in the tomb of Neferabet.

What seemed strange about this statement of Sonnini that was being endorsed by Heritage Malta was that the statuette was supposed to have been found around the 1770s inside the tomb complex of Deir el Medina that only started to be officially excavated in 1886.[43]

The tomb builders of the pharaohs are widely believed to have also been the tomb robbers. However they protected their own burial places very well against other robbers; as a consequence their tombs were not disturbed and in their majority were found "intact".[44]

One could certainly not exclude the possibility that modern day tomb robbers at the neighbouring village of Abd el Qurna had also known about Deir el-Medina before its official excavation. In mole-like fashion they would have dug up passages underground and robbed each and every sepulchre that they found. Several of these tomb robbers actually made their homes on the Qurna hill, right inside the tombs of the New Kingdom nobles. Others maintained silence about the tombs that lay right beneath the floors of their homes and they intermittently robbed them.

Could the statuette have ended up in Malta as a direct result of tomb-robbing in modern times?

Marta and I harboured rather different notions about the precise time that modern tomb robbing became established along the Upper Nile valley. We had each been impressed differently by the literature that we were independently perusing. When we reached the stage of trying to reach a conclusion about this, it became an exchange of quotes via e-mail from our own expert sources.

I sparked it off with an extract from Christine Hobson's publication: "One crucial point is that the site of Deir el Medina was unknown until 1815, and this is confirmed by other reliable sources. Abandoned in the reign of Rameses XI, it lay buried in the sands for centuries, totally forgotten and unseen by human eyes".[45]

Marta answered me on this by quoting from Morris Bierbrier. "The residential site of the village was covered by the desert sand but not the village temples. Those had been in use up to Ptolemaic times and in fact during the reign of Ptolemy IV a temple dedicated jointly to Hathor and Ma'at was erected on the site of the former village's temples. The complex was continually being enlarged and construction only stopped in the Roman period. Furthermore the village cemetery was being reutilised in the Late Period".[46]

I agreed with her completely on this, and quoted from yet another author that came up whilst I was reviewing some translations of New Kingdom inscriptions. "The site was still totally buried under the sands of time when Napoleon's team of surveyors visited the sites in the vicinity', and it was only after 1815 that the first antiquities were being discovered and 'sold to passing tourists.' Having been spared the spoiling of ancient tomb robbers, Deir el-Medina was 'unusually well preserved and systematically excavated'.[47]

I was obliged to concede that Neferabet's tomb would certainly have been disturbed in antiquity. Yet I was still mainly concerned with modern tomb looting that might have accounted for the statuette having been lifted from its context around the end of the eighteenth century as suggested by Sonnini's publication. Although occasional travellers to Upper Egypt were known in the seventeenth century, 'none of Luxor's early visitors' ever mentioned the existence of Deir el-Medina. And the scientific team that

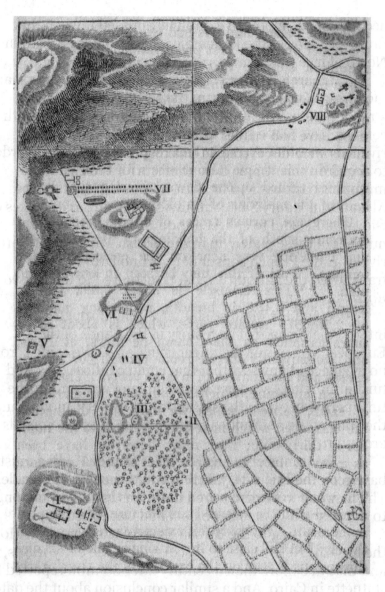

Figure 11. British Museum map of 1832 [Charles Knight, London]. The structures indicated are Medinet Habu [1], the Colossi of Memnon [II], site of temple [III], broken colossi on the ground [IV], 'temple of Isis' [V], the Ramesseum [VI], avenue of the sphinxes [VII] and the remains of 'Gournou' [VIII].

accompanied Napoleon completely missed it when they drew the plans of the Ptolemaic temple that lay just to the North of it.[48]

It therefore seemed plausible for us to assume that modern day tomb robbing in the Upper Nile valley was strictly established in the early decades of the nineteenth century. This was a time when the nations of Europe rivalled one other through their respective consuls in order to acquire ancient Egyptian artefacts for their national museums back home. The British Consul-General in Alexandria, Henry Salt commissioned agents of the likes of Giovanni Belzoni to collect antiquities for him, and a number of these ended up in the British Museum. His arch-rival was the French consul Bernardino Drovetti who transferred the antiquities that he acquired to the *Museo Egizio* in Turin.[49]

So had the Maltese statuette gone through an intermediate phase of its history in the hands of the European consuls or their agents in Cairo? We came across no evidence of any sort that that could confirm this. And furthermore this scenario would still not account for the time period between the statuette's 'discovery' in 1778 and the start of the antiquities trade by the European consuls around 1815.

The tombs of the workmen at Deir el Medina must have remained relatively immune to the antiquities trade. The first one to be discovered there was in 1886. It belonged to a craftsman named Senedjem and was found intact. [50]

According to the British Egyptologist Rosalind Moss, the tomb of Neferabet was discovered in the early 1880s,[51] and that was more than a century after Sonnini reported the statuette in Cairo. And a similar conclusion about the date of its discovery had also been reached earlier by Jacques Vandier, the French Egyptologist who thoroughly investigated the earlier literature on the tomb of Neferabet and then documented it fully in 1935.[52]

58

Systematic excavations started at Deir el Medina around 1905, and the Italian Ernesto Schiaparelli was among the first to do so, like Drovetti before him, for the *Museo Egizio*. Several mummies and other artefacts were transferred by him from Deir el Medina to the well-known Egyptology museum in Turin.

When I visited the museum in 2006 I was impressed with the amount of material that Schiaparelli had transported there from the workmen's village. The tomb of Kha and Merit had been transferred practically *in toto* and took up an entire corridor of the upper floor.[53]

It seemed to us that the Maltese statuette could not have been found inside Neferabet's tomb before 1778. Could it have been found *outside* of the tomb, such as in one of the designated sanctuaries at Deir el Medina? Was it placed in Neferabet's home or inside some workshop in the village?

Gozo or Thebes?

The main controversy relating to the statuette was clearly its archaeological context. The Maltese authorities of the *nineteenth* century had given it a *find* date of 1713, and, before the days of archaeology proper, the find *spot* was vaguely assigned to an 'archaeological site in Gozo'. But all this changed with the exhibition. The research that had just been carried out was demonstrating that it had actually been found in the area of Thebes in Egypt sometime in the late Eighteenth century.

Both contexts were somewhat vague, but that may have been due to the prevailing standards of 'archaeological' practice at the time. If the 'archaeological site in Gozo' was too hazy a context, then the vast expanses of the 'Thebaid' as proposed by Sonnini and Heritage Malta was certainly even vaguer. This 'Thebais' context as indicated by Sonnini and endorsed by *Heritage Malta* was providing no find spot in particular, no finder and no find year. Insofar as context is concerned, such a description is totally null and void. There was not even a name assigned to the monk who had given it to Sonnini's companion in 1778 and no explanation at all as to how the statuette could have ever ended up in Malta after it was received in Cairo.

Nevertheless, the engraving produced by Sonnini and published in 1798 bore an uncanny resemblance to the statuette on display at the Museum of Archaeology. The similarity between the engraving and the statuette was certainly there, and in fact the Maltese statuette had already been identified with Sonnini's drawing long before the exhibition of 2003.

Although there were a few discrepancies between the statuette and the engraving, we were not yet in a position to contest their identity with one another. Was Sonnini a reliable source for the statuette's context?

I discussed this with Marta. There were valid reasons why we were not in agreement with the statuette's context as stated at the Exhibition.

"For one thing," I started off, "the Maltese documentary material of the nineteenth century was stating otherwise. And furthermore there were serious problems about the reliability of the sources that were being relayed to Sonnini in Cairo in 1778".

The alleged source for the discovery of the statuette in Thebes in the late eighteenth century was a very dubious one. The story had been given by word of mouth by an anonymous priest in Cairo who had heard it from an equally anonymous entity. Furthermore, it had not been Thebes that had been put forward as the site of the discovery, by a third anonymous entity, but the 'Thebaid', and this was not strictly identical with 'Thebes'."

Marta agreed with all of this, adding that 'the Thebaid' was evidently referring to the region around Thebes. "However it was strictly not a very precise term to use", she added. "In ancient Egypt and in Egyptological terms Thebes is divided into the East Bank and the West

Bank. The East Bank comprised the Karnak and Luxor temple, the pharaonic administration and the living quarters from the upper class to the lowest in the relevant suburbs. On the West Bank were the cemeteries of the workmen, the Valley of the Kings, the Valley of the Queens, Abd el Qurna, Assasif and Dra Abu el Naga and the funerary temples of the pharaohs: Medinet Habu, the Ramesseum, Deir el Bahri and the rest. The Workmen's Village was located on the West Bank in isolation, despite the fact that it was a living quarter. Thus Neferabet's statuette could only have originally been placed on the West Bank: either in his tomb, his house, a local temple or a workshop. The term 'Thebaid' is inappropriate".

I pointed out that there was yet another problem that one could not explain, and that was how the statuette ended up in Malta once it was given to De Tott in Cairo *after* his visit to Malta in June 1777. He did not return to Malta at any time afterwards, and two years later, in 1779, he was back in France.[54] Nobody in his right mind in the late 18th century would return to Malta after having spent time in the Levant because of the strictest and harshest quarantine restrictions that then prevailed.

The priest with no name

I went through Sonnini's publication in some detail in an effort to try to establish the identity of the Italian monk of the *Propaganda Fide* whom Sonnini and the baron had met in Cairo, and I came across a few interesting facts.

Sonnini and the baron were not on the best of terms. Whilst in Malta, Sonnini might have been annoyed at the fact that when they were invited there at theGrandmaster's country residence in San Anton in Malta, whilst the barons of the entourage, de Tott and de Durfort were given places at the Grandmaster's table, he was not.[55]

By way of emphasising the baron's lack of general knowledge in basic matters of a scientific nature, Sonnini described the incident when he made a complete fool of de Tott in the presence of the Grand Master. De Tott never forgave Sonnini for this 'offence'.[56] And later on in the text Sonnini even ridiculed the nature of one of de Tott's official assignments that he had taken 'into his head' whilst in Cairo.[57]

Insofar as the monks were concerned, on the 12th March 1778 Sonnini narrative made the acquaintance of a French trader established in Cairo, a certain Charles Magalon who then introduced him to the 'President' of the *Propaganda Fide*[58] in Cairo, a Brother Gervaise d'Ermea. In his turn the latter presented Sonnini with a letter of recommendation for assistance during his travels up the river Nile.[59]

The letter was addressed to the 'President' of the Italian monks established in a convent in the *Thebaid*, the very reverend Father Gedeon de Baviera, at the town of Akhmin that lay half a league away from the Nile.

I looked at a contemporary [1782] map of Egypt by the French cartographer Bonne[60]. An extensive region in Middle and Upper Egypt was being referred to as the Thebais, or *Thebaid*. Within its territory it included the cities of Thebes and Akhmim and the convent of the Italian monks there. Sonnini's context for the statuette was even vaguer than I had originally imagined.

When Sonnini eventually reached the convent of the Italian monks in Akhmin, he was completely shocked by their crookedness and dishonesty [*leur malhonnete*]. Notwithstanding the letter of recommendation from Cairo, his reception there could not have been worse or ruder;[61] the monks were characterised by 'idleness and ignorance' [*ces moins Italiens, de l'un des orders que la fainantise et l'ignorance caracteristent*], and behaved like the 'lowest and most impure of people' [*de la portion du people la plus basse et la plus impure*], simply living off the toil of others through their constant begging and cash collections. These Italian monks were the source for the context of the Egyptian statuette as published by Sonnini.

These and other considerations must have contributed to the rejection of Sonnini's context by later scholars such as the Maltese prehistorian, Sir Themistocles Zammit and the British Egyptologists Rosalind Moss and Bertha Porter.[62]

The statuette's transfer from Cairo to Malta

If Sonnini's context was the correct one, how did the statuette reach Malta from Cairo? It was being suggested on the information panels at the exhibition that the Baron de Tott would have taken the statuette to Malta himself. However the statuette had only come into his possession in Cairo, the year *after* his sojourn in Malta.

After an exhaustive literature search in the relevant material that was available in the Maltese libraries, there was no evidence suggesting that de Tott was ever in Malta *after* this episode with the priest in Cairo in 1778. Nevertheless it was the contention of Heritage Malta and the organizers of the exhibition that the statuette eventually reached Malta from Cairo, even going to the extent of actually misquoting Morris Bierbrier as stating that the statuette reached Malta *directly* from Cairo[63]. Yet what Bierbrier had written was that "Sonnini's description ... confirmed that [the statuette] did not leave Egypt until the second half of the eighteenth century."[64]

The entire story according to Sonnini was readily available in his own published account. What was his travelogue stating? I opted for the original version in French. I went through the entire volume of Sonnini[65] in order to get a better picture of the Baron Françoise De Tott and attempt to figure out the details of the sequence of events relating to the acquisition of the statuette.

According to Sonnini's text the Baron travelled together with Sonnini from Toulon to Alexandria and thence to Cairo. *En route* to Alexandria, both De Tott and Sonnini sojourned together in Malta for seven days. The Grand Master Emmanuel de Rohan, a French Knight of the Order of St John, entertained the both of them one evening at his summer palace at San Anton. Whether the honour was due to the baron's diplomatic status or his family tree is uncertain. Strong rumours placed De Tott amongst the illegitimate sons of Pope Clement XIV before his pontificate[66].

Sonnini then wrote that he left Malta together with the baron in June 1777. The pair sailed to Alexandria and they reached Cairo together *without* the statuette at the beginning of 1778. It was during their sojourn in the Egyptian capital that De Tott allegedly received this statuette from an Italian monk. De Tott then proceeded, to Constantinople on his own, without Sonnini. The baron returned to France in 1779.[67]

There was no mention at all in the Maltese literature that suggested that de Tott stopped at Malta *en route* back to France. In fact, coming from Constantinople, de Tott would have done his utmost to avoid landing on Malta where he would have unconditionally been obliged to spend a number of weeks in quarantine[68] there if he as much as landed on the shores of Malta.

At that precise moment in time, the turn of the eighteenth century, the health and quarantine regulations prevailing in the Mediterranean were at their strictest. No traveller from the East would have been allowed to enter Malta without first spending a few weeks in isolation. This period was spent on an island with a designated quarantine hospital known as the *Lazaretto*. (Figs. 13 & 14)

These regulations and restrictions applied to anything on a boat coming from the East, whether this was human, animal, vegetable or mineral.

Figure 12. Outbreaks of infectious illness caused chaos in the hospital wards and led to a total disruption in the economy of the islands.

Figure 13. The Lazaretto (left) was situated next to the military fortress (right) that enforced maintenance of the strictest quarantine measures.

There were also instances when entry into Malta was refused outright on grounds of possible disease on board the vessel. In September 1796 the traveller Bertel Thorvaldsen and the crew of the *Thetis* that was transporting him were refused entry into Malta because they had been at an infected port in Algiers. The vessel was obliged to spend some time in Tripoli before returning to Malta and then spend the required period of time in quarantine at the Lazaretto there on Manoel Island.[69]

Social status did not bend the rules, no matter if it was Lord Byron, Cardinal Newman, Sir Walter Scott or Sir Moses and Lady Montefiore; all were obliged to go through their quarantine periods in Malta. Isolation at the Lazaretto was not merely a major inconvenience, but it also involved a high risk of contracting a fatal disease. Many a traveller died during isolation at the Lazaretto in Malta, some from the diseases that they carried back with them from the East and others from infections that they contracted from the other inmates.

Vessels undergoing quarantine were not even allowed to enter Grand Harbour but were obliged to enter the one at Marsamxett and anchor opposite the Lazaretto on Manoel Island.

Enforcing quarantine were several Guardians of Health, 'some of whom did duty afloat'. 'Watch boats had the duty of preventing any communication with ships undergoing quarantine. No other vessel was allowed to approach a ship held in quarantine, or to drop anchor near it. On no account were foodstuffs or other articles to be collected from such ships or dropped into the sea.' There were also 'patrol boats carrying gun crews and fully armed soldiers to police the harbour.'

Quarantine under the Knights of St John was so strictly imposed in Malta that failure to conform to procedure ran the risk of imprisonment and even the death penalty; gallows for the purpose were actually installed below the Lazaretto hospital on Manoel Island.[70]

FC

Figure 14. No vessels from the Levant were allowed entry into Malta's Grand Harbour (left); these were obliged to undergo quarantine in the Marsamxett harbour (right) at the Lazaretto on Manoel island (below). The Lazaretto site is arrowed

FC

When these measures were relaxed early on in the nineteenth century, plague soon reached the islands from Constantinople via Alexandria. Havoc reigned in 1813, the disease destroying hundreds of lives and crippling the economy when all business came at a standstill.

A few years later the renowned French scholar and decipherer of the Egyptian hieroglyphs, François Champollion was obliged to spent time in quarantine after his return from Egypt. He carried this out in Marseilles, but even there the experience was a terrible one and may in fact have contributed to his premature death.

The Lazaretto quarantine hospital in Malta today is in an extremely dilapidated state, but despite the dangers of the unstable structure I carried out an intensive search amongst the hundreds of graffiti with autographed names of inmates who spent time in quarantine there. These included the renowned personalities already mentioned above, as well several others of diverse nationalities. There was definitely no de Tott amongst these. The pompous person that he was, the baron would certainly have found the time to add his name to the repertoire if he had spent a few weeks there.

There is furthermore no documentary evidence of any sort that de Tott ever carried out quarantine in Malta at any time. There appears to be no record of a de Tott, or Sonnini for that matter at any time, and specifically for 1779, the year that de Tott returned to France.

The baron had already fulfilled his mission in Malta whilst *en route* to Egypt in 1777; it would have been a superfluous act on his part, and also one of unnecessary personal hardship merely to donate his statuette to the Grandmaster in Malta. Would de Tott have gone through all of this after dragging it along with him for the previous two years?

There was another significant factor militating against the hypothesis that the Baron donated his statuette to the Maltese authorities. De Tott had no connection at all

68

with Malta that would have prompted him to do such a thing. He was not even French but Hungarian by birth – at least it is so registered – and in fact he spent his last days in Hungary.

De Tott's memoirs

It seemed that a number of people were taking Sonnini's words for granted regarding the provenance of the Egyptian statuette, even though these conflicted with other versions of the story. Then Marta casually asked me one afternoon whether we could confirm the story with De Tott himself. Had his memoirs been published and did they mention the Maltese connection?

I could have kicked myself for not even having considered that option. That line of inquiry was not merely one worth pursuing, it was a crucial exercise, and I immediately set myself to the task. It did not take me long to discover that the baron had actually published his own memoirs after all, and part four of his second volume said it all.[71] Whilst I awaited my copy to reach me by slow mail, we availed ourselves of Google that had conveniently digitised the text and also made it available in the Library of the University of Michigan as a *pdf* file. I could not have asked for anything more.

According to the baron's own memoirs, he left France on the 2nd of May 1777 on board the *Atalanta* that was commanded by the baron de Durfort. There were a few noblemen who were to be dropped in Sicily. An eastern wind obliged them to 'put into Genoa for a few days' before sailing to Sicily, and then continuing with their voyage to Malta, where De Tott 'acquitted himself of a commission with the Grand Master'. The nature of this commission was not specified.[72]

The baron continued with his journey eastward to Egypt. An unexpected surprise was in store here for by the time that de Tott left Egypt there had never been any mention at all of his meeting up with a priest or his receipt of a statuette at any time. The only thing that the baron ever received from a priest en route to Constantinople was a 'blessing', and that did not even take place in Egypt.

Oddly enough, the baron did not even mention Sonnini at any time in his published memoirs. What he did repeatedly mention was his own constant preoccupation with the drawing of anything interesting that came his way, and these included several remains of pharaonic Egypt[73].

I skimmed through the remainder of the text until I reached the crucial part of the baron's memoirs, and this was the return journey of de Tott from Constantinople to France two years later. In his own words, after leaving 'Naples of Romania' the baron de Tott 'departed for Tunis where I was to finish my inspection. After reaching Malta [*touché à Malthe*][74], and putting into Lampedoose[75], we doubled Cape Bon and anchored opposite the new castle of the Gooletta, whence I sailed to Tunis'.[76]

The *Memoires* of the baron clearly demonstrate that their vessel had neither anchored nor even 'put into' Malta, but approached it and passed by it, possibly after receiving fresh water supplies from there,[77] and only 'put into Lampedusa'; they finally anchored in the bay of Tunisia where the baron terminated his mission for the French government.

If the baron set his foot upon Maltese soil a second time, he would have mentioned it in his *Memoires*, and he would also have lamented his obligatory quarantine period at the Lazaretto.

A contemporary Frenchman

I next searched avidly for a travelogue that was as close as possible in time to 1779, the year that De Tott returned to France, and one that involved travelling in the Mediterranean. I was extremely fortunate. During this same period of time, another Frenchman, a Monsieur De Non, gentleman in ordinary to the King of France, was on his way by sea to Malta *not* from the 'insalubrious' Levant, but from the relatively healthy shores of Sicily. Here is his personal account of the situation that prevailed at the time in the Maltese islands. The date was September the 5th, 1778.[78]

"We bore down on Gozo during the remainder of the day, but ... made *la Cumino*, a little island ... between Malta and Gozo ... my impatience to land in order to procure some relief and give a few moments respite to my stomach ... rendered this rugged of all shores, in my eyes, a most delightful grove... scarcely had we remained two hours in this situation, before I felt myself awakened by a man ... [who] ... made me comprehend that we must not remain there, unless we wished to perform quarantine ... we learnt from him that the isle of Gozo was in quarantine, a slave from the Levant having escaped, and concealed himself on the island, and though we had not landed there, should we be discovered by the barks of the police, we should be obliged to perform quarantine on our arrival at Malta. The idea of this made us all shudder; I dreaded the quarantine still more than the sea, and presently slippe[r]d a crown into the hand of our adviser."

"We returned on board in the dead of night, with all possible haste, and doubling the *Cuminotto*, a small desert rock, sailed along the low coast of Malta ... following all the windings of the shore, and passing under the different towers and forts which defend the bays and anchoring grounds of that part of the island, which alone is accessible; all the other side being sufficiently guarded by nature ..."

When De Non reached the main harbour area of mainland Malta he discovered that the entire crew of the *Cato* had been obliged to submit to quarantine after their return from Constantinople, the very same town that the baron de Tott had just been to

"We passed before the harbour of *Marsa Muscet*, where we found the French ship of war the *Cato*, which had carried M. de Saint Priest to Constantinople, and was performing complete quarantine, the most violent plague raging in, and depopulating, all the coasts of the Levant. We next arrived under the famous fort *Saint Elmo* ...

"We were stopped at the first guard-house, till the officer on guard relieved us...

"We were obliged to give up all thoughts of visiting Gozo, for fear of exposing ourselves to the plague, or at least to a very vigorous quarantine."

Quarantine measures on mainland Malta would have been even much stricter from the fact that plague was then present on the sister island of Gozo.

Having sailed North to Sicily from Malta a few days later, still in September 1778, they reached the port of Syracuse. Fears of the plague were so intense along the Mediterranean littoral, that despite the fact that they had not been to the Levant, they were obliged to perform quarantine there, probably because of the situation on Gozo. De Non's vessel was "compelled to land at a wretched hovel, called the Health Office ... a quarantine, that there is neither a lodging, nor a shed ... having suffered martyrdom for eight and twenty long days unjustly imposed on us; sleeping all this time without distinction among the sailors, drenched every night by the excessive rains of the season, scorched by the heat of the sun at noon, and exposed every evening to a wind that made our bones ache as in a fever; we at length got out of this infected hole, covered with vermin and sores, and with our clothes so torn from not having been off our backs for a whole month together, that they would scarcely hang on any longer."

Why would the baron have opted to delay the continuation of his mission to Tunisia through a sojourn of extreme discomfort in quarantine in Malta, and all this merely in order to donate a statuette to the Maltese authorities?

Comparing photographs with the engraving

At that stage we were still unsure as to the accuracy of Sonnini's engraving of the statuette in question. Was it justified to equate the two depictions of the statuette? In order to answer this, Marta and I thought that we would meet on the morrow and make a comparison of the engraving with the photographs that we had taken of the statuette during the exhibition.

As I started making the preparations for this exercise on the laptop in the afternoon of the following day, another active member of the local Egyptological Society joined me at my place in St Julians before Marta's arrival there. Rosman was a very practical man who spent long hours in the countryside looking for potentially archaeological sites. He investigated anything that related to the history of the Maltese islands, and he involved all his family members in these field trips.

I was impatient to carry on with the setting up of the images for comparison. Rosman asked if he could join in the exercise as I opened the file with the photographs that I had prepared. I placed these images side by side with the corresponding areas on the engraving. We alternated between one photograph and the other on Adobe Photoshop, and the two of us peeled our eyes for anything significant that we could detect as different between the two depictions.

The *Minolta* shots provided great photographical detail, and as the enlarged features on the statuette appeared upon the laptop screen Rosman came out with a crucial observation.

'In the engraving, the seated goddess[79] has two armbands and the male deity on the proper right of the statuette has one on the left arm. But there are no armbands in the photographs you took of the statuette!'

He was absolutely right! We checked this out again and again from all angles on the photographs and the

73

absence of armbands on the exhibited statuette was unambiguous.

Within minutes we had singled out the first feature of discordance between the statuette and its engraving by Sonnini. Was this simply a case of artistic license? Yet was Sonnini entitled to this form of license in a scientific theme? If he played around with his drawings then his copy of the hieroglyphs was not a reliable one.

Automatically and instinctively we set out hunting for more discrepancies.

The doorbell rang and Marta joined us at this point. Hardly had she seated herself and got told about the arm bands that she immediately picked up the second significant discrepancy. She concentrated upon the object that was being held in the left hand of the male deity. This was the *ankh* that Marta elaborated upon as a characteristic ancient Egyptian symbol denoting 'life'. This *ankh* was definitely present in the photographs we had taken of the statuette but it was unquestionably absent in Sonnini's engraving. If the addition of armbands reflected an element of artistic license, then the crucial detail of the *ankh* would certainly not have escaped the artist with the least inkling of Egyptology.

I had not contributed anything that far, and I peeled my eyes in search of something to pick up - it was my turn next. Finally there was something by way of a relatively minor dissimilarity. In the engraving, the feet of the dedicatee or standing figure were clearly inverted against the lower side of the pillar that supported the pedestal, but in the photographs the feet of the dedicatee were clearly set upon the base.

Within the lapse of twenty minutes each one of us had identified a feature that differentiated Sonnini's engraving from the statuette on display. It was unambiguously clear to the three of us that Sonnini's engraving of the statuette was not a perfect reproduction of the statuette of today.

AM

Figure 15. There is an *ankh* but no armbands on the statuette (above), whereas there is no *ankh* in the engraving published by Sonnini (below), and armbands have been added on to both seated deities.

The main differences between the two depictions involved the *ankh* and the arms bands. Sonnini's engraving had the armbands but not the *ankh*, whilst the statuette had the *ankh* but not the armbands. The positioning of the feet upon the base was also different.

If Sonnini's engraving was depicting the Maltese statuette, his precision in documentation certainly left a great deal to be desired. If he had resorted to artistic license, research upon his engraving was bound to be significantly flawed.

Reliability of Sonnini's context

Sonnini's account of the statuette's acquisition by the baron de Tott in Cairo is not supported by any other known documentation.

Apart from the fact that we only have Sonnini's testimony for the incident in Cairo, it is significant that the baron did not even include this episode in his own journal.[80]

As it turned out, it was the baron rather than Sonnini who was sketching everything interesting that came along their path during the trip, and that included ancient Egyptian artefacts. The likelihood that the baron had made a sketch of the statuette in Malta, Gozo or Cairo suddenly seemed to make more sense.

De Tott published the *Memoires* of his 1777-1779 travels in 1784. It is significant that he ignored Sonnini altogether in his publication.

In the meantime the latter was engaged in publications concerned with industrial inventions and discoveries particularly those related to agriculture. This literary activity of Sonnini featured both before and after his travels in 1777-78.

The baron de Tott passed away in 1793. Then the Grandmaster De Rohan passed away in 1797. Sonnini published his travelogue in 1798. There was nobody to contradict him then.

Instead of ignoring the baron, Sonnini paints an ugly picture of him and of the others who maltreated him, like the monks of the *Propaganda Fide* - they too ignored and were very rude to him at their convent in Ackhmin.

De Tott's paintings of ancient Egyptian material were never published. If Sonnini had ever come across a drawing of the statuette by de Tott, he would have assumed that it had been executed in Cairo, just like all the others.

If the hypothesis that Sonnini created an artificial context for the statuette is correct, using as he did the baron and a monk of the *Propaganda Fide* as the main actors, then it would have had to be an anonymous priest donor, an unknown statuette finder and unknown find spot if he was not to be found out. In fact it was just such a context that was used, with Sonnini attributing the find spot of the statuette to an incredibly vast area of the Nile regions that includes Upper and Middle Egypt.

This multiple anonymity surrounding the statuette contrasts significantly with the remainder of Sonnini's narrative which is highlighted by detail in every instance.

In our proposed scenario Sonnini's book is translated into English and eventually reaches the shores of Malta, then under the British administration. Vassallo is concerned and researches the statuette's context.

It is only when the manuscripts at the Bibliotheca are being compiled by Vassallo that it becomes possible to ascertain the context of some of the archaeological artefacts that were fortunately being preserved in the same building. Vassallo utilises what he can from the rotting archives[81] that had deteriorated so severely that they had to be burnt later on down the century. Through these sources Vassallo discovers the statuette's correct context.

In 1842 the German Egyptologist Carl Lepsius arrives in Malta en route to Egypt. Vassallo shows him the statuette during his sojourn there.

Lepsius would have been aware of Sonnini's context, but he is told a different version by Vassallo. Lepsius would have had to be sufficiently convinced by Vassallo's research on the statuette if he was to ignore Sonnini's context, which he did.[82]

Lepsius makes a sketch of the statuette together with its hieroglyphs, rather similar to the engraving that was published by Sonnini. However, there is a significant difference between the two depictions. We have the documentary evidence of both Dr Cesare Vassallo and Lepsius that the latter took his observations directly from the statuette. Consequently he executeds his drawing scientifically, from the frontal and side views, and unlike Sonnini, he neither adds on nor omits any details.

The likelihood that it was not Sonnini who originally sketched the statuette is rendered more probable through his fatal error in identification of the gender of the dedicatee on the Maltese statuette, designating him as a priest*ess* instead of a male functionary. Close inspection of the statuette leaves no doubt that the dedicatee is a male, whereas the gender is ambiguous in the engraving.

It is interesting to point out that in the title page of Sonnini's publication, the engravings are stated to have been "drawn on the spot" not by the author but "under the authors' *inspection*" [emphasis added].[83]

Other factors that support this hypothesis include Sonnini's inability to get an accurate measurement of the statuette, when precision would have been expected of him as a French naval officer. His failure to register the conspicuous *ankh* on the knee of the male deity and the spurious addition of bracelets to the arms of the female deity provide additional support.

And so the question remained unanswered. Did Sonnini merely copy a sketch of the statuette by the baron and then embellish his narrative by adding the monk episode when there was nobody around to contest his word?

What possible scenarios would account for the engraving published by Sonnini? Firstly, as already discussed above, the baron might have been shown the statuette whilst in Malta or Gozo. In his usual manner, de Tott would have made a sketch of it that Sonnini was aware of, and the latter might even have copied it and then used it after the baron's demise.

A second scenario would presume that whilst in Cairo, Sonnini and de Tott might have only seen a *drawing* of the statuette, rather than the statuette itself, in the hands of a priest of the *Propaganda Fide*. The bulky statuette would certainly have been awkward to carry around by a cleric on the move.

It was standard practice at the time for the Jesuits and Inquisition in Malta to send drawings of archaeological artefacts found on the island to their superiors in Sicily and Italy for further analysis. This sketch of the statuette would simply have been one of the several that were constantly being sent over by the Inquisition in Malta to their superiors overseas.[84] We are not even told by Sonnini whether the donor priest was on his way down from the Italian peninsula.

It would not have been an impossible task for Sonnini to have copied the drawing into his engraving and then embellished the story in the manner that he did.

The original context

So if the statuette had not been found in Thebes just before 1778, could it have been found on the Maltese island of Gozo in 1713 and then kept in low profile for over a century? What would its initial fate have been under these circumstances? What was happening to the archaeological artefacts that were intermittently being picked up on the Maltese islands during this period of time?

This particular phase of Malta's history coincided with the rule of the Knights of St John. These warrior monks represented the military arm of the Roman Pontiff, whereas the concurrent Inquisition in Malta functioned in the same manner as it did in Europe, by searching out and removing any possible source of interference with the Roman Faith. It ensured a thorough censorship of most if not all of the artefacts that were occasionally picked up and presented to the authorities. And archaeological artefacts with inscriptions that were written in mysterious 'pagan tongues' constituted such a threat[85].

During the time of the Knights of St John in Malta there were several contemporaneous accounts that amply demonstrated their negative attitude towards the Maltese archaeological heritage.[86] And the archivist and historian Dr A. A. Caruana was later able to confirm the severe losses that had been incurred through the caprices of the Inquisition and negligence on the parts of the Knights of St John during their tenure of the islands.[87]

The prehistoric monumental structures on Malta suffered severely at this time. Several of those lying along the coastline were sacrificed for the sixty kilometre long line of fortifications. In the Grand Harbour area around Valletta, an entire megalithic temple complex was lost. Those situated inland provided a readily available source of stone slabs and were quarried in the main.

By way of mobile artefacts, the numerous Phoenician inscriptions that were still to be found on the Maltese islands just before the arrival of the Knights there in 1530 have since all disappeared. These inscriptions were documented at the time by a Knight of the Order of St John who published the first history of the islands[88].

Fate of the artefacts discovered on Malta and Gozo

What was happening to the archaeological artefacts that were being discovered on the Maltese islands at around the same time that the statuette was reported as having been found, in 1713?

It would seem that the archaeological specimens discovered on Malta and Gozo during the time of the Knights of St John experienced different fortunes. Whilst those on Malta were under more rigid control by the Inquisition, the ones from the sister island tended to survive better.

Archaeological artefacts in Malta that survived into the mid-seventeenth century were first officially preserved at the mansion of the Vice-Chancellor of the Order of St John, the Villa Habela. This was situated at the Marsa, overlooking the main harbour area. Visiting scholars from overseas made it a point to visit the antiquities there.

The artefacts discovered on the sister island were kept by the Gozitan priest Pietru Agius de Soldanis.[89] It was apparently 'finders keepers' at the time[90].

When Abela's 'museum' was inherited by the Jesuits of Malta in 1655, the artefacts suffered great losses. Archaeological items went missing and others were reported as stolen. The near life-size statue of Hercules in Malta was accidentally beheaded whilst in their custody. They sent it to Naples for repairs but it was replaced by another statue.[91] The whereabouts of the original artefact remains unknown.

As a result of this constant loss the surviving archaeological artefacts were small in number and were initially preserved together with the archives. The artefacts moved with the archives. Where did the Knights of Malta been keep their records and archives?

A Library of the Order of St John was founded in 1650. This was initially located over the oratory in the Conventual Church of St John in Valletta, but was then removed to a hall on top of the sacristy.

In 1761 the books were taken to a house let to the Bali Ludovicus Guerin de Tencin, in the house called 'Il Forfantone' in 251 Strada San Giorgio, Valletta (now Republic Street), where a Public Library was instituted. Its first librarian was the Gozitan priest Agius de Soldanis[92].

If the statuette had been discovered in 1713 and brought over to Malta it would have been transferred to Tencin's house, 'Il Forfantone'.

After de Soldanis it was the Abate Gioacchino Navarro, a Conventual Chaplain of the Order of St. John who took over the care of this library; this was between 1770 and his retirement in 1812.

In 1798 the Knights of St John's were ousted by the French who took over the administration of the islands until 1800. During the British Protectorate that followed and lasted until 1814, a third building was put aside in Valletta to accommodate both the archives and the antiquities. This was the Bibliotheca in Treasury Square. Although it was primarily intended to house the volumes and antiquities then being held at the Tencin Library, it degenerated into a British officers' mess. In the meantime the ancient documents and books simply rotted away.[93]

In 1812 the archaeological artefacts and ancient documents eventually found their rightful place in the Bibliotheca, the site of today's National Library in front of St Anne Square. A Canon Giuseppe Bellanti succeeded the Abate Navarro and he maintained office until 1839 when he was replaced by Dr Cesare Vassallo.[94]

This was where the statuette first appeared in the Maltese records. It would have been transferred to the section there allotted to the antiquities, the *Gabinetto della Antichita*, at the time that the administration was assumed by a Dr Cesare Vassallo in 1839. One of the first scholars to see it amongst the Maltese antiquities was the German Egyptologist Carl Lepsius when he stopped in Malta *en route* to Egypt in September 1842.

Significant losses to the archives still continued to occur through inadequate funding by the authorities. The condition of hundreds of old volumes had deteriorated to the extent that they had to be incinerated.

In the meantime the Bibliotheca continued to house the archaeological artefacts together with published books and manuscript archives under one roof until the turn of the twentieth century.

The first archaeological museum proper in Malta was created in the Xara Palace in 1901. The artefacts were moved to another building, the Auberge d'Italie in 1922 and subsequently to its present site in the Auberge de Provence in 1955.[95] All three museum buildings were situated in the capital city of Malta, Valletta.

Several of the antiquities found on the sister island of Gozo remained there in various institutions, and some of these are still preserved today at the Museum of Archaeology at the Cittadella in the capital city, Victoria. Yet this was only set up in 1960.

These artefacts found on Gozo include the 'Romulus and Remus with the she-wolf statuette' and a number of 'Egyptianising' amulets that had been picked up from various Phoenician tombs in Gozo[96]. Some of these and others were transferred to Malta and are known to have been kept at the Grandmaster's palace. They were subsequently preserved with the archives when the Knights of St John left the islands in 1798.

There were a few private museums on the islands, such as the one kept by the Marquis Barbaro. Unfortunately a large number of Maltese archaeological artefacts were lost when his entire collection was sold to a Mr Winkelson in 1795[97]. And there were other sad losses of antiquities.

The fate of a number of archaeological artefacts that were picked up on the islands at around the same time as the statuette might throw some light on its possible fate. The earthquake on Malta in 1692 may have been partially responsible for the unearthing of at least a few of this cluster. Soon after the earthquake a hoard of ancient gold coins was found in the ground beneath the Mdina Cathedral in the ancient Maltese capital.

In 1694 the Inquisition was investigating two important bilingual inscriptions that were found in an archaeological site in South East Malta. After a brief period of research that included sending copies of the inscriptions to Naples, it was decided to re-bury both artefacts deep in the soil of the Jesuits' Villa in Marsa. It was only through pure chance that these artefacts were re-discovered a few decades later. One of the pair was later donated by the Grandmaster to the French monarch. The equivalent of the 'Rosetta Stone' for Egyptian hieroglyphs, these invaluable inscriptions turned out to be the key for the decipherment of the Phoenician language.

Also in the second half of the seventeenth century, the Bichi family in Malta buried four ancient Egyptian funerary steles beneath the foundations of their palace overlooking the Grand Harbour; these steles had been found earlier on the island. The Bichi clan included the notorious Inquisitor who later made it to Pope Alexander VII. Fortunately these steles were later recovered by the British army as they were dismantling the foundations of the villa in 1829, in preparation for the building of their new naval hospital on the island[98].

Whilst a few of the disposed of artefacts were re-discovered, others were lost forever. The British author and visitor to Malta, William Tallack recounted the fact that in '1694, some golden plates, covered with Egyptian hieroglyphs, were found in Malta. These have long since left the island, having been presented to the Archbishop of Naples'.[99]

But what about the ancient archaeological objects discovered on the sister island of Gozo? This was where our Egyptian statuette was reported to have been found. Were these artefacts evading the eyes of the Inquisition?

The Gozitan historian De Soldanis documents the discovery of a gigantic molar tooth in Malta "in 1658, and because of its extraordinary size was given as a gift to Grand Master De Redin who in turn thought of sending it as a gift to Pope Alexander III".[100]

The following extracts from De Soldanis's publication provide a few clues as to what the archaeological finds were going through.

"I was lucky to see a marble statuette of Hercules. It was four feet high and was broken. This statue was found by Felic Manduca Piscopi, Count of Montalto. I have also seen a one foot three-inch alabaster statue of the goddess Flora with a boy next to her on her right side. This was a very refined statuette discovered in 1720 hidden in an underground cave in a field called *Ta'l-Imqajjem* on the side of Zebbug called *It-Taflija*. Some thought this statuette represented Spring". The fate of these artefacts is unknown.

De Soldanis also recounts that "among other treasure discoveries we have that of Antonio Vella, a Gozitan nicknamed *Ta' Dmieghi* who while digging with his son in a field at Zebbug Valley unearthed 33 golden rods at *Ta' Tlajfa*. These rods were given to Grand Master De Wignacourt [between 1690 and 1697]. This happened a little before this Grand Master extended the water supply to Valletta".[101] Similarly the fate of these rods is unknown.

The Gozitan priest gives us further examples of how other artefacts discovered on Gozo ended up. "In the year 1720, a statue of a she wolf suckling two babies Romulus and Remus was found among ruins in the street that leads to *Ghajn il-Kbira* (The Great Fountain), at Rabat Gozo. It is made of alabaster and very artistic. It is approximately one foot long. This statue was at Grand Master Manoel [de Vilhena]'s residence but now belongs to Grand Master Pinto. The Grand Master did me the great favour of allowing me to see this statue in 1746. It is very well kept together with a bronze statue of a beautiful ram found in Sicily and a great collection of coins of all metals. Everything is kept at his apartment at the Palace of the Grand Master. And since this Grand Master is a Great Prince both in power and kindness he not only gave me permission to see the statue found at *Ghajn Il-Kbira Street* for a second time but he even allowed me to take its measurements".[102] This statue was eventually returned to Gozo and is presently exhibited in the Museum of Archaeology there. (Fig. 16b)

The episode that is most often recounted is the one where de Soldanis gives an account of a golden calf. "In the same year 1729, Antonio Pace, a Gozitan who is still alive found in a cave located near the ruins of St Nicholas' Chapel near Dwejra, a statuette of a bull made of solid gold, with a gem on his head. It stood on a pedestal that was also made of gold. It was over a foot long. At the time I was living in Malta and when I heard people mentioning this discovery I almost could not believe that on Gozo, which is such a tiny island, a golden bull could have been found. Soon the Siniskalk De Stadel published a booklet where he explained how it was quite possible that Gozo possessed the golden bull".[103] Back in Gozo the historian was able to interview the farmer directly and extract the details.

Taking the lead from the reference mentioned by De Soldanis I looked up the publication by the 'Siniskalk De Stadel' but was initially unable to find a copy of De Stadel's booklet.

However a chance visit to the National Library in Valletta yielded a document that was far better. *Mss 155* (1737) turned out to be the original manuscript where the Bali Fra Ferdinand Ernest de Stadel described the event in question in folios 225 and 226.

It seems that it had been a poor Gozitan farmer by the name of Anthony Pace who discovered the statuette of the golden calf in his field in 1729, and that he sold it to one of the local jurors in Gozo soon afterwards. The discovery and sale of the artefact reached the ears of the Grandmaster Antonio Manoel de Vilhena, and the latter immediately set up an intensive inquiry in order to recover the statuette. The *giurato* was questioned inexorably and tortured until he died without giving away the secret of the calf's whereabouts.[104]

The question I asked myself was what would the Grand master have done with the golden calf if he had found it? Would he have kept it in his palace, as he had done with the 'Romulus and Remus with the she-wolf statuette' mentioned above? Would he have send it over to the Pope as a gift as had happened with the gigantic molar tooth? Would he have sent it to the French King as had been the case with the bilingual inscription?

If the Grandmaster kept it in his palace, he would then have been in a position to show it off to his visitors, as a beautiful *objet d'art* of antiquity.

The fate of yet another artefact that was discovered in Gozo provided an interesting analogy. A private museum collection in 18th century Malta was maintained by a certain Count Abela Giovann Antonio Ciantar, who also published a historical account of the islands in 1772. One particular artefact described by him was found in 1771, at the coastal village of Ghajnsielem, next to the main harbour at Mgarr in Gozo. I went to visit the exhibition when it was available to the general public at the offices of Heritage Malta there.

The artefact in question was a bronze statuette of a seated male youth with 'awkward intertwined legs' and holding a vessel in his outstretched right hand. It was being attributed to the Early Christian or Byzantine era, to around 535 AD. The uniqueness of this artefact was the mysterious writing that covered the statuette. A few characters were Greek but the others are unknown to this day. (Fig. 16a)

Research upon this artefact has been extremely limited over the past three centuries. Various hypotheses have been put forward in an attempt to identify the figure, the more popular among which are a beggar or a cripple. Had this artefact been discovered in Malta and by the Inquisition, it would have most likely been spirited away through the very nature of its undeciphered characters.

According to one of the information panels at the exhibition, the bronze statuette was seen in 1791 by the French voyager, the Comte de Saint-Priest at the museum of the Public Library in Valletta;[105] two years later it was in the collection of the Grandmaster, Emanuel de Rohan de Polduc (1775-97). It was seen there and mentioned by another visitor to Malta, the Italian connoisseur Carlo Castone della Torre di Rezzonico[106].

There were other archaeological artefacts that were kept by the Grand Master[107], and these too eventually ended up in the 'Cabinet for the preservation of the local Antiquities' that De Rohan set up at the National Library in Valletta. [108]

This analogy raised the possibility in our minds that the Egyptian statuette, also found on Gozo in the eighteenth century, might have gone through the same drill as the bronze statuette, and for a time formed part of the Grandmaster's collection.

And it is therefore quite conceivable to hypothesise at this stage that the baron de Tott saw the Egyptian statuette in Malta or in Gozo[109], and in his standard manner of behaviour the baron made a drawing of it. The engraving published by Sonnini would then have been more likely executed in Malta rather than in Cairo. The baron's companion Sonnini would have had access to the engraving and used as his own in 'another context' after the baron's demise.

This hypothesis was even more likely when consideration is taken of the similar history experienced by the Egyptian statuette and the bronze cripple. Both were discovered in Gozo in the 18th century and spent some time there. When the Knights left at the turn of the nineteenth century they were preserved in the museum of the Public Library throughout the French occupation and the British takeover. Both artefacts remained there at least until the end of the nineteenth century. Then in 1882 the two statuettes were photographed for the first time and included

Courtesy of Heritage Malta   AM

Figure 16. The cripple (above) and the alabaster 'Romulus and Remus with the she-wolf' (below) were found in Gozo.

Courtesy of Heritage Malta   AM

in the museum catalogue by Dr A. A. Caruana. Then in 1894 both were included in W. K. R. Bedford's 'Malta and the Knights Hospitallers'[110].

The movements of the two statuettes were not documented after this date, and both artefacts resurfaced on exhibition more than a century later, respectively in 2003 and 2009.

Another article by an archaeologist

In the meantime, there was another development during this early phase of our investigation. Another local newspaper, *The Sunday Times* of 2 November 2003, carried an article with the title "From Thebes to Malta: Neferabet at the National Museum of Archaeology". This time around, the correspondent was an archaeologist by training. She therefore submitted her comments from her professional point of view.

Once again, the message that was conveyed to the general public was that the statuette in question had not been found in Gozo in 1713 as previously assumed, but that it was an imported artefact from Thebes in modern times. Reference was made once again to the study of the hieroglyphs on the statuette by a number of scholars, and the writer asserted that this had resulted in the identification of a certain workman Neferabet from Deir el-Medina as the dedicatee of the statuette.

Like that in *The Malta Independent* of a few days earlier, the article stressed the participation and contributions of several scholars and added a few more details, including the participation of some foreign individuals and institutions of repute.

Besides the National Library of Malta, a number of museums and other organizations abroad had contributed towards the exhibition, and these included the *Institut Français d'Archeologie Orientale*, the Egyptian Museum in

Cairo, and the Ashmolean Museum in Oxford. This was truly an impressive group of scholars, a formidable array of researchers. The results of their combined research would surely be interpreted by all and sundry as impressive.

The justification that was offered by Heritage Malta for the alteration in the accepted context of the statuette was an original one. Although the statuette had been documented as having been discovered at an archaeological site in Gozo in 1713, it seemed that the only reference to this provenance that was available to the museum authorities was from Dr A. A. Caruana in 1882.[111] This seemed to be far too distant in time from 1713, the year when it was reported to have been found. After a lapse of seventeen decades between discovery and report, the credibility of Caruana was considered highly suspect. These circumstances weighed heavily against Caruana, and his reliability in this regard was thus cast into serious doubt.

Furthermore, the *Sunday Times* article suggested that, since the only person who had declared its provenance in Gozo was not an archaeologist but an archivist; he must therefore have been mistaken. Who was this individual, and what authority was he wielding in this assertion of his?

Librarian curator of antiquities

In the late nineteenth century, Dr A. A. Caruana was the curator and chief librarian at the Bibliotheca of Malta. This was the institution that held the large number of archives, documents and publications of the Knights of St John, in whose time the statuette was reported as having been discovered. Dr Caruana would most certainly have confirmed this evidence of his from these archives, which were immediately at his disposal whenever he wanted.

Furthermore, Caruana was not the first person to have stated the fact about the statuette's provenance from Gozo in 1713. His immediate predecessor at the Bibliotheca had already published the same find context more than three decades before him.

The main protagonist in the play had in fact been missed out altogether. His role was a crucial one in the story, and yet it seemed that he had been totally ignored in the exhibition. He was the person whom Dr Caruana was quoting in 1882 for the provenance of the statuette.

In the late 1830s, the British Governor-General in Malta[112] decided to bring some form of order into the archives, records, antiquities, and books in the Bibliotheca, or Public Library of Malta.[113] For this purpose, he commissioned a certain Dr Cesare Vassallo[114] as Head of Antiquities and the Government Archives.

On the assumption of his post on 1 January 1839,[115] this humble and unpretentious lawyer was assigned the near-impossible task of compiling and cataloguing the tremendous amount of volumes and manuscripts at the newly acquired building in St Anne Square, the Bibliotheca. These documents had been neglected over the previous decades of political turmoil in the islands. [116]

As the first librarian and antiquarian under British colonial rule, Vassallo exploited the archives in his research on the Maltese monuments and artefacts. He then published these findings in his Cenni Storici.[117]

During his meticulous cataloguing and archiving, Vassallo was able, for example, to detect the unexplained disappearance of a certain volume by the chaplain of the order, Fra Jean Quintinus, that gave a description of Malta immediately before the advent of the Knights of St John in 1530.

Vassallo also involved himself in the archaeological excavations that the British Army was then conducting in Malta. Vassallo was able to give a detailed description of a Negroid human skull that had been excavated from one of the Maltese Neolithic temples, that of Hagar Qim, in the 1820s. Since this skull has now disappeared from public view, his record provides us with its unique documentation and description.

Vassallo's main task at the Bibliotheca was to sort out the documents into an organized catalogue, and accordingly he started off by compiling the volumes first. These ran into several tens of thousands.

By 1843–44, Vassallo was able to publish this catalogue, which he categorized in a number of subject matters, with each individual volume bearing its identification number and classification type – Scienze et arti; Teologia e giuriprudenza; Istoria; Belle-Lettere, etc.[118]

Once he had finished with the compilation of the volumes at the Bibliotheca, Vassallo set about cataloguing the several manuscripts, most of which had lain dormant there for centuries and several of which had undergone severe decay.

The process of compilation of these manuscripts at the Bibliotheca had long been overdue. The number then surviving totalled 497; these were catalogued by Vassallo and published in 1856.

These hand-written texts were crucial in that they contained material that had been refused publication during the time of the Knights of St John in the islands. As Caruana put it, these manuscripts were particularly valuable since they were "memoirs, narratives of events which were denied publication by the Government of the Knights, records of local traditions, and historical documents referring to the islands of Malta, the Order of St John, the Inquisition, and the local Ecclesiastical history".[119]

Scholars outside the Maltese islands were under a similar impression about their great historical value. For example, in his 'Nouvelles recherché Historique sur le principauté français de Morée', a certain M. Buchon was able to show for the first time in 1843 that these manuscripts at the Bibliotheca also contained crucial historical material for the history of the islands. [120]

The renowned German Egyptologist Carl Lepsius was in Malta in September 1842, at a time when Vassallo was already three years into the cataloguing process of the Bibliotheca archives. Before the publication of Vassallo's catalogue, Lepsius documented the Egyptian statuette in his notebook, declaring for the first time that it had been found on the Maltese islands over forty years previously, "or even longer than this". [121] Lepsius must therefore have obtained his information about the statuette's context directly from the librarian-curator himself, Dr Cesare Vassallo, just as he had obtained the information for the other artefacts at the Bibliotheca. [122]

A few years later, the English traveller and author William Tallack also saw the archaeological collection at the Bibliotheca. He was acquainted with the provenance of the Egyptian statuette, that is, Gozo in 1713, and he praised the Governor-General and Vassallo for their highly commendable efforts in organizing the antiquities at the Bibliotheca. Quoting from his own words, "if every country had been as diligent in the promotion of the study and exhibition of objects of local interest as the Maltese naturalists and antiquarians have been, there would have accrued a vast addition to the aggregate amount of the world's knowledge". [123]

Another significant contributor who documented the statuette's provenance was an executive committee member of the Bibliotheca, the Reverend W. K. Bedford. He published his own volume on the history of Malta, and he included the context of the statuette in question as "in Gozo in 1713". Like William Tallack before him, Bedford spoke of Dr Cesare Vassallo as "a learned, courteous, and in every way admirable librarian"; he then went on to confirm that there was a lack of funding with the retirement of Vassallo, everything started going steadily downhill and a large number of documents had rotted away and had to be burnt up. These volumes had belonged to the Knights of St John;

they comprised their personal records, and thus a great loss was sustained through their extinction.[124]

When compiling the Bibliotheca's archives, Vassallo would have had ready access to these archives that had suffered deterioration and decay and were inevitably lost. The content of the archives would have included the details of the artefacts that were discovered in Malta. The archaeological artefacts were then being preserved in the same building as the archives, and the latter would certainly have included the details and other relevant data for the Egyptian statuette.

The efforts of Vassallo were thus doubly important, for he took the trouble to research into these documents and extract what information he could in order to tie up Maltese historical facts together before they were lost forever.

Further research, compiling, documentation, and reference to the ancient documents in the archives eventually led Vassallo to publish the first official guide to the Maltese archaeological artefacts in Malta and Gozo in two languages – in Italian in 1861, with an English translation in 1862.

In all of these publications, Dr Cesare Vassallo gave the archaeological context of the Egyptian statuette as having been discovered in 1713 at an "abandoned archaeological site in Gozo" but had not specified its precise context. At that time, there were no official excavations in progress; they had not even started. Archaeological sites were simply quarried for their masonry by the locals, whereas during their official excavations in the early nineteenth century, the British military were simply clearing away these archaeological sites of their artefacts. [125]

Vassallo spent forty years amongst the archives of the Bibliotheca. His experience and first-hand contact with the historical documentation of the Knights of St John[126] was a vast one. He retired on 14 December 1880, and Caruana took over his duties the day after. As chief librarian and antiquarian at the Bibliotheca, Cesare Vassallo had set up an exemplary behaviour pattern that was then taken up by his successors. When Caruana retired on the last day of 1896, a Dr Filippo Vassallo assumed these duties until his demise on 17 March 1897. [127]

So why had the organizers of the exhibition absolutely ignored Cesare Vassallo's valuable contributions to Maltese archaeology in general and the statuette in particular? All his publications were readily available at the time at the main institutions of Malta – the National Library in Malta, the National Library in Gozo, and the Melitensia section of the Malta University at Tal-Qroqq.

Caruana had been proper and scientific in his manner. When he attributed the Egyptian statuette in question to Gozo with a discovery date of 1713, he was quoting from the reliable sources of his predecessor, Dr Cesare Vassallo.

My letter to the Sunday Times of Malta

Once the relevant material had been thoroughly investigated, I felt that the matter of the statuette's *context* had to be clarified to the general public. I had a letter published in the *Sunday Times of Malta* on the Sunday following the opening of the exhibition. [128] In a nutshell, I delineated a number of inaccuracies in the exhibition. These included the first reported accounts of it in Malta, the first photographic documentation, and particularly the fact that one cannot loot a tomb without disturbing it. In 1778 the tomb of Neferabet was still intact, and it remained so for more than a century after this. The statuette in question could not have been discovered in Neferabet's *tomb* at Deir el-Medina in the late 18th century. [129]

I stressed the fact that "the investigating team had totally ignored the documentation of the statuette in 1842, 1851, 1861, 1871, 1872, 1876, 1894, 1897, 1901, and that the photographs of 1882, 1894, and 1897 were missed".

I could not fail to mention a significant omission in the exhibition. "The major obstacle to Gouder's new hypothesis was the fact that the documentation of the statuette had not started with Caruana in 1882, but had occurred much earlier than this – at least forty years earlier, and there had been at least six references to it during this period of time that had tantamount been regarded by the Museum authorities and the panel of experts as the statuette's 'Dark Age'. And furthermore, all of these six references between Sonnini and Caruana had unanimously attributed the context of the Maltese statuette as the Maltese islands in the eighteenth century – specifically, this was in an abandoned archaeological site in Gozo in 1713."[130]

I had also been upset by the stigma that was pasted on to the earlier curators of our national heritage, Dr. Themistocles Zammit, Dr. Annetto Caruana and, indirectly, on Dr. Cesare Vassallo.[131] Through a sustained series of strategic omissions, ambiguous statements of fact and subliminally delivered degrading remarks about the Maltese curators of the 19th and early 20th centuries, a completely inaccurate picture of the real scenario behind the statuette had been offered to the public of Malta and Gozo.

Furthermore the whereabouts of the chevalier's statuette were still unclear, and grave doubts on the authenticity of the statuette on display had already started to be seriously entertained. The artefact placed on exhibition might have only been a copy of the original statuette.

A substitution of the statuette was hardly an unlikely proposition. A Phoenician inscription known as the *Melitensia Quinta* was found in the megalithic temple of Ggantija in Gozo around 1855[132] and became the property of a British family, the Stricklands, then resident in Malta. It was subsequently bequeathed to the Museum in the early 1940s. Yet a copy of it had already been made before this donation to the museum and has constantly been exhibited in preference to the original that has not been seen for some time.[133] Could the Egyptian statuette have met with a similar fate?

Research by an Austrian Egyptologist

Were there other ancient Egyptian artefacts that had reached the Maltese shores over the years, over the centuries, perhaps even over the millennia? Was there anything else by way of artefacts on Malta that was possibly associated with Neferabet?

In 1989 the Austrian scholar Günther Hölbl[134] published a catalogue of the ancient Egyptian objects that were found on the Maltese islands.[135] The list is extensive but not a fully comprehensive one. However Hölbl simply assumed that most if not all of the Egyptian artefacts that were found in Malta were brought over to the islands by the Phoenicians or the Carthaginians.

The scholarly authority of Hölbl weighs heavily upon the local archaeological establishment, and yet his sources have not constantly been reliable and trustworthy. Regarding the statuette in question, it appears that he dismissed its significance and context much too lightly and without adequate justification[136].

We therefore sought out the Egyptian artefacts in the local museums and started with the small collection held at the St Agatha Museum at Rabat in Malta.

An excursion of our Egyptology society was accordingly organised in this direction. The Reverend Victor Camilleri was a very dedicated individual who managed the museum extremely well and was extremely courteous and obliging in our regard.

The vast majority of the items on display were *ushabtis* and, according to Fr Camilleri, all were discovered on Malta. Yet we were far from convinced of the authenticity of these artefacts, apart from three at the most.

Marta and I investigated one artefact that we considered to be a genuine item. This was a funerary cone. In the end we prepared a printed caption for him that he appreciated and incorporated it in the cabinet presentation.

Several Egyptianising artefacts were discovered in Phoenician tombs in Malta, and these *ushabtis* could very well have been some of these items. They could even have been manufactured by Phoenicians as imitations and then incorporated them in their tombs.

Then an opportunity presented itself to view the Egyptian antiquities in the reserve collection at the National Museum of Archaeology in Valletta.

Other ancient Egyptian artefacts on Malta

Suzannah Depasquale brought out box after box of ancient Egyptian artefacts and placed them right there on the table in front of us. She was the curator at the National Museum of Archaeology in Valletta, and Helen Foster had arranged the appointment with her for that day the 13th June.

The purpose of this visit was to permit the members of the local Egyptology society to view some of the Egyptian artefacts that were to be found on the Maltese Islands, most of which, however, had not been discovered locally. The ones that were about to be shown to us had been the property of Lord Francis Wallace Grenfell. He had brought them over to Malta with him and then donated them to the Museum of Archaeology of Malta at the termination of his governorship of the Maltese Islands in 1903.

Oddly enough, it was around the time that Grenfell donated his artefacts to Malta in 1903 that the statuette in question disappeared from public exhibition for an entire century. At least that was what was reported in both newspaper articles that covered the exhibition.

Suzannah wore latex gloves and handled the artefacts for us as we requested her to inspect them one after the

99

other. All the members of the group had a heyday, and we were very generously attended to for over an hour. The collection consisted of some *ushabtis*; but there was also an *ushabti* box and a number of votive bronze figurines, the largest of which measured no more than three inches in height.

As later research demonstrated, the Egyptian collection that we were then examining was comprised not merely of the 1903 donation of Lord Grenfell, but also of a number of other ancient Egyptian artefacts that were discovered and published in the Maltese islands before the time of Lord Grenfell's governorship. (Fig. 18)

As the meeting was drawing to a close, Susannah went on to outline for us the forthcoming plans for the museum. These included the exhibition of the ancient Egyptian artefacts in a museum context. Now that was good news for the society members!

She did add that at the present time there was no evidence at all that linked ancient Malta with Egypt; she also confirmed that the Egyptian statuette with the triad was in storage. It had just been exhibited for several weeks a few months previously and was not brought out for us that morning to see.

The American Egyptologist's study on Neferabet

The research for the exhibition had been initiated by Alicia Meza and we decided to get in touch with her. It was through little effort that I managed to contact her by e-mail in a very short space of time.

I asked Alicia for a copy of her article and she very kindly supplied me with an offprint.[137] Meza acknowledges the fact that it had been the *Sunday Times of Malta* article of the 16th June 2002 to which I had contributed that triggered her off to research the Maltese statuette.[138] And the article led to the exhibition. In its turn the exhibition

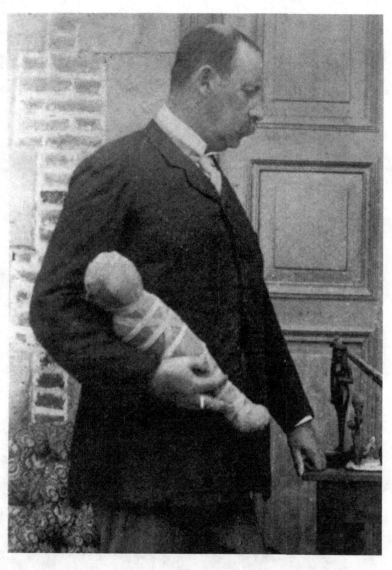

Figure 17. Lord Francis Wallace Grenfell.

Figure 18. Ancient Egyptian / Egyptianising artefacts discovered on Malta, (three of the above, arrowed), and on Gozo (below) before the time of Lord Grenfell.

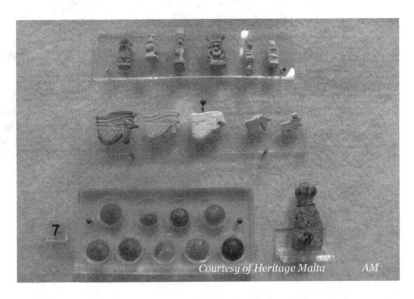

had led to the formation of the Egyptology Society of Malta. So after all, I thought, my contribution towards that article had paid off rather well.

I could confirm that Meza's article had provided the basic material for the information panels at the Valletta exhibition of the statuette in 2003.

The earlier descriptions and photographs of the statuette are not mentioned by Meza. The contributions by Cesare Vassallo, Karl Lepsius and William Tallack are also missing, and so are the drawings by Lepsius and the earlier photographs of it by Caruana and Bedford.

The bit at the exhibition about the statuette having 'been transported directly from Cairo to Valletta' according to Morris Bierbrier was also hers.[139] It seemed to me that Meza was extrapolating when making that statement; Bierbrier never said that.

After perusing the article more thoroughly a few facts started to crystallize that were definitely not in agreement with what had been stated in the exhibition panels at the Valletta Museum. There were a few technicalities in Meza's investigation that were causing significant concern.

For one thing, Meza confirms that the hieroglyphs had not been transliterated and translated from the Maltese statuette on display. A part of these derived from Sonnini's engraving and the remainder came from a number of digital photographs. According to Meza, Dr James Allen had not seen the statuette itself except on photography. So basically James Allen had relied on Sonnini and the photographs. Sonnini had not been precise over details in his reproduction of the statuette, and photographs are never as good as the real thing.

Secondly, there was the detail about the actual spelling of the dedicatee's name. The 'aAbt' glyph forming the end part of Neferabet's name is also known as Gardiner's trilateral sign M 19.[140] Marta pointed out that the capital 'A' represents a consonantal sound that is non-existent in the Latin alphabet.

We still needed to verify whether that the 'A' in Gardiner's table really represents a consonant, a glottal stop or possibly the vowel 'a'. Though the 'Egyptian vulture' sign is normally transliterated into an inverted letter 'E' and represents an 'aleph',[141] it seems that the Egyptologist tends to read it as an 'a'."[142]

Had Allen simplified matters by transcribing the name of the statuette's dedicatee as Neferabet instead of NeferaAbet? As the present consensus seems to favour the former version we have adopted that form of the name.

Thirdly, Meza does not identify the central cobra of the triad with Wadjet, the goddess of Lower Egypt, as had been proposed by Heritage Malta for the exhibition.

Fourthly, whilst naming Neferabet as the statuette's owner, Meza makes the statement that the statuette in question had been dedicated by Neferrenpet for his father Neferabet[143]. We could not find any evidence to support this.

According to the hieroglyphs engraved upon it, it seemed to us that it was Neferabet who was the dedicatee, the commissioner and owner of the statuette. Through the mention of his deceased son Neferrenpet and other close family relatives, Neferabet would have caused them to partake of any benefits that could be obtained through the statuette.

The main offering formula was the one on the back pillar, where Neferabet was asking the Lady of Isheru to give him everything good and pure for his *ka*. If his son Neferrenpet had made the statuette for his father, the offering formula would have been different. Before the mention of the recipient Neferabet there would have been the words to the effect that 'Neferrenpet made it for his father'. One example that comes to mind is Tutankhamen's dedication of a surveying instrument for his 'father's father ['s father],' Tuthmosis IV.

Meza also mentions two steles that had been commissioned by Neferabet, the one at the British Museum [BM 589] and the other in Turin [No. 102].

We were already aware at the time that there were even more of these steles of Neferabet distributed around the various museums, and we planned to trace them all and accord each its own significance.

Summing up

In the meantime we considered the various hypotheses brought forward by the organizers of the exhibition of Neferabet's statuette. The points were outlined in summary form and those we disagreed upon were annotated together with our reasons for doing so.

What was the context of the statuette that was being presented by Heritage Malta? The following statements had been made at the exhibition through the information panels.

1. The statuette had been found in the late eighteenth century by an unnamed person in Thebes, and it derived from the tomb TT5 of Neferabu also known as Neferabet.

2. The unnamed finder of the statuette gave it to an unnamed Italian priest who was resident at the *Propaganda Fide* outpost in Akhmim in Middle Egypt. The priest travelled to Cairo in 1778, and he donated it to the Baron de Tott, then in the company of the traveller Charles Sonnini. The latter published this episode twenty years later, a few years after the death of the baron.[144]

3. De Tott had then somehow donated the statuette to the Maltese before returning to France in 1779, but no indication of how this might have happened was furnished by Heritage Malta.

4. The statuette was unheard of until 1882, when the government curator-librarian, Dr. A. A. Caruana provided it with an allegedly fabricated context, an archaeological site in Gozo in 1713.

5. The statuette was first photographed in 1931.

6. The report by Morris Bierbrier that the statuette had gone missing for a while was being justified at the Exhibition by the statement that the statuette was being investigated and researched during the time in question, namely the latter half of the twentieth century.

There were a number of reasons why these statements by Heritage Malta were unacceptable. Marta and I made a list of our objections.

1. The statuette could not have been discovered in Neferabet's Tomb (TT5) before 1778, because tomb TT5 was discovered and excavated more than a century later. It was found in a context that was last disturbed by the ancient Copts, and had been unrifled and undisturbed in modern times. When the area of Neferabet's tomb was explored by Weidemann between 1883 and 1886 it still lay buried and hidden beneath the sands.[145]

2. There was no documentation of the name either of the discoverer of the statuette, nor of the priest who reported on its Theban context. Furthermore Sonnini himself has shown the reliability of the priest in Cairo to have been seriously suspect in view of the *malhonnete* that characterised the entire community of priests of the *Propaganda Fide* at Akhmin.[146]

3. It has been shown from the sequence of Sonnini's travelogue that the baron De Tott allegedly received the statuette from the priest *after* his visit to Malta. The baron was not yet in possession of the statuette when he was in Malta and there are no records at all that indicate that De Tott ever returned to Malta a second time. Furthermore, the prevailing quarantine regulations would not have permitted the Baron de Tott to have returned to Malta from Constantinople in 1779 and donate *anything*, even a piece of paper in his possession, to the Maltese.

The science of micro-biology was still unknown at the time, and these objects were considered to be potentially hazardous agents for transmitting diseases that were then endemic in the East.[147]

Visitors were obliged to spend a period of around four weeks there on the least suspicion of having come over to Malta from an infected country, typically Constantinople, precisely where the baron had been.

There are no records of any presentation of an Egyptian statuette to the Maltese, and visitors to Malta who were shown its antiquities shortly after this time have constantly failed to point it out. It must still have been preserved during this time either in Gozo or possibly in the Grandmaster's possession, and was only transferred to the Bibliotheca at the time of the British Governor-General, Sir Henry Bouverie, and the recently installed archivist Dr Cesare Vassallo.

4. The statuette had definitely been well documented before 1882. It has been shown above that it had been documented in the personal journal of the German Egyptologist Carl Lepsius forty years before the date stated on the Exhibition panels, and that it also appeared in print in at least five publications *before 1882*. It was also not the case that it was first photographed in 1931, for frontal and side views of the statuette are still available from fifty years before this. And a scale drawing produced by Lepsius in 1842 is still extant in Berlin.

5. Finally, the period indicated by Morris Bierbrier as to when the statuette disappeared from public view, at the turn and beginning of the nineteenth century, was totally out of phase with the period when it was being researched during the twentieth century. This anachronism was in the order of well over a century.

These were serious problems that were not backing up the thesis then being brought forward for the Exhibition of the Egyptian statuette. An alternative scenario that explained all these discrepancies was our objective.

107

Location of the statuette in antiquity

The precise function of the statuette also seemed to be in question. Was it a funerary one or was it votive? Had it been part of Neferabet's tomb furniture or had it been positioned somewhere else outside his tomb?

The two locations that were being proposed by Heritage Malta for the placing of the statuette were either Neferabet's tomb or, according to the writing upon one of the panels at the exhibition, in front of an altar "perhaps at the chapel located above his tomb."

It seemed to us that Heritage Malta was restricting the statuette's context to a funerary one, either the tomb itself or the 'chapel' above it. Why was it disregarding the presence of chapels in the Place of Truth other than those that surmounted the tombs?

During discussion over the most likely positioning of the statuette in question, Marta had her reservations about the discovery of the statuette inside a niche that was situated *inside* the tomb of Neferabet. But she favourably considered the strong possibility that it may well have originated from one of the chapels or small temples that were attached to the village.

As she explained, "it was customary for a statuette of the deceased to be placed in a niche on one of the walls of this chapel. An ancient Egyptian could endow such a temple and be allowed to place a small statue of himself within the temple precinct so that his *ka* – or 'post-mortem existence' - could benefit from the offerings of food and drink that the priests were presenting daily for the cult statue of the deity".

The village cemetery with the tombs and overlying chapels lay at the base of the hill that separated the workmen's village from their place of work at the Valley of the Kings. Yet there were other chapels in the village that were not of a funerary nature, and these were laid out close to the accommodation area provided for the workmen. These chapels or temples of the workmen were immediately outside the walls of the village proper. The surviving Ptolemaic temple, for example, was erected on the remains of a New Kingdom temple and was situated about fifty metres away from the village wall[148].

There was yet another sanctuary that provided an alternative placement for the statuette. Along the path that stretched between the workmen's village and the Valley of the Queens there was also the cave sanctuary that was dedicated to Ptah and Meretseger. (Fig. 19) Neferabet set up two steles that related to his temporary blindness,[149] and these were dedicated specifically to Ptah and to Meretseger. It seems very likely that these steles deposited in this cave sanctuary rather than anywhere else. Was the statuette also placed there?

The other question that required an answer was, when did the statuette leave the West Bank, and how did it finally end up in Malta, and when?

Figure 19. Deir el Medina is situated to the extreme right in the drawing, and the Valley of the Queens to the extreme left. The sanctuary of Ptah and Meretseger lies on the small hill in between [arrowed].

Visitors to the antiquities of Malta

In an effort to establish the statuette's earliest link with
Malta, we next tackled its documented presence in the
Maltese islands over the last few centuries. It had caught the
eye of a number of scholars who were in Malta during this
time. I embarked upon an analysis of their published
reports, with particular reference to the Egyptian statuette.

If the baron De Tott did donate the Egyptian
statuette to the Maltese authorities in 1779, then the
travellers who visited the Maltese antiquities in the
following years would have mentioned it.

Sonnini mentions the public library in Valletta that
housed the books and where 'several objects of natural
history' were exhibited. Sonnini was fascinated by a
fossilised femur, probably of elephant or hippopotamus,
and he sent a drawing of it to an authority abroad by the
name of Buffon. A private museum of a Mr 'Barbaroux' is
also described by Sonnini, [150] and this contained 'several
beautiful shells and petrifications ... pearls ... medallions'.
Oddly enough, no archaeological artefacts proper are
described by Sonnini in the two 'museum' sites of Malta that
he mentions. [151]

In June 1790 Sir Richard Colt Hoare was shown the
ancient Maltese artefacts during his visit to the islands. He
mentions the very significant fact that the Grandmaster kept
a 'museum of antiquities' in his Valletta palace and Colt
Hoare describes his being shown 'large bas-reliefs, bronze
and clay idols, earthenware and Siculo-Greek vases and a
marble group representing Romulus and Remus' by the
Grandmaster. At the Public Library Colt Hoare was also
shown the ancient artefacts by the person in charge there,
the Abate Gioacchino Navarro. There was a 'figure of
Hercules, two antique candelabras with Punic inscriptions,
and various medals.' Colt Hoare did not mention the
Egyptian statuette. [152] The Grandmaster was the same
Emmanuel de Rohan (1775-1797) who entertained Sonnini

and the baron de Tott[153] – he had bronze and clay idols on exhibition but did not have any statuettes made out of limestone as the Egyptian statuette was.

The Comte de Saint-Priest and Carlo Castone della Torre di Rezzonico have already been mentioned above. They both saw the bronze cripple statuette from Gozo but not the Egyptian statuette when they visited the islands, respectively in 1791 and 1793. It was between these two dates that the bronze statuette was transferred from the Grandmaster's palace to the Public Library. Was this an isolated move, or was it reflecting a generalised transfer of archaeological artefacts?

Another early visitor to the library was the Danish sculptor, Bertel Thorvaldsen. He visited the library and archaeological specimens on Friday the 6th January 1797.[154] He made mention amongst other things of the large collection of books that numbered some 30,000 and were shelved in six rooms; he also made reference to some French literature, several coins, some geological specimens, pottery and the statue of Hercules; but once again, no mention was made of the Egyptian statuette.

The Knight Louis De Boisgelin described the Maltese antiquities in 1804; the statuette was neither included in the collections of the Grandmaster nor in the Public Library. [155]

Once again the antiquarian Monsignor Onorato Bres did not include the Egyptian statuette amongst the Maltese antiquities in his publication of 1816. [156]

Eleven years later, in January 1827, the British traveller Andrew Bigelow visited the library but did not make mention of the statuette amongst the ancient artefacts that he saw exhibited there[157].

In the wake of Napoleon's campaign, Egyptologists of international renown were visiting the Maltese islands during the early decades of the nineteenth century, at a time when ships *en route* to Egypt made an obligatory stop in Malta for supplies. Several of these visiting Egyptologists made it a point to examine the Maltese archaeological

111

heritage during their sojourn there, and they evidently involved themselves in the Egyptian artefacts that had been discovered there in Malta.

The renowned British Egyptologist John Gardner Wilkinson did not see the statuette during his visit to Malta in 1829-30, but he saw and described other Egyptian artefacts, such as the four funerary steles that had just been found buried beneath the 'Villa of the Bichis' on a promontory in Malta's Grand Harbour.[158]

By 1838 the Egyptian statuette was still not being displayed in the National Library of Malta, for the British author George Percy Badger does not comment upon its presence amongst the several other archaeological items there during his visit[159]. Until this time there had still been absolutely no mention of the Egyptian statuette in Malta.

Then the Governor-General William Reid initiated a number of significant improvements to the archives and antiquities on the islands. A private library was set up in the sister island of Gozo in 1839, at the same time that Dr Cesare Vassallo was commissioned to take charge and compile all the antiquities and volumes on the islands. He brought all the antiquities that he was aware of under one roof, at the Bibliotheca; these included the cripple, the ram, the Egyptian bronze figurines and the Egyptian statuette. Gozo was included in Vassallo's jurisdiction, and it must have been around this time in 1839 that the Egyptian statuette travelled from Gozo to the Public Library in Malta.

So when on 14th September 1842 the German Egyptologist Carl Richard Lepsius visited Malta whilst *en route* to Egypt, he was no doubt assisted in his documentation of the artefacts at the Bibliotheca by the newly appointed Dr Cesare Vassallo. In his *Notizbuch* (or notebook) Lepsius recorded the presence of a number of ancient Egyptian and other interesting archaeological artefacts that were discovered in Malta.[160]

Amongst all the ancient artefacts that he saw on Malta, Lepsius's particular attention was drawn towards the

Egyptian statuette in question. He included two drawings of it on his notebook, one view of the front and another of the left side, and he included some of the hieroglyphs that were engraved upon its surfaces. He also gave an abridged translation of these inscriptions, together with a brief note about the function of the statuette and its provenance. [161]

However Lepsius dedicated some more of his time on the statuette that would prove crucial to our study. Under the fascinated eyes of the Maltese curator, he took casts of all the hieroglyphs that covered the statuette's surface and he promised Dr Vassallo a full translation of them. But his monumental work in Egypt that followed would have distracted him from this translation, and the statuette simply remained documented only in his notebook. This was the first known instance, in 1842, that a visitor to Malta mentioned it as being exhibited in the Bibliotheca. Lepsius was also the first to attribute the context of the statuette to Gozo in the eighteenth century[162].

If, as it was generally attested until 1982[163], the statuette had been discovered in 1713 in Gozo, it would most probably have initially remained there for a while. In view of the attitude of the Inquisition towards the discovery of archaeological artefacts,[164] it would only have escaped their eyes if it had been kept hidden away in some private residence or closet from 1713 until the date that it was brought over to Malta, most likely through the efforts of Dr Cesare Vassallo.

And as already mentioned, since the Maltese antiquities included the ones discovered on Gozo, Dr Cesare Vassallo would have brought the Egyptian statuette over to Malta soon after his assumption of the duties of librarian and antiquities curator in 1839.

After Lepsius, subsequent visitors of the likes of the author William Tallack described it as still being exhibited at the library, along with 'several other statuettes ... ornamented with hieroglyphs'. Tallack also mentioned the

Figure 20. Lepsius's *Notizbuch* with drawings of the statuette, 1842.

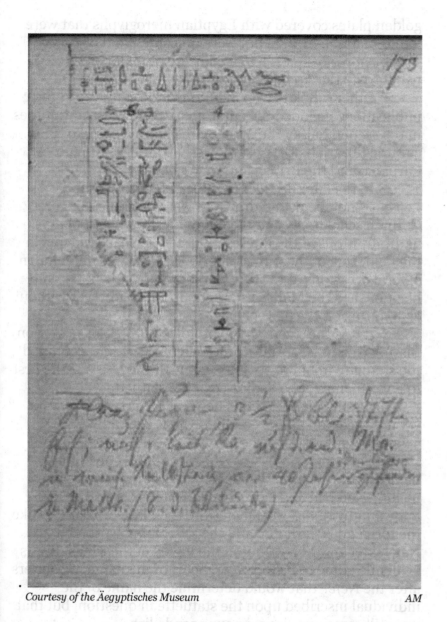

Figure 21. Lepsius's *Notizbuch* with more details of the statuette.

golden plates covered with Egyptian hieroglyphs that were found in Malta in 1694 but were presented to the Archbishop of Naples.'[165] The diocese of Malta was a tributary to the Archdiocese of Naples at the time.

Other scholars who mentioned the statuette in their publications included the curators of the Maltese antiquities in the second half of the nineteenth century, the two curator-librarians Dr. Cesare Vassallo and Dr. Annetto A. Caruana, and the British author W. Bedford.

In the later decades of the nineteenth century, Lepsius's notebook and drawings were published by three German scholars,[166] and the Egyptian statuette in Malta naturally aroused the interest of other German students in the field. One of these was Albert Mayr. He was in Malta on several occasions at the turn of the twentieth century, and he published the Maltese statuette in 1901, however without elaborating on the hieroglyphs.

It was the Austrian Egyptologist, Professor F. W. von Bissing who had a go at the hieroglyphs when he examined the statuette in Malta six years later. In 1907 he was the first to give a name to the dedicatee of the statuette.

Bissing identified this name as Nefertanpet[167]. And yet it is the craftsman Neferabet who is generally acknowledged as the owner of the statuette in question[168].

The prefix *Nefer* was a very common one in the names of the ancient Egyptians. A few of the famous ones include Nefertiti and Nefertari. But there were other less known individuals, workmen from the Place of Truth,[169] like the foreman Neferhotep and the royal tomb workmen Nefersatet and Nefersenut in the Valley of the Kings. It was evidently going to be the second part of the name, the letters after the *Nefer* that would determine the name of the individual inscribed upon the statuette in question, but that was still some way down in our agenda list.

The statuette was still being preserved in Malta's Bibliotheca, the National Library, during the remainder of the nineteenth century and had apparently disappeared from public view after it was examined by Professor von Bissing in 1907[170].

In the meantime an archaeology museum proper for the archaeological artefacts was set up in 1901. This building[171] was separate from the Bibliotheca that henceforth housed only the books and archives.

It was at the turn of the twentieth century that the statuette was displayed under a glass cupola on a column and was placed next to the statue of Hercules.

During the 1920s the statuette must have disappeared from public view for a while[172] whilst the archaeological specimens were being transferred from the Xara Palace to a new museum site.

However there was at this time a fruitful visit by the Danish Egyptologist Dr Erik Iversen from the Royal Library in Copenhagen. An expert in the field of papyrus, philological and lexicographical studies, Iversen made it a point to seek out this kind of documentation outside the shores of Egypt. He studied the statuette in Malta, made his measurements and notes on it and then handed these over to the British Egyptologist Rosalind Moss.

In 1949 Moss published an article 'An Egyptian statuette in Malta,' in the *Journal of Egyptian Archaeology*[173]. She reproduced the entire repertoire of hieroglyphs that were engraved over the statuette's surfaces together with their translation. Ross also published four photographs of the statuette – the frontal one identical to that published by Zammit in 1931 (Fig. 8)

There were some important facts in this article that were significant to our investigation of the statuette's context *vis-á-vis* the information panels at the statuette's exhibition in Valletta in 2003. One vital piece of information that had been filtered out of the equation during the 2003 exhibition in Valletta was that, although she was aware of it, Moss completely ignores Sonnini's context for the statuette.

Another piece of information that had been ignored in the exhibition was that according to Ross the statuette must have originally derived from a Theban temple rather than from the Deir el Medina cemetery. She was stating this on the basis of the findings of the excavator of Neferabet's tomb, Jacques Vandier in 1935.[174].

After a reappraisal of all the available literature and other evidence, Vandier concluded that the tomb of Neferabet must have been discovered sometime between 1883 and 1908, and that several artefacts relating to Neferabet had not been originally placed inside his tomb as funerary items but rather outside of it inside a shrine. This sanctuary was not buried underground and was therefore more available to looters. It would have been rifled before the tomb, such as in the very similar instance in relation to the other craftsman from the Place of Truth, Penchenabu.[175]

The information panels at the 2003 exhibition had limited themselves to the publication by Rosalind Moss that she co-authored with Bertha Porter, namely *Ancient Egyptian Bibliography,* and specifically to the section on Private tombs in section 7 of the 'Theban Necropolis' in volume 1. Here Moss was said to have identified the source of the Egyptian statuette as Deir el Medina, and that she also provided some data about Neferabet's tomb.

When we researched this statement we came across a number of significant data that were even more useful to our enquiry.

Rosalind Moss was an anthropologist and field archaeologist and she was the co-worker and co-author of Bertha Porter, the armchair Egyptologist who conducted most of the literary research. Porter had teamed up with the Rosalind Moss in 1924, and these two British scholars co-authored the *Topographical Bibliography of ancient Egyptian Hieroglyphic Texts, Reliefs, and Paintings.*

The first volume in their series was *The Theban Necropolis* in 1927. There was a revised second edition of this first volume in 1960 and 1964, this time with the assistance of a third scholar Ethel W. Burney. Subsequent editions continued to appear. This first volume has provided a significant amount of information upon Neferabet's tomb.

Rosalind Moss was clearly and unmistakably in favour of the statuette's provenance in Gozo in 1713; any identification with Sonnini's context was neither an issue nor an option insofar as Moss was concerned. Moss concluded that since the tomb of Neferabet had been discovered between 1883 and 1886, the statuette must have originally derived from a Theban votive chapel, shrine or temple.[176]

We then looked into the publication mentioned in the exhibition, Moss and Porter's *Ancient Egyptian Bibliography*, specifically the chapter on 'Private tombs' in Section 7 of the 'Theban Necropolis' in volume 1. Once again, contrary to what was being stated in the exhibition, the published context of the statuette was that it was unambiguously found in Gozo in 1713.

There was another curious detail that puzzled us in Moss's article of 1949. Although aware that the original statuette had measured 35.56 cm [14 inches] in height in the late nineteenth century, the measurement taken by Moss was different from this reading, by a significant seven centimetres[177]. With such a striking difference in measurement, the inevitable question cropped up once more. Was the statuette on display the original one or was it not?

PART TWO

A TOMB PAINTER

Preliminary research on the painter Neferabet

Who was Neferabet, the owner of the several artefacts at the Place of Truth that are now spread out in various museums, including those of Turin and London?

Marta had already conducted some research of her own, and she submitted a number of points to me when we met one mid-morning that we were both relatively free.

We devoted all the time to an exchange of the information we had gathered individually since the previous society meeting. The session was basically a discussion on the statuette and the person to whom it would have been dedicated. Marta started the conversation as she sipped her tea. Stimulated by a piping hot espresso, I listened attentively to what she had to say.

We were still hoping to be able to investigate the family of Neferabet through the inscriptions in his tomb at Deir el-Medina. We were probing the possibility of acquiring a publication of those inscriptions that came directly from the pen of the excavator.

"It is necessary for us to take a look at the steles of Neferabet and identify his name upon them, see what hieroglyphs were being utilised for his name, and then compare them with those on the statuette," said Marta.

"Romer mentioned the fact that Neferabet 'set up several steles'; should we be thinking that 'several' signifies more than two steles, even perhaps more than one copy of each? I do not know whether the others are preserved in some museum or institution, whether they are entire artefacts or else in fragments, since no provenance is quoted in any of my reference books".

Our first lines of investigation clearly indicated that Neferabet's family had been a very successful one in the social field. His was a long career as a painter of the royal tombs at the workmen's village, and his family members seem to have been equally prestigious.

The family tree of Neferabet as presented by Heritage Malta required some modification.

For instance, his wife Taese's father was listed as Amenmose on the information panels of the Valletta exhibition of 2003, yet this was the name of Neferabet's grandfather according to Jacques Vandier, the scholar who was reading the hieroglyphs in Neferabet's tomb.

On the other hand, Neferabet's grandfather was listed as Tenhaynu in the 2003 exhibition, whereas this should have been Amenmose. So it would seem that the names had been substituted, Amenmose being the grandfather and Tenhaynu the father-in-law of Neferabet.

We were hoping to fill in the names of Neferabet's siblings who were not included in the exhibition, including that of his brother 'Anhotep; on the other hand this brother's name was amongst the hieroglyphic inscriptions on the information panels.

There are five known generations in the Neferabet line. The earliest of these was a "charmer of scorpions". From Deir el-Medina records have survived that confirm the presence of scorpion charmers amongst the community there. The *kherep serqet* was the one "who had the power over the scorpion goddess". It was a title generally assumed by the village doctor or the lector priest. His role was the prevention of bites and stings, and this was intricately related to the function of the snake charmer.

A number of spells survive that mention this problem amongst the community at the Place of Truth. Living in an environment that hosted snakes and scorpions, the ancient Egyptians developed a number of remedies to deal with the effects of their stings and bites.[178]

A spell of Amenmose survives at University College London. Written in hieratic, the *ostrakon* is in limestone, UC39606. It contains a short letter from Amenmose to a priest of the Ramesseum. He asks the priest for the ingredients of a remedy for a sick man.

"The scorpion charmer Amen-mose and the temple scribe, prophet Piay of the mansion of King Weser-Ma'at-Re Setep-en-Re, l.p.h. (the Ramesseum) in the House of Amen (on) the West of Thebes".

To the effect that: the prophet is ill. When my letter reaches [you, you] will send him one grain, one jar of syrup, one festival date-juice (?)[179].

AM

Figure 22. The palettes used by the scribe and painter in ancient Egypt. The scribal palette (front) has two depressions, for the red and black paints, with a slot for the reed brushes. The painter's palette (back) required more depressions for more colours.

THE FAMILY TREE
(as elucidated by the Vandiers)

1. AMENMOSE, the charmer of Scorpions – grandfather of our Neferabet.

2. NEFERRENPET, son of Amenmose, and his wife MAHI - parents of our Neferabet and his siblings

3. NEFERABET, 'ANHOTEP, IPUY, AMENEMOPE,[180] MERYMA'A, MERYSAKHME, I[181], NEBENTER, HOUI and PAY – sons of Neferrenpet and Mahi.[182]

TAESE, MUTNOFRET, ISETNOFRET, TENAMENTE, TENTHAY, TAYSENOFRET – daughters of Neferrenpet.[183] The mother of Taese was not Mahi but Tenthay, and so it seems that Neferrenpet had at least two wives.

4. MERON, NEDJEMGER, NEFERRENPET, PASHED, LOT and RAMOSE – sons of Neferabet.

IY, MAHI, MUTMOPE, HENTAWY, HENTTA, HETEPI, ISETNOFRET, TENTHAY, HENTONE – daughters of Neferabet.

5. RA'MERET[184] – most probably the daughter of Nedjemger, thus granddaughter of Neferabet

The other artefacts dedicated by Neferabet

The statuette that was being attributed to the workman Neferabet was evidently just one out of several artefacts that he had dedicated to his favourite deities in the Egyptian pantheon. The search for these other artefacts that had once belonged to Neferabet took us to Deir el Medina, as the Place of Truth is known today. What had the excavations there revealed and uncovered? The Italians and the French had been there at the turn of the twentieth century.

Ernesto Schiaparelli[185] excavated at Deir el Medina in Upper Egypt at the turn of the twentieth century, and he furnished us with the first photograph of the tomb of Neferabet underground. (Fig 24) Apart from this, there is unfortunately no record remaining of this excavation.

Then between 1922 and 1951 the Frenchman Bernard Bruyère led the excavations at Deir el Medina[186], and the inventory that he drew up of the artefacts relating to Neferabet provided us with what we required for our search. It significantly facilitated our investigation by telling us where to go and what to look for. There were several artefacts of Neferabet that were still around, and these were distributed in various museums and institutions that we could visit. The list furnished to us by Bruyère was a substantial one.

At the British Museum

1. A fragment of an offering table in limestone is catalogued as BM 552 [421], and is in the name of Neferabet. It is decorated with depictions of bread and cakes etc. On one of the sides of the gutter there is the name of one of the children of the deceased, Neferrenpet, and on the other side the name of one of his daughters, Mahi.[187]

2. The stele in limestone BM 693 [305] measures 64 by 42 centimetres and was set up by Neferrenpet, the son of

the deceased Neferabet. It derives from the collection of Henry Salt. It has an arched summit and bears the name of Neferabet. It is divided into four registers. In the first, five females, two standing and three sitting, perform the 'wailing task' in front of four mummies, whilst two functionaries carry out the opening of the mouth ceremony upon the deceased. Behind them are two wailers and a small girl. The scene of the embalmment appears in the second register, whilst two sons and two daughters of the deceased present the offerings. The fourth register contains extracts from Chapter I of the Book of the Dead.

The mention of several individuals has rendered this stele in particular as significantly instrumental in the elucidation of the family tree of Neferabet. We made note of this artefact as a priority item to examine when at the British Museum.

3. Another limestone stele BM 742 [150] measures 1.83 by 1.24 metres and, according to Bernard Bruyère[188], most probably derived from the chapel of Neferabet that surmounted his tomb. It incorporates five registers. On the arch at the top, two kneeling men venerate Meretseger, the serpent with the head of a female and a vessel with plumes or feathers. Eight blocks of hieroglyphs translate into "*to worship Meretseger, to scent the ground before the Peak of the West, for the ka of the śdm-'š in the Place of Truth, Neferabet, justified; his father Neferrenpet, justified; his mother the lady Mahi, justified*".

Towards the left is a destroyed picture scene of the opening of the mouth ceremony in front of a pyramid; towards the right are the wailers. The text gives a few proper names that are tackled below.

The third register shows the carriage of the coffin by the relatives and friends of the deceased and by some oxen. Here once again, and in the following registers the text includes the mention of a few other proper names.

The fourth register shows the transport of the chest of canopic jars and the case of *ushabtis*; the fifth illustrates the porters of the funerary furniture.

This stele was providing additional support for Neferabet's veneration of the goddess Meretseger and we planned to have a look at it if the opportunity came up during our planned visit to the British Museum.

4. BM limestone stele 786 [589] measures 40 by 26 centimetres and derives from the so-called Belmore collection. It has an arched top and bears the name of Neferabet. Ptah sits inside a *naos*, under a canopy in front of a table of offerings. Also depicted are four ears, symbolic of the god hearing the prayer, and the sign of *ka* and two eyes. Neferabet is shown in a kneeling position next to an engraved hymn of praises to Ptah. On the rear face of the stele are ten lines of text in honour of Ptah.

A facsimile of the stele was published by Hawkins in 1843.[189] Then Maspero translated it once again and published it in 1880.[190] The German scholar Erman retranslated it in 1911[191] and once again another translation was furnished by Gunn in 1916.[192] The standard translation that is used nowadays is that of Miriam Lichtheim and we utilised that version for our research[193].

This stele was clearly dedicated to Ptah, most likely in relation to Neferabet's episode of temporary blindness, and we earmarked it as another priority item to examine once we visited the British Museum.

5. The fifth item that Bruyère listed as preserved at the British Museum was a mural fragment in limestone, or possibly the base of a large stele, that measures fifteen by fifty centimetres. The inscription had been copied from the original by Jaroslav Černý in 1929 and comprises a register with porters of furniture. There are seven men depicted, the first four representing the four sons of Neferabet, namely Neferrenpet, Ramose, Nedjemger and Meron. The relationship with Neferabet of the sixth and seventh individuals, the painters Ipuy[194] and Pashed, was not

indicated. The seventh individual was a sculptor but his name is no longer visible.

Since Ipuy is in Neferabet's funerary procession one can safely assume that Neferabet pre-deceased him. This Ipuy was most likely his brother, the painter who later became foreman.

At the *Museo Egizio* in Turin

Bruyère's catalogue also indicated a number of artefacts from the Egyptian Museum in Turin that related to Neferabet and to the goddess Meretseger. These looked very promising and prompted a visit in the very near future.

1. The upright or post of a door, and this bears the names of Ipuy, Nebamente and Neferabet.

2. Artefact 6151 measures 80 by 30 centimetres and is a fragment of a square limestone pillar or an obelisk with the name of Neferabet.

3. Stele 102 is a votive monument that was dedicated to Meretseger.

4. The base of a limestone stele, catalogue number 9510, depicts a large quantity of offerings to Meretseger by Neferabet and by Prahotep[195].

In the Museum of Egyptian Antiquities in Cairo

During our previous visits to the Cairo Museum of antiquities we had not identified any of the artefacts listed by Bruyère as being held there. They would either have been in storage at the time; or else we could have very easily passed them by and missed them. We would look out for them should another opportunity to visit the museum present itself. There were three items altogether that related to our Neferabet.

1. A wooden latch that was acquired in Gournah in 1916 and gives the names of Neferabet and his son Neferrenpet; this is listed in the Cairo Museum with catalogue number 44514.

2. and 3. These are two fragments of limestone painted in golden yellow and measuring 20 centimetres in height and respectively 40 and 50 centimetres in width. They were acquired in Luxor in 1929 and represent the same scene, namely a cortege of standing men and women bearing offerings to a sitting couple, Neferrenpet with his wife on the first fragment, and Neferabet with his wife on the second. These fragments would have either derived from a lintel or simply represented the registers of a stele.

Marta attempted to read the hieroglyphs from the photographs published by Vandier,[196] but the only translation that could be made out was a partial one, 'his son ... daughter, mistress of the house'.

The Museum of Rennes

We had not visited this museum that holds a fragment of an upright of a door, with Catalogue number 104. It derives from the ancient collection of the *Bibliotheque Nationale*, and is catalogued by Ledrain as No. 27. It depicts two kneeling males, and the text reads "*the śdm-'š (servant) in the Place of Truth, Neferabet, justified ...*"

The Museum in Brussels

We had not visited this museum either. A limestone fragment of a statue's base measuring 11 by 6 by 4 centimetres gives the name of "*the śdm-'š in the Place of Truth, Neferabet, justified*" and of Neferrenpet. It is listed in Speelers Catalogue as E 291.

Figure 23. The Skylight stele would have been positioned in the niche of the pyramidal structure above the chapel.

Deir el Medina

A small number of artefacts have come to light directly from the Place of Truth.; the modern tomb raiders had left them there. These were excavated by Bruyère shortly before Vandier's publication in 1935. They would have been preserved with the finds of the French Archaeological team at the time and later presented to the Egyptian Museum. A few have ended up in the Louvre. It has not been possible to elucidate the present whereabouts of all these artefacts from Bruyère's excavations.

1. The Skylight Stele in limestone, measuring 60 by 40 centimetres[197], was found by Bruyère in 1929 at the bottom of the shaft No. 1195. The stele is today preserved at the Louvre[198]. Inside the arch is the solar boat and below this a register, *"Meretseger, the Peak, serpent goddess with the head of a woman, is venerated by the śdm-ˁś in the Place of Truth, Neferabet"*. Damaged segments of another two registers are also visible.

2. A fragment of the left half of the lintel of a door giving the name of Neferabet and his wife Taese.

3. Two fragments deriving from the base of a statue. The first fragment is from the central part and gives the name of Neferabet followed by that of his father Neferrenpet. The second fragment is from the left side of the base and gives the name of Mahi, the mother of Neferabet.

4. The last two fragments derive from the excavations of Deir el Medina and were found in the magazines without a note of their provenance. They formed parts of a doorpost, but although deriving respectively from the left and right sides, they do not seem to match one another, and none of them appear to match the one preserved at the Museum in Rennes. There were therefore at least three pairs of doorposts bearing the name of Neferabet.

5. At the time that Vandier was finalising his publication in 1935, a fragment of an offering table at Deir el

Medina also gave the name of Neferabet. Its whereabouts have not been elucidated.

During the excavations by Bruyère an amount of pottery was found engraved with the marks of ownership by Neferabet. There were two options available to explain these. If they were excavated from anywhere close to the tomb they would have derived from the pillaged funerary offerings. On the other hand, if they were excavated from inside the village itself, or from the garbage post, they would have originated from his household.

There was yet another artefact worth mentioning. In her article of 1949 Moss pointed out an artefact that once formed part of a statue or column and was inscribed with the name of "Neferabet, Servant at the Place of Truth".

This derived from the notebook of the renowned British Egyptologist, J. Gardner Wilkinson, already mentioned above. The artefact had formed part of the Giovanni d'Athanasi's collection of antiquities.[199]

There are the cartouches of Amenhotep I, Ahmose Nefertari and her daughter Meritamen on the same artefact.[200]

As Marta explained, "this inscription shows that the patrons at the Place of Truth had deified and worshipped Queen Ahmose Nefertari and her two children, the Pharaoh Amenhotep I and sister wife Meritamen".

There were a number of other institutions that preserved artefacts of Neferabet at Deir el Medina. By the time of publication we had not had the opportunity of observing and examining all of these because of the nature of their conservation. A few were in the act of being restored, others were on loan and a number were still being processed by the authorities who were responsible for them. Yet the documentary evidence was available and we scanned this in our search for further details on our painter.

We planned visits to the institutions that preserved some of these artefacts, and we started off with the ones that were closest to home.

There were at least three museums that held ancient Egyptian artefacts in northern Italy, and so when my old friend Frank invited me to Florence for a few days, I planned to visit all three of them. These were the *Museo Archeologico di Etruria* in Florence, the *Museo Egizio* in Turin, and the section on ancient Egypt in the *Museo di Bologna*. The *Museo Egizio* housed a number of artefacts from the tomb-workers' village at the Place of Truth.

We hoped to be able to investigate the family of Neferabet further through the inscriptions on the steles held at these institutions. The key artefact was the one held at the Museo Egizio in Turin. This was Neferabet's dedicatory stele to Meretseger.

The opportunity to visit the museums in northern Italy came up rather unexpectedly.

Florence, Bologna and Turin

I had no choice in the matter. Frank called one day to tell me that I was booked with *Ryanair*. The flight to Pisa was to happen on the 9th November, with a return to Malta five days later.

This arrangement suited me just fine. If I managed to visit all three of these museums, then the trip would really be worth the while. The *Museo Egizio* was the one that we knew held the artefacts of Neferabet and Meretseger, but the other two could very possibly yield something interesting for the other research projects that we had lined up.

Frank volunteered to pick me up on the 9th, but the airport at Pisa was covered with dense mist and the landing lights were insufficient to guide the aircraft to a safe landing. So we were diverted to Genova.

I got through to Frank on his mobile immediately after landing and acquainted him with developments. He had already driven the one hundred kilometre stretch of motorway from Florence to Pisa. His initial suggestion was for me to take the train to Milan and await him there on the morrow. But I was restricted for time and the morrow was reserved for the Museum of Archaeology in Florence.

Mist was fast accumulating along the motorways and it would be much worse in a few hours, explained Frank. So we agreed to meet in about four hours in Florence at the railway or coach station there. Frank took the motorway back to Florence and awaited me, initially at the flat, where he prepared *lasagne*, and then at the station in Florence. It took us till 22.30 to reach Pisa by Pullman coach, by which time the last train from Pisa to Florence had already left.

Alternative transport arrangements were provided by the *Terravision* airport transfer coach and it was at midnight when we reached Florence. Frank was there at the station, having abstained from the *lasagne* on my account so that we could partake of it together. It was at two in the morning that this was finally realisable - a fantastic meal that went very well with the red wine of year 2000. Frank had purposely brought it over from his cellar in Milan just for the occasion. All the inconveniences of the evening were cast aside and our moods brightened up in anticipation of the photography sessions that we were planning together of the archaeological artefacts in the North of Italy.

Egyptology in Florence

I was up the next morning by 06.30 and after a quick breakfast we were off together by walk along the *Via Pier Luigi da Palestrina* and the *Via delle Porte Nuove* until we reached the junction of the two main avenues – the *Viale Belfiore* and the *Viale Fratelli Rosselli* - at the *Porta al Prato*. Here we parted. Frank was all geared to wrap up his week at the office and I was to start my excursions in Florence.

There were two targets for me that morning, and I had to see to both before Frank called me back to his flat for the drive to Milan. It was a fantastic morning, and I was in Florence for the first time in my life. This was the city of the Renaissance, the land of the Medici dynasty, the home of the Neo-Platonic school and the great masters – Leonardo da Vinci, Raphael and Michelangelo.

Walking would have consumed vital time and so I took a taxi to the *Piazza della Santissima Annunziata*. The *Museo Archeologico di Etruria* was right there in the corner on the *Via della Colonna*, number 9. The 'Lonely Planet' guide book had told me it would be open at nine, but a notice on the door informed me otherwise – for some reason it would open its doors to the public at 10.15, and that was forty-five minutes away, so I walked round the square and scanned the environs.

It was a few minutes after 10.30 that we could hear the doors being unbolted from the inside. A four-euro ticket got me in, and I immediately purchased a small catalogue of the archaeological collection there, basically to cater for the eventuality that I would not be allowed to take photographs. As it turned out non-flash photography was allowed and I availed myself of it freely.

The ground floor was reserved for the classical period, but I did not spend too much time there and was soon going up the stairs to the first floor to view the Egyptian collection. I was impressed by the determination of a seven-year old girl who, despite a serious gait problem, was managing very well to keep up with her school mates as they went up the wooden stairway.

A number of Egyptian artefacts were being exhibited along the hallways on the first floor, but the main collection was housed in a number of sizeable exhibition halls, or 'Sale', that were numbered in reverse order from XI to I.

There was a splendid chariot in pristine condition that attracted the immediate attention of everyone who came in its proximity. This would have been similar to one of the chariots used by Tutankhamen before he presumably fell off it and fractured his femur. So many of the pharaohs would have led their armies and shot their arrows at the enemy as they sped along on a chariot such as the one on exhibition.

The last *Sala* contained the oldest artefacts, and these included two fantastic vases with Naqada boats that necessitated a long sequence of photographs from all angles to get the boats adequately documented. These I was very keen to photograph as fully as I could for later research as well as for our archives. We were planning to use the Naqada boats for one of our forthcoming publications.

There were no artefacts relating to our Neferabet or any of his colleagues from Deir el Medina, and I had known well beforehand that I would most probably have to wait until I got to Turin before finding something in this vein. Nevertheless the collection was an extremely valuable one and provided a large amount of material for our other themes in Egyptology.

The weather was very nice, and after leaving the museum I walked back towards Frank's flat at a leisurely pace, with a detour for me to visit the famous *Piazza della Signoria* with its renowned statuary by Michelangelo, Raphael and other famous artists of the Renaissance, and of course its centrepiece, Poseidon's[201] fountain. Several of the original works of art had been transferred indoors in museums and other institutions for safe keeping, but the copies that replaced them outdoors were very good facsimiles.

I was particularly fascinated by the figures comprising the fountain. There was a larger than life statue of Poseidon at the very top, and four elf-like creatures were spread around the rim of the fountain. In between were two female statues at the feet of Poseidon that were meant by the sculptor Ammanati to represent two of the Nereids in Poseidon's retinue.

Whilst I was engaged in photography of the fountain, I received a mobile call from Frank urging me to be at the flat at the earliest for us to go to Milan and avoid the weekend traffic congestion. So I hurriedly left the piazza and walked at a fast pace until I eventually reached the *Porta al Prato*, then the *Via delle Porte Nuove* and finally the apartment in *Via Pier Luigi da Palestrina*.

Within twenty minutes we were in Frank's *Audi A4*, racing off along the motorway in a northwesterly direction towards his home and family in Milan. I had not seen Pascale and the children, Mark and Dominique, for a while and I looked forward to meeting up with them again. There was a fantastic dinner prepared in my honour and I was flattered.

Frank knew about my plans and the 2002 red wine that he selected from his cellar placed him in an exceptionally generous mood. He very kindly suggested during dessert that on the morrow the five of us should go southwest from Milan to Turin to see the Egyptian museum there. This was much more than I had ever hoped for.

Frank had furthermore promised me that he would drop me in Bologna on the Monday on his way back to Florence. I thought that if I made it to the museum there on the Monday morning, I would have managed to visit the top three Egyptian museums in the North of Italy in a matter of five days, literally over an extended weekend.

The *Museo Egizio*

We initially planned to go to Turin by train, but by the morning Frank decided to go there at our leisure in his *Audi*.

The autostrada got us there in no time at all. In the centre of the main roundabout leading to the town centre a giant statue of a sphinx announced the Egyptological Museum. Once in the *Via Giulio Cesare* we looked out for parking and within a few minutes managed to find a slot in the *Parcheggio San Stefano*. A short walk towards the *Via Giuseppe Garibaldi* took us to the large square with the museum at its corner. Two larger than life *Sekhmet* statues flanked the sides of its main entrance.

The *Muzeo Egizio* was out of this world. No wonder it is rated as second only to the Museum of Antiquities in Cairo. The Italian excavator Ernesto Schiaparelli[202] had been a major contributor of the finds from ancient Egypt that are displayed there, and a bronze statue of him at the entrance commemorated this.

The good news was that Schiaparelli had taken the earliest photograph of Neferabet's tomb; that was in 1908. This had shown no artefacts visible inside the tomb and I therefore presumed that he had transported what he had found there to the museum in Turin. I was already aware of the stele to Meretseger, Turin Museum 102 (50058), that was known to be preserved there. The prospect of finding other artefacts from Neferabet's tomb seemed all the more likely.

Schiaparelli had found a number of intact tombs at Deir el Medina, and these included that of the foreman Kha and his wife Merit. The contents were transported *in toto* to the museum there.[203] Other excavators from other countries discovered other mummies and they took these to their own museums back home. The tomb workmen's mummies are therefore now spread out all over the globe. Families have been split up. Whilst the mummy of Senedjem is in Cairo, that of his wife is in the Metropolitan in New York and that of his daughter-in-law is preserved in Berlin.

The museum entrance led into the first hall, a large area that was circular in shape. It was beautifully laid out with display cabinets with very well illustrated artefacts. Once again the Naqada boats on pottery fascinated me and there were several examples on exhibit. However this time

AM

Figure 24. The southern wall of the second chamber. This is the first photograph of Neferabet's tomb; it was taken by Ernesto Schiaparelli in 1908.

round these painted ceramics were surpassed by the remarkable boat paintings on the papyrus fragments that had been found in Middle Egypt at Gebelein and were being exhibited in one of the halls in the basement. Photography was availed of to document all that I could, and the illumination inside the halls was sufficient to get good quality photographs without the need for additional lighting through flash; this was prohibited as in the norm.

Once again I did not miss the opportunity of photographing any artefact that might be valuable for our future research on themes other than Neferabet. In one hall to the left were displayed the remarkable remains of the world-renowned Turin papyrus that had sadly suffered in recent times after surviving the millennia. This papyrus with the Ramessid Canon of kings had allegedly been discovered

141

at Deir el-Medina. In its brilliantly restored and repaired state it still forms a crucial part of the documentation for the ancient Egyptian dynasties and pharaohs. In the same hall copies of the Palermo stone and the Abydos list represented the other sources for the documentation of the Egyptian dynasties.

The magnificent hall that held the life size statuary was out of this world. The lightly but strategically illuminated hall provided a divine atmosphere that alas was not ideal for photography.

The topmost floor was dedicated principally to the mummies that were brought over to Italy by some of the Italian excavators at the turn of the twentieth century. Besides the numbers of Graeco-Roman sarcophagi and mummies there were also a few from the Late Period and some from the New Kingdom.

I was struck with the appearance of one particular mummy face that was visible inside its sarcophagus and wondered what sort of degradation processes would still be going on slowly inside the tissues. The environmental temperature and humidity were not being monitored or maintained at a constant level as in the Royal Mummy Room in Cairo, and yet all seemed to be well preserved.

There were a number of lengthy papyri that were framed and made to hang next to one another upon the walls. Some of these had derived from Deir el Medina, and one in particular bore the name of the 'Turin Strike Papyrus'. It had been composed by one of Neferabet's nephews in his position as village scribe. It is singular in being the first document to register workmen's strikes in the Valley of the Kings.

Another discovery from Deir el-Medina that was displayed there was the 19th Dynasty limestone stele of Parahotep, a servant at the 'Place of Truth'. This showed the cult of the deified pharaoh Amenhotep I together with the gods Amen-Re and Meretseger[204].

It is a well known fact that it had been Amenhotep I and his mother Ahmose Nefertari who had established the village of the royal craftsmen at the 'Place of Truth'. The cult of this deified couple was very popular there, as could be gauged from the several representations that were found of them in the village.

Also on this top floor of the museum I came across a most revealing artefact[205] that provided us with a near perfect analogy for our statuette. I had not fully appreciated this very interesting parallel at the time that I was there. The similarities to the statue of Neferabet were superficially noted and registered, yet it was Marta who exploited it to the maximum as we were later perusing the gallery of photographs from the *Museo Egizio*. (Fig. 25)

The dedicatee was Penchenabu[206], a craftsman at the Place of Truth, and he was kneeling in front of an offering table surmounted by the head of Amen-Re in his guise as a Ram. There were representations of deities on his upper arms. These were painted over, or possibly tattooed; on his right shoulder was Amen-Re and on his left the deified Ahmose Nefertari, the patroness of the Place of Truth. The inscribed hieroglyphs dated the statue of Penchenabu to the time of Rameses II.[207] According to Lise Manniche commenting upon this artefact, it was important for these 'simple private people, who were non-royal and non-official, to prove their devotion towards one or the other numerous deities or divinities of the Egyptian pantheon'[208].

It was approximately double the size of the Maltese statuette of Neferabet, and was similarly made out of limestone, but it was painted all over, mainly in white and black. The wig was similar to that of Neferabet. We had seen traces of residual black paint upon the wig of Neferabet, and it was most probable that the statue of the latter had also been painted all over. Both statues are dated to the reign of Rameses II and this has been based upon stylistic grounds of the wig and kilt styles. During this period the wigs were sculpted with more fluidity than usual.[209]

The provenance of Penchenabu's statue was in many ways similar to that of Neferabet. They had both been discovered approximately a century before their respective tombs were discovered. Penchenabu's statue was acquired by the *Museo Egizio* in 1824, a century before the discovery of TT322 at Deir el Medina. Both statues had most probably been discovered in a chapel or small temple context and were thus looted before the discovery of the respective tombs of their owners.

The statuette commissioned by Neferabet seems to have been the only one with a triad of gods that has survived from amongst those set up by the workmen at the Place of Truth. But there have been other statuettes that derived from the workmen's village and its environs and these too provide us with a glimpse of their dedicants.

Some of the workmen at the Place of Truth were exceptional artisans and some of the very best were even commissioned by officials from Thebes visiting the village to manufacture statuettes for them. These public officers were usually represented on these statuettes together with their consorts. Contrasting sharply with those of the village workmen, these commissioned statuettes were very precisely carved either in limestone or in wood, and a fine example of the latter is the statuette of an 'inspector' of the craftsmen at the Place of Truth at the beginning of the 19th Dynasty. His name was Amenemopet. His proper designation was to be seen in the hieroglyphs that ran down the front of his skirt. Marta read them as 'Amenemopet ... for the *ka* of the king's scribe.' Like the vizier, his function at the village was in a supervising capacity, and since he was not a craftsman, he did not reside in the village. [210]

The Peak of the West

Towards the end of my tour of the top floor I entered a side corridor and finally came upon Meretseger. She was being

AM

Figure 25. The workman Penchenabu presents a single
deity, the ram, symbolic of Amen-Re.

displayed in a number of well illuminated showcases with excellent labels.

But just then a problem came up that threatened to bring the visit to the *Museo Egizio* to a premature conclusion. By that time we had already spent two hours in the museum, and that was a relatively long time when considering that there were two impatient adolescents in the group. Mark and Dominque had just about had enough by the time I found the 'Goddess of the Peak'.

I had to negotiate and do it fast if I wanted to have sufficient extra time for Meretseger. On the spur of the moment I first promised them that the side corridor in question would definitely be the last item on my agenda for that morning, and secondly I invited them all to lunch at a restaurant of their choice. They liked my proposition immediately and I made the most of it while they discussed the options.

One portion of an exhibition case was totally dedicated to the goddess Meretseger, identified in antiquity with a pyramid-shaped mountain that dominated the Valley of the Kings. This mountain peak in the Valley is one amongst several others on the West Bank of Thebes. The inhabitants of the 'Place of Truth' worshipped this patroness of their village with small monuments, some of which they carved and painted themselves. As already hinted at, Meretseger was venerated along with Ptah in a cave sanctuary near the Workmen's village, along the path towards the Valley of the Queens.

The association between Meretseger and the serpent was unavoidably demonstrable in the artefacts that were being displayed there.

The most conspicuous amongst these was a limestone statue of a few feet in height that depicted the goddess with a female head and the body of a cobra. According to the information board, she was the 'protector' goddess of the village of Deir el-Medina, but was also 'ferocious in her punishment of those who disobeyed her'.

Courtesy of the Museo Egizio, Turin   AM

Figure 26. The statue of Meretseger, the 'Goddess of the Peak'.

This statue of hers was dated to between the 18th and 20th Dynasty, and would most likely have been around the village at the time of Neferabet. (Fig. 26)

To the right of the statue of the goddess was a limestone stele of Wab (Fig. 27), one of the workmen at the village during the 19th Dynasty. The deceased was in the kneeling position and in the act of veneration. In front of him were twelve serpents that were placed one above the other. All of these represented Meretseger.

There were three other artefacts that derived from Deir el-Medina and these were displayed upon the shelf right above these two representations of Meretseger; all were dated to the 19th dynasty. The first on our left was a small painted stele fragment where Meretseger was represented as a standing cobra.

Next, in the centre of the display cabinet was the limestone stele of Nebre, the painter of Amen at the 'Place of Truth'. Nebre was kneeling in the act of veneration in front of Meretseger and yet another serpent goddess, Renenutet. It seems that the latter goddess was represented in a variety of forms, this time round as a serpent on a podium in the form of a temple.

Right next to the stele of Nebre, on my right as I faced the display case, was another limestone stele where the goddess Meretseger was shown in two registers in the form of two cobras.

Neferabet's stele

Insofar as I was concerned, the stele of Neferabet's prayer to Meretseger was the star of the show. (Fig. 29) It was preserved as artefact number 102, Catalogue number 50058. It had derived from Deir el-Medina and I had finally found it. Its exact provenance is not known and this is owing to the plundering of artefacts from the site in the early nineteenth century.

Stele di Uab. La defunta è inginocchiata in adorazione di dodici serpenti sovrapposti, tutte rappresentazioni di Meretseger, venerata in una grotta presso Deir el-Medina. Calcare. Deir el-Medina. Nuovo Regno, XIX dinastia (1292-1186 a.C.). C. 1533

Stele of Wab. The deceased is kneeling in adoration before twelve serpents one above the other, all representations of Meretseger, venerated in a cave near Deir el-Medina. Limestone. Deir el-Medina. New Kingdom, Dynasty XIX (1292-1186 BC). C. 1533

Figure 27. The Stele of Wab dedicated to Meretseger

149

Rather than the inside of the tomb itself, the modern consensus of opinion favours the source of the stele in question as one of the small designated temples at the Place of Truth.[211] Neferabet himself would have actually handled this very stone and selected its placing alongside that to Ptah, possibly within the cave sanctuary outside the village along the footpath. He would also have instructed the engraver on its layout and what the contents of the hieroglyphs upon it should read.

It took the form of a rectangular limestone slab measuring 54 centimetres by 20. Meretseger was depicted on the right side of the stele as a serpent with one human and two serpent heads. She lay beneath a legend that identified her as 'Meretseger, Lady of heaven, Mistress of the Two Lands, whose good name is Peak of the West'.

In front of Meretseger was an offering stand, and to her left was the hymn in seventeen columns that covered the remaining entire surface of the stele.

The English translation provided by Miriam Lichtheim[212] has been utilised here.

"Giving praise to the Peak of the West,
Kissing the ground to her *ka*,
I give praise, hear my call,
I was a truthful man on earth!
Made by the servant in the Place-of-Truth, Neferabu, justified.

"I was an ignorant man and foolish,
Who knew not good from evil;
I did the transgression against the Peak,
And she taught a lesson to me.
I was in her hand by night as by day,
I sat on bricks like the woman in labour,
I called to the wind; it came not to me,
I libated to the Peak of the West, great of strength,
And to every god and goddess.

VF

Figure 28. One of the present authors in 2002, under the conspicuous 'Peak of the West' in the Valley of the Kings.

Courtesy of Museo Egizio   *AM*

Figure 29. Turin stele 102. Neferabet's hymn to Meretseger.

"Behold, I will say to the great and small,
Who are in the troop: Beware of the Peak!
For there is a lion within her!
The Peak strikes with the stroke of a savage lion,
She is after him who offends her!
"I called upon my mistress,
I found her coming to me as sweet breeze;
She was merciful to me,
Having made me see her hand.
"She returned to me appeased,
She made my malady forgotten;
For the Peak of the West is appeased,
If one calls upon her. So says Neferabu, justified.
He says: Behold, let hear every ear that lives upon earth:
Beware the Peak of the West!"

According to Bierbrier, Neferabet had set up his stele to Meretseger, as well as that dedicated to Ptah, in the cave sanctuary that was established for the use of the inhabitants of the Workmen's Village.[213]

In all probability this was the shrine that was known as 'Ptah, South of His Wall'. Ptah was god of the crafts, and thus patron of all craftsmen. This was precisely what the population at Deir el Medina was.

Neferabet's stele to Ptah was no longer close to that to Meretseger. This was then still being preserved at the British Museum and we planned to examine it at some later date.

I had managed to complete my task in Meretseger's corridor. By that time Frank's children had predictably selected MacDonald's for lunch. We spent about an hour there, most of this time spent going over the photographs with Frank who had taken his own set. Several of these were even better than my own, and, as we normally do, we agreed to exchange copies.

We drove back to Milan after this, reaching the city at 17.30. There was sufficient time for some shopping at the centre and I joined them, getting a birthday present for my daughter Tabitha in the form of a *Carpisa* shoulder bag that she had much wished for and indirectly asked me to get her. I spent the remainder of the time at the IPER complex going through the various items of electronic equipment, yet totally resisting all temptation to purchase anything and adding to my restricted luggage weight on my return journey to Malta by *Ryanair*.

Once we were back at Frank's apartment I had sufficient time to charge all the photographic equipment. Frank and I exchanged the photographs we had individually taken. Between the both of us we had each covered practically everything inside the museum, and furthermore we each had taken a few remarkable shots that we gloated over as we went over them on the laptop.

Whilst Pascale prepared dinner, Frank and I checked on the museum at Bologna for opening days and hours. Our suspicions had been correct – it was not open on Mondays. We then checked on the Florence museum where I had already been a few days earlier. This was open between 14.00 and 19.00 on Mondays. We would probably reach Florence late morning on the Monday, and another visit to the Etruria museum there would be well worth the while, if only to see the Etruscan Amazon sarcophagus that I had only picked up on the catalogue after my first visit there.

But was there any possibility at all that I could visit the museum at Bologna at some time in the morning of the Tuesday? The flight back to Malta was at 15.30, and I would be loaded with my luggage. Frank suggested that I could leave the luggage in front of the train station in Bologna with persons he knew there, so that solved a bit of the problem for me.

The other difficulty was finding sufficient time to see the artefacts in the museum after nine in the morning on the Tuesday when I would have to be at Pisa at 13.00 for checking-in. There was a train from Bologna to Pisa at 10.30, and if I could take the 7.00 train to Bologna and be there well before 9.00, I would walk as fast as I could to the museum and make it there in about twenty minutes. I could photograph Neptune's fountain in the square before opening time at 9.00, visit the museum and then walk back in time to reach the 10.30 train to Pisa. That left me with barely an hour. Was it worth it? I thought it was. I could always get the catalogue for what artefacts I would not have had the time to see and photograph.

Frank agreed that if an hour at the museum was sufficient for me, then the plan should work. He would drop me at the train station in Florence on Monday morning, and I would be able to sort out all the tickets there before visiting the museum.

Once again it was a fantastic meal with fabulous red wine selected by Frank for the occasion. The morrow was planned for Milan with lunch close to the *Duomo*. We managed to see all the interesting sights in the town centre and my hosts even allowed me to fulfil part of my obligations and pay for lunch.

Florence once again and Bologna

The return drive from Milan to Florence was in the early morning, and this time the 'mista nebbia' was making driving difficult. At times there was barely 20 metres visibility, especially when close to the cultivated fields all around us. When we stopped for fuel, we managed to get a city map of Bologna in order for me to find the museum and its orientation in relation to the train station. Once I had identified the train station in the *Piazza Medaglie d'Oro* and the Archaeology Museum in the *Via del Archiginnasio*, it was mere child's play to link them up – very simply through the long but straight *Via dell'Indipendenza* that directly connects them through the *Piazza Nettuno* and *Piazza Maggiore*.

In the square opposite the museum, the *Piazza Nettuno*, there was that other fountain of Poseidon, similar

154

to the one I had seen in Florence[214], and this was definitely worth visiting. I could do that precisely just before museum opening time. The walk from the station would take me approximately twenty minutes if I were not loaded with my *Reebok* backpack. The plan at the time was for me to leave this with Frank's acquaintance at the Star Hotel in the *Piazza Medaglie d'Oro* right in front of the train station in Bologna.

As we were entering Florence a mobile call informed Frank that there was an urgent meeting convened for him at 10.30, and he was thus obliged to drop me off before reaching his apartment in Florence. So I asked him to hold on to my *Reebok* as I alighted on the *Viale Belfiore* at its intersection with the *Via G. Monaco*. The instructions from Frank were simply to walk along the road and that would lead me to the train station through the *Via Luigi Alamanni*.

At the *Informazione* desk of the train station I asked for the possibility of getting from Florence to Bologna by train and then from Bologna to Pisa on the morrow, the Tuesday. The lady behind the counter very kindly gave me a printout of the schedules. So I proceeded to the *Biglietteria* and got a ticket for 07.00 hours from *Firenze Santa Maria Novella* to *Bologna Centrale*, and another for the 10.30 train from *Bologna Centrale* to *Pisa Aeroporto*. I calculated that I should be at the airport in Pisa at 12.55, and that gave me ample time to check in for the 15.30 flight. The young woman issuing the tickets reminded me to have them *convalidati* through the small yellow contraptions before boarding the train.

I toured Florence that morning until I reached the Museum of Archaeology and I visited all its halls once again. The Etruscan sarcophagus occupied most of my time there. I required it for another project and so I took a number of photographs to document it as best I could.

In the evening Frank took me to Pisa airport in order to deposit my luggage there and save myself carrying it around with me the following morning at the museum in Bologna. He also prepared a fantastic plate of pasta.

The next morning I accompanied Frank to his office and then continued by walk to the train station. I was well in time and took a few of my typewritten notes out to edit *en route*.

The train reached the station at Bologna on time at 8.14. Frank had already logged in at the office and then sent me a short text message informing me that according to most recent update on the return flight from Pisa to Malta by *Ryanair* that day, the time of departure from Pisa had been re-scheduled to 17.10. That gave me another two hours in Bologna if I wanted, but I thought that I would rather keep to my plan of travel and time of my arrival at Pisa airport.

The walk to the museum from the station was a very straightforward one. It was a simple traipse down the *Via della Indipendenza*, unfortunately beneath the arches that prevented me from getting a GPS signal on my wrist-held *Garmin*. I reached the *Piazza Nettuno* in a few minutes and Giambologna's fountain of Poseidon occupied my Sony camera until it was opening time.

The museum lay across the square at the start of the *Via dell'Archiginnasio*. Entrance was free, and all the staff was extremely obliging and charming. The section on the Egyptian antiquities was one floor below ground, and was distributed along a wide and massive corridor with the display cabinets on either side. There was a clearly marked separation of the main divisions of the Egyptian dynasties. The Old, Middle, New and Late Kingdoms followed one other in a harmonious arrangement of artefacts. The first corridor was entirely dedicated to Horemheb's[215] tomb, and in fact the star items of this museum were the five limestone reliefs that were discovered at his tomb in Saqqara by a 19 year old Amalia Nizzoli[216].

All the artefacts on display were immaculately labelled. Photography was allowed as in all the other museums in northern Italy.

It was in the New Kingdom section that one of the *ushabtis* in a group labelled as number 15 caught my attention. The function of these funerary statuettes was to perform tasks in the Underworld on behalf of the deceased. These *ushabtis* on display had derived from the 'Palagi Collection'. Palagi was the person to whom the husband of the above mentioned Amalia had sold his Egyptian collection. They were all dated to between the 18th and 20th dynasties. One of these *ushabtis* bore a striking similarity to the prototype of the dedicatee of the triad in Malta, both in the headpiece as well as in his attire. The vertical register of hieroglyphs that ran down the lower half of the statuette would later occupy sometime of ours to decipher.

The other item that was of interest to our research was a varied collection of funerary cones. We had one in Malta that had evidently been imported and was displayed at the St Agatha museum next to the Old Capital, in Rabat on mainland Malta. Marta and I had researched it and with the varied range of funerary cones that I photographed there I envisaged an interesting comparative exercise.

I managed to cover the entire repertoire of artefacts at the museum and I was ready to leave for the station at 10.20 but I just missed the 10.30 train. So I sorted out the tickets at the *Biglietteria* in the train station, knowing full well that I would still be in time for the 17.10 flight, and took the 11.45 train to Pisa via Florence.

The train to Pisa

As the train rolled on through the densely foliated and multi-coloured plains of northern Italy, I had all the time in the world to review all that I had seen by way of artefacts that were related to our present theme. Dedicatees presenting triads of gods were not very common but we had seen a handful. The one in Malta was the only one of its kind insofar as its source was concerned. The one of Penchenabu that I had seen in Turin from the same site in the Place of Truth was limited to one deity, that of Amen.

I had also seen similar statuettes with triads though the dedicants in these cases were all of a senior status than the tomb workmen.

My mind went backward in time to one of my 2001 visit to the Museum of Egyptian Antiquities in Cairo and the Luxor Museum of Ancient Egyptian Art where I had come across two similar statuettes presenting triads[217].

Both statuettes had derived from Karnak in Thebes. The former had been found in the temple context rather than in a tomb, and the same probably applied to the latter. Thus the positioning of the statuette of Neferabet in a temple context rather than in a funerary one would satisfactorily explain the otherwise impossible situation where the statuette would have been discovered in a funerary context that had not yet been exposed at the time.

I was in Pisa airport just over an hour before flight time but this was not sufficient for *Ryanair* to accept me on board. The papers had already been sent to the captain. I had lost my flight and was obliged to return to Florence to a surprised Frank. I thought that I should make the most of the two-day delay, and so I planned my itinerary that evening as Frank and I once again indulged in another good meal with an excellent Italian red wine.

I was back in Pisa on the morrow and saw the leaning tower of Galileo and then travelled by train to Milan to baby sit Frank's children overnight whilst Pascale flew to Poland. The delay had not been that useless after all.

Once back in Malta I scanned the photographs with Marta, particularly the ones with Meretseger. The statue of Penchenabu was also important for it gave us a better idea of how the statuette of Neferabet might have looked like in its pristine condition.

The British Museum

The steles of Neferabet at the British Museum were preserved in the Department of Egypt and Sudan[218]. Marta and I decided to see these together. The main artefact there was Neferabet's stele to Ptah that, according to Morris Bierbrier, would have been positioned in the shrine of "Ptah, south of his wall" next to that to Meretseger.

I had already been to the DES in 2003 when Nigel Strudwick very kindly made arrangements for me to examine the four funerary steles that were discovered buried together in Malta late in 1829. Three of them were dated to the Twelfth Dynasty and the fourth to the Eighteenth. They had also been studied by British Egyptologist Margaret Murray when she was analysing the ancient Egyptian material that had been found on Malta.

So five years down the line I contacted Nigel once again and asked him to let me see the steles of Neferabet and possibly also the four Bighi steles once again. He very generously volunteered to fish them out of storage for us, also offering us the facility to examine them all at our leisure. Once we provided him with the catalogue numbers, the process for him to trace and pick them out was not an elaborate one.

Our appointment was set up for 31 March 2008. We flew to London for the day and reached the Information Desk of the British Museum at the appointed hour; they then got us in touch with the DES. A kind gentleman at the other end informed us that Dr Strudwick was in the United States, but a Dr O'Connell was in charge in his absence and was expecting us if we were the people from Malta.

We signed the visitors' book at the DES and followed the kindly gentleman who greeted us; he eventually introduced himself as Neal Spencer. He led us up to a large hall. There the artefacts that we had requested had been brought together on a large table. The illumination through the large windows was excellent. We later found out that Dr Neal Spencer was the assistant keeper at the DES.

Six slabs of stone lay upon a layer of white fabric on the large mahogany table. Hieroglyphic engraving was evident on all of the artefacts – four of these would be the steles from Bighi, and the other two were therefore the steles with the name of Neferabet – but were there two unavailable, BM 305 and 742? Yes they were, but fortunately for us Neferabet's stele to Ptah was there.

The schedule for examining the artefacts that were laid out on the big table for us was readily sorted out. Marta was to study the engraved hieroglyphs on the steles whilst I carried out the measurements and took the photographs.

We had forty-five minutes at our disposal before the midday break. We started with the stele that lay furthest to our right on the large examination table – it was labelled as EA 589. Neferabet had dedicated it to Ptah and had it placed in his cave sanctuary along with the other stele to Meretseger. This was the prayer of Neferabet to the god he had offended, Ptah, the lord of righteousness. Neferabet admitted that he had taken a false oath and that he had been punished for this sin by blindness.

This was clearly the largest of the steles in the group there. It measured 40 centimetres in height and 27 across – it was 5.5 cm thick. Its form was the standard round-topped shape that characterised the vast majority of such funerary artefacts.

At the top end of the obverse, the god Ptah was seen seated in a kiosk, facing an offering table with a legend above it that read, "Ptah, Lord of Ma'at, King of the Two Lands, the fair-faced on his sacred seat". Neferabet, the person making the dedication, was kneeling on the right side of the lower register.

I had brought along some notes on these steles. The text of the hymn started on the obverse, and was described as having been engraved in vertical columns on both sides of the stele. So we asked Neal, who sat at the desk next to us, to

AM

Figure 30. One of the present authors examining the stele of
Neferabet to Ptah at the Department of Egypt and Sudan,
The British Museum.

kindly turn it over for us and he readily obliged. On its reverse side there were another ten vertically disposed registers.

As Marta skimmed over the individual hieroglyphs and murmured the translation, I was looking out for the rendering of the name of the dedicatee, Neferabet, and how it was spelt in the hieroglyph text. In the very last register of text, Marta came across the actual hieroglyphs for the name of the dedicatee – Neferabet. (Fig. 32)

The full translation of this inscription has been published by Miriam Lichtheim[219] and is used here. On the obverse -

"Praise giving to Ptah, Lord of Ma'at, King of the Two Lands,
Fair of face on his great seat, The One God among the Ennead,
Beloved as King of the Two Lands.
May he give life, prosperity, health,
Alertness, favours, and affection,
And that my eyes may see Amen every day,
As is done for a righteous man,
Who had set Amen in his heart!

"So says the servant in the Place-of-Truth, Neferabet, justified".

The composite hieroglyph for the *abet* sign was immediately identified, and Marta drew the characters that made up the name for later comparison with those on the statuette in Malta.

On the reverse face of the stele, the text translated by Lichtheim continues –

"Beginning of the recital of the might of Ptah, South of his Wall, by the servant in the Place-of-Truth on the West of Thebes, Neferabu, justified. He says:
I am a man who swore falsely by Ptah, Lord of Ma'at,
And he made me see darkness by day.
I will declare his might to the fool and the wise,

162

Figure 31. Details from obverse side of Neferabet's stele to Ptah, BM EA 589, showing Neferabet in prayer (above) in front of Ptah (below). One version of Neferabet's name arrowed (above)

To the small and great:
Beware of Ptah, Lord of Ma'at!
Behold, he does not overlook anyone's deed!
Refrain from uttering Ptah's name falsely,
Lo, he who utters it falsely, lo he falls.

"He caused me to be as the dogs of the street,
I being in his hand;
He made men and gods observe me,
I, being as a man who has sinned against his Lord.
Righteous was Ptah, Lord of Ma'at, toward me,
When he taught a lesson to me!
Be merciful to me, look on me in mercy!

"So says the servant in the Place-of-Truth on the West of Thebes, Neferabet, justified before the great god".

The name of Neferabet had apparently been engraved on both sides of the stele, yet we had only recognised it on the reverse. Had we missed it on the obverse? Or had it simply been spelt differently? To complicate things further, the "abet" sign used to be read as "abu" by the earlier Egyptologists.

We were therefore obliged to ask Neal to have the stele turned over on to its obverse side once again and we identified the characters that made up the name of the dedicatee between the forearms of Neferabet's engraved image. It was being spelt differently. (Fig. 31)

We had thus come across two versions of the name of the dedicatee on the same stele. [220] Had that been our sole discovery, this development would have made the trip to London worth all the effort. Once back in Malta we would see how these two spellings of the name compare with that on the statuette [221]

We had spent a considerable amount of time on the first artefact. It had certainly been well worth the while, but we were not keeping up with our planned time schedule. So we moved on to the stele that lay next to it.

This smaller artefact was one of the four steles that had been discovered beneath the foundations of a

AM

Figure 32. Second version of Neferabet's name on the reverse side of the stele to Ptah, BM EA 589, tenth column. Translated into 'Neferabet true of voice before the great god'.

seventeenth century villa on the Bighi promontory of Grand Harbour in Malta. [222] There were four of these steles from Bighi. The first time I had seen them was in 2003, and they had all been enclosed within their case, which had made their study slightly more difficult. This time in 2008 we had been granted permission to view them outside their cases and at close range. They were not part of the Neferabet study, but once we were there and had the opportunity for examining these artefacts we did so for the purpose of another projected publication of ours.

Once finished with the Bighi steles, we moved on to the next artefact on our agenda. This was not a stele but an *ostrakon*, a huge flat fragment of chipped-off limestone that was used as a writing pad by the scribes at the Great Place, today's Valley of the Kings. This piece of flat limestone would have been picked up by one of the scribes at the Place of Truth and used as an attendance register of the workmen there. Upon it the scribe noted that 'Neferabu' had submitted a request for a few days' leave in order to bury his recently deceased brother.

The characters that were painted in black and red were in hieratic, and this script was unfamiliar to both Marta and me. So we limited ourselves to its measurements and the photography. Like the BM 589, its characters were spread out over both its surfaces, technically in *verso* and in *recto*.

There were other ancient Egyptian artefacts for us to examine. These were not related to Neferabet and so we postponed them for after the staff lunch break that was coming up. We availed ourselves of the open-air cafeteria at the museum to have a snack and go over two of the artefacts preserved there, the *ostrakon* and a stele that was not available there at the time. We just managed a corner of a long table and started off with the last item we had seen.

Morris Bierbrier quotes from this ostrakon, BM 5634, as an example of a kind of an attendance register of the workmen at the Place of Truth. He mentions the

AM

Figure 33. The *ostrakon* BM 5634.

workman Neferabu at the Place of Truth, who, in year forty of Rameses II, took time off in order to embalm his brother.[223] Bierbrier limits Neferabu's lifespan to the reign of Rameses II. [224] Further on down the text, he again mentions Neferabu in relation to the statuette with the triad of gods that were described by Sonnini in 1798.

Yet John Romer mentions Neferabu[225] in the middle of the reign of Rameses III. [226] Marta came up with a valid query. Could Neferabet's lifespan have been that long?

One or two individuals?

Our very first impression was that this individual on the *ostrakon* could not possibly have been the same person as the dedicatee on the Maltese statuette with the triad of gods. After calculating the time interval that would have been necessary to make this a feasible proposition, it seemed improbable that the two individuals could have been one and the same. But we could have been mistaken.

There were two options. There may have been two Neferabets, separated in time by slightly more than half a century. [227] Otherwise Neferabet had reached an advanced old age and maintained sufficient health to remain in active service for the pharaoh.

Marta started off by breaking down Neferabet's life span into the individual regnal periods of the pharaohs involved.

"The attendance register on the *ostrakon* in question has been dated to regnal year forty of Rameses II. The youngest possible age for Neferabet to have started to work at the Place of Truth would have been around sixteen. That leaves twenty-six years until the end of Rameses II's reign, plus the reign of Merenptah (ten years), plus that of Amenmesse (three years), Seti II (six years), Siptah (six years), Tausert (two years), and Sethnakht (two years). Neferabet died around year eleven of the reign of Rameses

III. I deduced this from his brother Ipuy's death following his promotion to foreman, but it may not necessarily be a correct assumption. [228] If we count all these up, we come up with a hypothetical total of eighty-two years for Neferabet's age at his time of death." This was certainly not an impossible proposition.

There was a proviso, namely that the reigns of Amenmesse and Seti II and of Siptah and Tausert may have been contemporary, perhaps only in part, and this would make Neferabet slightly younger at his time of death.

Would an average Egyptian workman have survived that long? Provided with the best nutrition and medical care available in ancient Egypt at the time, Rameses II made it to approximately the same age of around eighty-two years at the time of his death.

Marta and I discussed nutrition, health, and longevity in terms of the evidently different lifestyles of Neferabet and Rameses II.

I started by pointing out that the pharaoh would have indulged in the best possible food available at the time, and this would not necessarily have been the healthiest and most suited for longevity. High calories in delicacies and sweets would have predisposed him to dental problems and metabolic disorders such as diabetes, resulting in a reduced life span.

These dietary factors need not have been the case with the painter Neferabet, who would certainly not have afforded such expensive tastes in food, especially with his large family.

Medical attention and surgery would have been more readily available to the pharaoh at all periods of his life. Neferabet's father-in-law, who was the village physician, would have given him that extra bit of medical attention. But at the time when Neferabet would have needed him most, in his advanced age, his father-in-law would most likely not have been around.

I agreed with the way Marta put it to me. "I would take the age of around eighty years as the maximum age achievable in ancient Egypt. This makes it just possible for the Neferabet indicated in the attendance register from year forty of Rameses II to be the same as Neferabet the painter blinded by the god Ptah, then healed by the goddess Meretseger, and almost certainly becoming a village elder once he achieved such a remarkable age. That would also make him the brother of Ipuy who became foreman of the right gang at the workmen's village in year eleven of Rameses III and who died after only a few years in office. It would seem from Romer's chart that Ipuy was foreman for approximately a three-year period."

Neferrenpet

The lunch break was coming to a close, and we discussed the stele we had missed examining at the DES. At the very start of our visit, Neal had informed us that the missing stele BM 305 was on loan for an exhibition in California. I had fortunately brought over a photograph from Bierbrier's book, [229] and we looked at it together over a quick tea.

There were four coffins described on the stele, those of Neferabet, his wife, and his parents. Marta studied the stele and the four coffins in its top left-hand sector. She could not agree with Bierbrier's description of these objects as four standing coffins and suggested that they were not coffins at all but bandaged mummies with *cartonnage* funerary masks. Wood was a precious and expensive commodity in ancient Egypt, and it is very doubtful whether any craftsman could have afforded a solid wooden coffin. It seems that only priests, nobles and royalty were able to afford this type of coffin; the rest had to make do with *papier maché* and gypsum plaster.

Marta further remarked that it would have been unlikely for these individuals to have all died at the same time. Unless there had been a tragic combination of deaths or a bad epidemic, it would have been unlikely that his parents would have lived as long as Neferabet. The stele would more likely have had a symbolic meaning, both in relation to the four bandaged mummies and to the opening of the mouth ceremony.

It was Neferrenpet who was performing the opening of the mouth ceremony for Neferabet, a ritual that was carried out by the eldest son. But Neferrenpet was also described as "justified" on Neferabet's statuette in Malta – this would imply that he pre-deceased his father. Could it have therefore been the *brother* Neferrenpet who had pre-deceased Neferabet? This had to be looked into, and we awaited other sources to solve this.

There were also other interesting points to consider in relation to Neferabet's statuette in Malta. As Marta pointed out, BM 305 was set up by Neferrenpet, as reported by Bruyère. [230] Now if Neferrenpet, the son of Neferabet, was listed as deceased on the statuette of Neferabet, then we have two possible scenarios. First, that Neferrenpet commissioned the funerary stele for his father while his father was still alive. But Neferrenpet died before Neferabet commissioned his statuette holding the triad. Thus on the statuette in Malta Neferabet listed his son as deceased.

We still had not definitely established that the statuette in question belonged to Neferabet. Everybody was assuming it. But there was a problem with the name of the dedicatee of the original statuette. We did have photographs of the one exhibited in 2003 at very close range, and the hieroglyphs there clearly read *Neferabet*. And yet the first attempt at identifying the name of the dedicatee had yielded a slightly different name for him. According to the Austrian Egyptologist Professor F. W. von Bissing, the dedicatee in the person of the standing figure[231] holding the triad was *Nefertanpet* rather than *Neferabet*. Was it merely a misinterpretation, or had it been a different statuette? This option remained an open one.

There was the theoretical possibility that the Malta statuette did not belong to Neferabet after all, but to another individual who may have had a son named Neferrenpet who predeceased him.

The name Neferrenpet was certainly not an uncommon one; the name is translated as "good year". We investigated the frequency and occurrence of the name and came up with a few other unlikely candidates.

There was a Neferrenpet who is known to have had a tomb, TT 178[232], in the Valley of the Nobles. Neferrenpet was the name he used in his public life. He served as the Chief Scribe of the Treasury of Amen Re and Scribe of the Divine Offerings of the Temple of Amen, in the reign of Rameses II. In his private life he was called Kenro, probably the name his mother gave him at birth or possibly a nickname given by his family or friends. At the present time this is now considered an obsolete reading, and Kener or Kenel have been proposed - these appear to be Canaanite. Yet his parents have Egyptian names. His father was Piay, Priest Pacifier of Amen and his mother, Wiay. He was married to Mutemwia, Chantress of Amen.

Besides the owner of Theban Tomb TT178 there was yet another Neferrenpet who also owned a Theban tomb, TT147,[233] located in the Dra Abu el-Naga region of the Theban Necropolis. The tomb was reutilised several times, but the original owner Neferrenpet lived and was buried in this tomb in the reign of Amenhotep III. His official title obtained from the cones that were applied to the façade of his tomb was 'Scribe accountant of the Cattle of Amen'. From within the tomb he is called 'Chief elder of the portal at Karnak (Ipet-Isut)'.

The name Neferrenpet occurs frequently in the reign of Rameses II. We came across another individual in the cemetery of the Nobles at Qurna hill. He was Neferrenpet, the Chief of Weavers in the Mortuary Temple of Rameses II. His tomb is TT133.[234]

There were evidently no family connections whatsoever to be drawn between our Neferabet the painter and these three individuals. These were all buried at the Theban Necropolis, and this was the privilege of the nobility. Furthermore, they appeared on the scene earlier than the date that we were proposing for Neferabet. [235]

The lunch break was definitely over. It was time to resume our documentation of the remaining artefacts at the DES, and we concluded this part well in time and according to schedule. We also had that little extra time to browse through some of the Egyptian artefacts at the Museum.

We visited the British Museum on another occasion for the Nebamun Exhibition late in 2009, and we came across the same *ostrakon,* BM 5634, when it was included amongst the artefacts. We were still then searching for more documentary or archaeological evidence in favour of the 'single Neferabet' hypothesis.

It was by pure chance that we then came across a reference that gave a different interpretation of the regnal year on the *ostrakon.* According to the illustration given by Vandier of the relevant hieratic signs on the ostrakon in question,[236] Marta confirmed the alternative date as year forty-six[237] rather than forty. This development made it even more possible for our Neferabet to have survived the period in question, namely between Rameses II and III. He need only have reached the age of seventy-six.

West of the Nile at Thebes

Intensive activity on the West Bank was not confined to the Valleys of the Kings and Queens of ancient Egypt. There were also colossal works being carried on the mortuary temples of the pharaohs. During the time of Neferabet it was the Ramesseum. There were other groups of workmen employed there.

The Ramesseum was less than a kilometre distant and therefore well within walking distance from the workmen's village. Yet visits there by the workers at the Place of Truth would not have been possible unless it was to leave offerings in the first court. However there would not have been any need for them to go there for this purpose when there was a small temple to Amen-Re at the village.

The funerary temple was more important for the pharaoh than his tomb which would eventually be camouflaged to remain hidden for eternity. If the tomb was robbed and the royal mummy destroyed, he would still live in the Afterlife if his name was spoken in the temple. The rituals in the funerary temple secured the pharaoh's repose in the other world. The same applied to the nobles' tombs. They had their funerary chapels built on top of their tombs, and the chapels were open for worship.

The West Bank was not the exclusive burial place of the pharaoh and his family members. The nobility and the workmen at the Valley of the Kings were also buried there, but they were obliged to sort out the arrangements on their own steam. The workmen prepared their own tombs, but it was not their direct responsibility to cater for the demands of the nobility. If they did so, the arrangement would have been on a private basis.

The earliest non-royal tombs of the Eighteenth Dynasty were dug at the Dra Abu el-Naga site, close to the temple of Rameses IV on the West Bank, whereas the later ones lay more to the south-west at Sheikh Abd el-Qurna, between the temple of Hatchepsut and Tuthmose III to the

174

Northwest and those of, Rameses II, and Tuthmosis IV towards the Southeast.[238]

Amongst the non-royal tombs on the West Bank of Thebes, those of the nobles provide a striking contrast with those of the workmen at Deir el-Medina. It is plain to see that the tomb of the nobleman was much more endowed than that of the ordinary workman.

Whereas throughout their lifetime Neferabet and his colleagues were limited in their means and would barely have scratched along, Nebamun and his equals could afford ample leisure time for sporting activities, such as hunting together with their families.

Nebamun's residence was lavishly furnished and so was his tomb. Through Nebamun's tomb we have a fair idea of what a nobleman's lifestyle was like in ancient Egypt during the New Kingdom. Similarly, a glimpse into the tomb of Neferabet would perhaps give us an indication of the lifestyle of an ordinary workman in the Valleys of the Kings and Queens.

Discovery of TT5

The tomb of Neferabet was excavated at the turn of the twentieth century by the Italian Ernesto Schiaparelli, then by the Frenchman Bernard Bruyère, and finally by the Vandiers in 1934. It was designated Theban Tomb 5 and abutted the Ptolemaic temple situated to the North of the village on the western bank of the Nile at Thebes.

An aura of mystery surrounds the circumstances relating to the discovery of his tomb. Nothing much is known with certainty. If we take Gaston Maspero's word for it, "it was discovered in Thebes at the beginning of the nineteenth century, and it furnished the agents of the European consuls of the likes of Drovetti, Salt and Minutoli with a number of artefacts that are today dispersed in several European collections and that have remained unknown and undocumented, as are the greater part of these monuments that are shut up inside these collections".[239]

Maspero's point of reference in terms of dating the discovery and its context was a stele in the possession of the Earl of Belmore and now in the British Museum. When Vandier checked this out, he found a very badly executed copy of the stele in question but without any information about its context.[240] A note said that it had been found in a Theban tomb by the Earl of Belmore in 1818.[241] It was assumed that the Theban tomb was that of Neferabet, but there was no confirmatory documentation to this effect. Yet it was presumed at the time that this was the time year the tomb of Neferabet was discovered.

This evidence is far too circumstantial in the light of the following points highlighted by Vandier.

Firstly, another artefact that was discovered at Deir el-Medina from Neferabet's tomb was the so-called Skylight stele. In 1929, Bruyère discovered it at the bottom of a shaft numbered 1195.[242] Just as this stele was not found in Neferabet's tomb, so also the Belmore stele might have been found elsewhere in 1818.

However, the tomb had already been discovered and excavated when the Skylight stele was found in 1929, so that the stele might have been mislaid after the official or clandestine excavations or might even have been lost when the constructions were destroyed. As it was on the exterior part of the tomb, it could have easily lost its supporting structure.

The Belmore stele at the British Museum is a votive one and would not have been placed in a funerary context but in one of the popular sanctuaries in Thebes. To the south-west of Deir el-Medina, one of these sanctuaries was dedicated to the serpent goddess Meretseger and to Ptah.[243] Neferabet's stele dedicated to Ptah would also have been placed there in antiquity.

Even if the votive stele of Neferabet had been placed in the tomb, it would have been positioned in the chapel, and this is on the exterior part of the tomb and would have met the same fate as the Skylight stele mentioned above.[244]

Secondly, when Weidemann described the tombs of the Nineteenth Dynasty at Deir el-Medina in 1886, he did not mention the tomb of Neferabet.[245]

It would not have been impossible for the tomb of Neferabet to have been discovered in 1818 and then buried rapidly once again beneath the sands. There are incidents of this happening. TT 3 was copied by Hay between 1825 and 1838 and was re-discovered by Carter in 1910. The tomb of Anhourkhaoui was partially documented by Lepsius in the mid-nineteenth century and was re-discovered in 1930 by Bruyère.

In 1908, Schiaparelli[246] excavated the tomb of Neferabet and even photographed parts of it; the tomb had been cleared by this time, for the photographs do not show the artefacts inside it. He was not able to clarify the queries put to him by Bruyère regarding the tomb's discovery. The discovery and discoverer of TT5 remain obscure.

The logical conclusion is that the discovery must have taken place between Wiedemann's travels and publication years, respectively 1883 and 1886, and the date of Schiaparelli's photographs in 1908.

The Vandiers

Jacques and Jeanne Vandier[247] spent several of their first years together at Deir el-Medina. They worked in Egypt under the auspices of the *Institut Français d'Archeologie Orientale* that was based in Cairo between 1932 and 1936. The institute had been maintaining excavation campaigns at the ancient settlement site of Deir el-Medina since 1922 under the direction of Bernard Bruyère. [248] Together with J. J. Clere and others, the Vandiers concentrated their efforts on the tombs of the royal artisans. In 1935, Jacques Vandier published *La Tombe de Nefer-Abou* for which Jeanne had done the drawings. [249]

An obscure reference to this publication led to some research upon its possible availability, but a copy was only obtainable from a few dealers of rare books. The initial sources requested several hundred Euros, but then my French son-in-law, Guillaume, came across one available from his native France, from *Cybele*, for a couple hundred. It was still in a very well-preserved condition when we received it a few days later.

A vast corpus of information suddenly became available to us. Once again, when it came to translate from the French, I found the assistance of Guillaume invaluable.

An added bonus was an analysis of the family tree together with a number of tables, including a particularly useful one with the orthographic variety of the hieroglyphs for *Nefer-abou*.

Only the pharaoh and the nobility could afford to employ artisans and other craftsmen to hew and decorate their tombs. The remainder of the populace was obliged to carry out the work themselves with the assistance of family members and friends.

The documentation of Neferabet's tomb by the Vandiers gives us an insight into what Neferabet was involved in during the periods when he was not engaged in work on the tomb of the pharaoh. For eight days at a stretch, he would spend very long hours absorbed in decorating the pharaoh's tomb and then spend every night in the settlement at the Valley of the Kings. The next two days would be spent in the Place of Truth, yet on both these days Neferabet would walk the short distance from the village up the slope of the hill and dedicate all the time he could afford to the preparation of his own eternal resting place.

The majority of the workmen's tombs were situated in the sloping ground that led up to the small hill to the

West of the village. The site selected by Neferabet for his own tomb was situated towards the northern end of the cemetery, not very far from the Ptolemaic temple.

Since there was work to be done even during the weekend breaks from the Valley of the Kings, it seems that tomb painting was a full-time occupation for Neferabet. After the family reunion in the village during this time off, Neferabet's priority was the preparation and decoration of his own final resting place. Thus his two days off per week had to suffice both for time spent together with his wife and children and also for the preparation of his tomb.

Neferabet would literally be working at a stone's throw from his home, and it was therefore possible for him to plan his own hours of work and rest. He was not required to be on his own, and just as he had done himself in his childhood, once his older children were of age; they would accompany him and render him their assistance in his enterprise. At the same time they would be acquiring their apprenticeship. In the end, they would most likely be doing the same work that their father did.

Neferabet could not afford a new tomb. He re-utilised a previous one and refurbished it to his own tastes. In fact, the original shaft to the underground chambers is situated at a distance of approximately two metres from the present one. In the 1930s one could still see, in the court of the chapel, the southern wall of the ancient shaft that had been constructed with sun-baked brick.

As a tomb painter for the pharaoh's tomb, Neferabet would have been more than amply qualified to decorate his own. If he had done do, his resources would not have allowed him to employ a draughtsman to design the decoration beforehand. He would have had to rely solely on his own artistic talents and skills for this sort of preparation, and might even have been obliged to go straight to painting without a control drawing beforehand. This seems to have been the case at least in the first chamber.

Neferabet's economical constraints also restricted the spectrum of colours for his palette. These were limited to white, black, yellow, and traces of red. The blues and greens were costly and beyond his means. Any close similarity to the decorations in the tomb of the pharaoh and those of the nobles on the other side of the hill was far beyond his wildest dreams.

It is the authors' contention that instead of investing heavily in the decoration of his tomb, Neferabet might have opted to concentrate instead on the stone artefacts. The steles that we saw at the British Museum and Turin seemed to us to be of very good quality indeed.

The workmen's tombs

The tombs of the workmen were carved in the rising ground that was located next to their village. The entire slope to the West of the Place of Truth was in fact taken up by the cemetery.

The younger the individual the closer to the village was his interment. Thus burials of the elder members of the community were placed up the slope whilst the younger people lay in the foreground; those of the very young remained inside the village.[250]

The cemetery at the Place of Truth was situated to the West and was only separated from the residential area by the main road of the village. The presence of small pyramids that surmounted the individual tombs made its identification very simple. It was situated on the village side of the *Gebel*, the hill that separated it from the royal tombs in the Valley of the Kings[251].

All the tombs in the Place of Truth were different from the other necropolis tombs because of their style, small size, and to a certain extent, to their subjects and colouring. They were all painted, whereas the steles, lintels and jambs were carved in stone.[252]

180

These tombs ranged in type from simple chambers that were dug out into the rock to elaborate constructions with external superstructures requiring great technical and architectural skills. The quality varied from a trial project to a masterpiece.

An ideal tomb of this type consisted of a rectangular court enclosed by walls and entered through a pylon structure that was orientated towards the East. At the other end of the court, on the western side of the structure, stood a colonnaded chapel with a pyramidal structure centred above it, and this was crowned with a pyramidion in limestone. (Fig 60)[253]

A stele recessed into the back wall of the chapel identified the tomb owner, and a statue of the deceased was positioned into a niche on the triangular face of the pyramid that faced the courtyard.[254]

The chambers were partly carved into the rock and partly built in bricks. The tomb itself was accessed from a shaft in the forecourt that was also decorated. This shaft or an inclined passageway was sometimes stepped. Only the underground chambers with vaulted roofs were decorated, with scenes of the Afterlife contributing to the standard decorative elements.

Other rooms were dug into the cliff face behind the workmen's village and these were used as 'offering chapels' where steles, statuettes or other votive offerings would be placed.

In the early decades of the twentieth century the French team under Bernard Bruyère carried out extensive excavations at the eastern cemetery of Deir el Medina[255]. It was established then that this necropolis had been meant for the lower class residents of the village[256]. It was dated to the first part of the 18th Dynasty and this dating was based on scarabs found with the burials and the architectural style of the tombs.

After a period of approximately two centuries from when the pyramid ceased to be the symbolic marker of deceased royalty, the structure reappeared in a relatively miniature form towards the end of the 18th Dynasty. It was no longer the prerogative of the pharaoh, for the high officials, artisans and other craftsmen at the Place of Truth started to decorate their own tombs with a small pyramid that was also capped by a pyramidion.

This sharply-pointed mudbrick pyramid and a pyramidion crowning the roof of the funerary chapel were architectural innovations of the New Kingdom.[257] This style was the one that was most frequently adopted during the 19th and 20th dynasties.

During the New Kingdom the tomb had become a sacred place where the deceased not merely worshipped the gods but also performed the funerary rituals there. And the statues themselves were no longer the simple recipients of the funerary offerings but also became objects of a memorial cult involving all the people represented in the scene.[258]

Bereavement in the family

Neferabet's absence from work was occasionally necessitated when a member of his family passed away. He would naturally have been expected to involve himself with his relatives in the funerary arrangements. However leave from work in order to assist in the mummification process of family members would only have entailed the occasional few days extra off during the embalming process.[259]

In the forty-sixth year of Rameses's reign, one of Neferabet's brothers passed away. This would most likely have been 'Anhotep. Neferabet would have had to go over the funerary details and make plans with his family and other relatives for his brother's embalming over the next few weeks.

A few of Neferabet's fellow workmen were also going to be absent during that same period of time that 'Anhotep died. One other tomb workman named Heknekhu lost his mother and he too was involving himself in her funerary preparations. She was then in the stage of bandaging and Heknekhu had also applied and taken leave in order to see to it. Another of the workmen had passed away and had no relatives to mummify him, so the task fell on yet another of his fellow workmen. These absences from work are all recorded by one scribe on one *ostrakon*.[260]

For his brother 'Anhotep's burial, Neferabet would have joined all the other family members in the cortege that followed the mummy sledge of. It was a short journey that started from the family residence in the Place of Truth and carried on across the main street of the village towards the family's tomb chapel.

Once the offerings for the spirit of 'Anhotep were made, his *cartonnaged* mummy would be lowered through the shaft in the courtyard in front of the chapel into the funerary vault underground.[261]

Deaths in the family were a constant reminder of the ultimate outcome, and like his fellow workers Neferabet probably set to work upon his own tomb early on in life. [262]

The style of tomb he selected was fairly popular at the Place of Truth and is today also seen in several of the other burial vaults there. The similarity in decoration is sufficiently close to hypothesise that they were very probably painted by the same artist. Whether Neferabet decorated his own tomb or else commissioned another artist is a moot point. If he did decorate his own then he would probably also have also participated in the decoration of the others that are similar to it. Notably these are the tombs of the notorious Paneb (numbered 211), of NebenMa'at (219), of Pashedu (323), of Nakhtamen (335), of yet another Neferrenpet (336), and of Amenenwia (356)[263].

The collapse of the cliff face has exposed the interior of the upper parts of the tomb to the open air. Although the external parts are damaged in the main, it is still possible to reconstruct the original edifice from the remains and the descriptions of other similar tombs.

The tomb complex is basically divided into two sections, a subterranean part that was exclusively reserved for the deceased and an external section that was accessible to the relatives and friends, and reserved for the cult of the dead.

The court is quadrilateral in form with each side measuring approximately six and a half metres, and it is encircled by a wall made up of stone slabs and sun-baked mudbrick.

Whereas most other workmen's entrances face the East, the entrance to Neferabet's is situated towards the South, though access to the court is similarly through two small pylons fashioned out of mudbrick[264].

At the very back of the court is the chapel structure topped by the pyramid[265]. This is built out of baked bricks and stone and measures two by just over three metres.

The wide door opens into the courtyard towards the South, and on the opposite wall stands the large niche that would have held the funerary stele and the table of offerings.

The ceiling of the chapel above the tomb would have been vaulted and spread out along an East-West axis that was parallel to the façade. The walls of the chapel would have been decorated with personages in a variety of tones and depicted upon a yellow background.

The walls of the chapel also serve as the base for the mudbrick pyramid whose external surfaces are covered over with a white wash. In order to reduce its weight and consequent stress upon the chapel below it, the pyramid is hollowed out on the inside.

There is a niche on its southern face, and this would have been the location for the arched Skylight stele that was found by Bruyère in 1929 in the neighbouring shaft number 1195.[266]

The other artefacts commissioned by Neferabet or his family members could have been placed virtually anywhere at the Place of Truth, in a temple, his home or inside the tomb itself. The wide distribution of these artefacts today suggests that they would have been originally placed in a number of locations.

The chapel pyramid is surmounted by its pyramidion in painted limestone and this is engraved with representations of the sun and the evolution of its diurnal phases.

Approximately two metres in front of the chapel area in the courtyard is the shaft that leads into the tomb. This is dug out vertically into the ground, and is just sufficient to permit a person to go down its depth through the extent of four metres.

A flight of steps leads into the first chamber, on the walls of which the dead man and his relatives are depicted worshipping the Hathor cow emerging from the hill on the right, and the Horus falcon on the left. (Fig. 63)

A second flight of steps leads to a second chamber that is decorated with religious scenes: Horus and Thoth pouring the purifying water over the dead man; Amenhotep I praying to Meretseger, the snake-headed goddess of the dead, and to Hathor; the sun, borne by two lions. On the rear wall, beneath the mouth of the shaft, are depicted the mummies of the dead man and his wife. Nephthys opens her wings above them.

As would be expected in the tomb of a royal tomb decorator, both funerary halls are painted all over their surface. The decoration on the greater part of the walls is still in a perfect state of preservation. It is only upon the ceiling and along the northern wall of the first chamber that the effects of charring and blackening are evident.

However there are a number of bosses, cracks and crevices immediately visible all over the chambers. Although the Vandiers suggest that these reflect a hasty process or a fund-sparing one, the cracks in the walls could easily have resulted from earth tremors. However, if this had not been the case, then cheap plastering would have been a far more likely cause of these defects rather than shabby

185

workmanship. This was not a rich man's tomb, but that of a workman who was scratching a living from his monthly rations; Neferabet would not have been able to afford the more costly plastering materials.

The standard practice was for the walls to have been coated with grossly pounded limestone. A second coat of minced plaster of limestone would then be applied upon it. All the walls as well as the vault would also have been covered over with a layer of baked bricks upon which a coat of mud would then be applied in as smooth a layer as possible. Once the walls had been so prepared they would have been finished with a lime wash that formed the white foundation for the depiction of the figures and scenes.

The artist adopts a series of independent vignettes as his main motif for decoration. These are separated from one another by bands with large hieroglyphs that are painted in black over a yellow background. The subjects of the vignettes themselves are depicted as yellow figures on a white background and emphasized with red and black.

Since the only colours that are employed in the tomb were white, yellow, red ochre, and black, the end result is an effect of order and clarity that is very agreeable to the eye.

Yet it seemed to the Vandiers that the style was too lax, and despite the great ability of the artist, one perceived a free and popular style and a work that seemed to have been a trifle hasty.

In the first chamber, the family members making up the defile are of a careless draughtsmanship, and the figures are truly plain. The bodily proportions are not elegant, and the sketches of the feet and hands are non-existent, whilst the gestures are awkward and without any suppleness.

However, it seems that the artist intended to make a greater effort for the second chamber; the individuals on the plinth, all much resembling those in the first chamber, are of a draughtsmanship that is far more elegant, and the faces are significantly less plain.

186

Although executed without any draft preparation, the hieroglyphs designed in black inside the yellow bands betray a sureness of hand and exceptional skill.

Tomb painters

Neferabet would have acquired his artistic skills from his long experience in the decoration of the pharaoh's tomb. As a child he would have started off as an apprentice when he used to accompany his father there on a fairly regular basis. It must have seemed to Neferabet that Rameses was immortal and would live forever and that the work upon his final resting place would never cease.

It could all have been a long-standing family affair, as Marta explained. "Neferabet's family members would have been painters at the village from the reign of Rameses II, if not from before that, and carried on right down to Rameses III. During the Nineteenth Dynasty there were no overlaps of reigns, or perhaps a mere four years when Amenmesse usurped the throne from Seti II after Merenptah's reign. So probably the orthodox chronology is right in assigning about ninety to one hundred years to this period, inclusive of Rameses II's reign of sixty-seven years."

Together with his brothers, Neferabet had most likely also assisted his father in decorating his own tomb. No doubt Neferrenpet expected all his sons to follow in his footsteps, and as the eldest son, Neferabet was the first to join his father as a novice painter at the Great Place, today's Valley of the Kings. As he gained experience, he was taken into the workforce, a move no doubt facilitated through the influence of his father, who had not merely secured his position there but also that of his two other brothers, Ipuy and Amenemopet. As the eldest brother in the family, Neferabet aspired to attain someday the position of his father as the *śḏm-ʿš* in the Place of Truth.[267]

Three of Neferabet's uncles had served as painters in the same royal tomb, and these were his father's younger brothers, Rahotep, Maaninakhtef, and Ipuy.[268]

Neferabet's brothers were still too young to be workmen, yet two of them, Ipuy and Amenemopet, were already in training. It would not be long before they would join their brother and get employment in one of the gangs. In the meantime, however, they were the children of the tomb, and they carried out errands, such as taking food and provisions to their father and brother at the work camp in the Great Place.[269]

Within a few years of starting to work there in an official capacity, Neferabet would have been thinking of getting married and raising a family of his own. He eventually decided that he would be sharing the rest of his life with Taese, [270] the local physician's daughter.[271]

Once their fathers were established workmen at the Place of Truth, both Taese and Neferabet would have been born and grown up in the same village there. They would have played together as children, but had decided one day that they were meant for each other and that they would start a family of their own. But this was still way ahead in the future. Whereas the pharaoh would have been suitable for marriage by the age of sixteen years, an age when he would have been considered fit to rule, this was not the case for a commoner like Neferabet. He could only get married if he had the means to sustain himself, his wife, and the brood of children that came along. It is therefore very doubtful that Neferabet married as a novice painter.[272]

As a tomb painter, Neferabet had his regular pay in food rations. On the twenty-eighth day of each month, he would receive four *khar* of wheat and another one and a half of barley, a *khar* being equivalent to 76.8 litres. This amount would produce eleven pounds of bread per day. Barley to the amount of one and a half sacks per month was included in the wage packet, and as an additional bonus, loaves and cakes were also occasionally provided.

The barley was used to make beer, notwithstanding the fact that two and a half quarts[273] of beer was provided to them anyway on a monthly basis. A daily ration of ten pounds of fish per workman provided their principal protein intake. Other provisions that were granted on a daily basis included milk, vegetables, fruits, oil, fat, and water.[274]

At the time there would have been no shortage of residences at the village for Neferabet and Taese, for there were forty-eight workmen families and a total complement of seventy accommodation sites.[275]

Neferabet's father-in-law would certainly have helped them set themselves up. Though the physician's pay at the Place of Truth was a minimal one, he earned substantial amounts from his patients, one example quoting twenty-two *deben* of the much sought after copper. A *deben* was the equivalent of 91 grams. In fact, most of the income earned by most classes of workmen at the Place of Truth was actually earned during off hours.[276]

Painters and draughtsmen

Miriam Lichtheim[277] describes Neferabet as a "draftsman ... of some prominence and wealth. He raised a large family and built himself a fine tomb."[278]

A few Egyptologists like John Romer assert that Neferabet and most of his family were painters rather than draughtsmen. However, it is known that the draughtsmen at the Place of Truth involved themselves also in painting.[279] The positions were different. The draughtsman came in first and sketched the decoration in red ink on to the plastered wall. Then it was the village scribe's turn to inspect to check the draughtsman's work; he carried out his modifications in black ink. Next in line was the painter who filled in the various colours.

When bas-relief sculpture formed part of the decoration, the protocol was different. Once the smoothed white walls were covered over by the ritual scenes, the outline draughtsmen utilised strands of strings impregnated with paint to create a network of lines, a grid that guided the decorative process. The sculptors were then able to start on the relief work, which was finished off in its fine detail by the other craftsmen with smaller chisels. The colour artists came in next, initially to colour the sculpted depictions and subsequently to enhance the images by drawing a border around every one of them, whether this was a hieroglyph, an image, or a figure.[280]

However, not all the royal tombs had images that were first carved and then painted. Several, such as that of Tutankhamen, had painted scenes applied directly on to plaster.

The pigments that were used for the beautifully executed depictions on the walls of the tomb were mainly in bright blue, red, and yellow. The texts were always done in black. Neferabet would have already been instructed as to how the pigments were to be prepared and the proportions of each to be used.

The basic colours were derived from various minerals. Carbon was used for black and calcium salts for the white coloration; for the red pigments, both ferric oxide and red ochre were utilized, whilst yellow ochre supplied the yellow paints. For the blue and green, azurite and malachite were respectively exploited. Combinations of the individual minerals provided the various shades, and this required experience and expertise on the part of the painter.[281]

As Marta commented to me in discussion, ancient Egyptian art is not much renowned for its shades of colours. It was rather uniform in style, and only the five essential colours were used. One rarely sees dark blue or light green, if at all. Yet in one of the nobles' tombs at Amarna, Marta remembers seeing an image of the Aten with a light green halo. But then Akhenaten was breaking away from the established convention; whatever was going on during his reign stopped after his death, and everything reverted to the orthodox tradition.

The śḏm-ꜥš

Both Neferabet and his father bore the same title, that of śḏm-ꜥš in the Place of Truth, a title also held by the other workmen who lived in the village and who were interred in the cemetery there. Neferabet had attained the status of his father as "hearer" at the Place of Truth, and also "hearer" for the master of the Two Lands.[282]

Eight metres away from KV55, an ancient graffito survives with the hieroglyphs of Neferabet and his father Neferrenpet, both bearing the title of śḏm-ꜥš in the Place of Truth. As Marta pointed out to me when I indicated this find to her, the KV55 is quite close to Tutankhamen's KV62 and Rameses II's KV8. Neferabet has been chronologically linked with Rameses II, and it seems that the life span of both individuals was a significantly long one. However Neferabet outlived him and survived into the reign of Rameses III.

There is some controversy amongst scholars about the role of the śḏm-ꜥš in the Place of Truth. The title was certainly not simply limited to the role of a painter of the royal tomb. For example, in the stele of Nebre, a documented draughtsman at Deir el-Medina, the hieroglyphs for his occupation were not transliterated as śḏm-ꜥš, as was Neferabet's.[283]

Was Neferabet a simple workman as Gunn and Bierbrier state,[284] or had he been privileged with a higher role towards the end of his life as a village elder, as the Egyptologist John Romer asserts?[285]

Romer describes Neferabet as a painter and a village elder in his later years, and he was certainly qualified for such a title if only from the ripe old age that he had attained. His longevity was a feature that appeared as a positive characteristic more than once in his funerary inscriptions, one that enhanced the prospects of his being justified before the gods of the West.[286]

As Marta explained, the designation of śdm-ˁš refers to an individual who hears. This can be the title of a judge, or in the case of Neferabet, a village elder. Some Egyptologists dispute this and interpret the 'hearing' as that of an order from a superior and they therefore translate śdm-ˁš as "servant" – one who hears the order. The hearer was the one who heard the command, that is, a servant. Thus theoretically anybody from the Place of Truth could bear that title.

The present authors believe that the title of śdm-ˁš or servant in the Place of Truth referred to the privileged and valued workmen who were preparing the tombs of the pharaohs, and that the title should be considered as such without the need to extrapolate for a hidden meaning.[287]

The title "servant of the lord of the two lands", that is, "servant of the king of Egypt" was not unexpected for a workman at the Place of Truth. It was the full title of his occupation there.

One privilege of the workmen in the Place of Truth was that in principle they answered directly to the Pharaoh, and their rations came from the royal storehouse. In this respect they were unlike the rest of the workforce of ancient Egypt, who had various supervisors, overseers, and managers above them.

However, it is unlikely that there were many cases, if any, where the Pharaoh communicated directly with the folk at the Place of Truth. But the vizier certainly did, and he visited the village on a regular basis.

Priest and guardian

In her *JARCE* article Meza suggests the possibility of Neferabet being a priest and guardian of the sanctuary of the gods in one of the local temples at the Place of Truth, possibly in a temple or temples belonging to the god and goddesses he carried. However, her argument rests on the basis of the epithet of Neferabet's title as śḏm-ꜥš.[288] Since other workmen at the Place of Truth bore this same title, Meza's argument leaves the present authors unconvinced. In such a limited community as the Place of Truth, how would religious things fare if every other workman was also a priest?

At any rate, the dedicatee presenting the triad of gods on the Maltese statuette was doing so in a private capacity and not as a priest. Neferabet was bestowing the offerings for himself rather than for the cult.

Although we are not in agreement with Meza's hypothesis that the title of śḏm-ꜥš designates a priestly function, we reached a rather similar conclusion through yet another title.

The fragment of an upright of a door from Neferabet's tomb is presently preserved at Rennes.[289] This artefact includes a useful inscription that I showed to Marta, and we studied it together. We used the *Collier and Manley Dictionary* for reference and in the 'Titles' section we found it listed amongst the "generic terms for office holding and status amongst the elite". The first two hieroglyphs on the left are transliterated and translated as *bꜣk and* "servant." This title was "often used as a means of stressing the dependent relationship of one person on another and could be used of people who otherwise had high status".[290]

The remainder of the hieroglyphic strip on the Rennes artefact translated as "Amen-Re". Neferabet's title of "servant of Amen-Re" would therefore have indicated that he served as a priest in the small Amen-Re temple at the Place of Truth.

However, this role would not have entitled him to use this title in the big temples. He was a priest of Amen-Re purely out of necessity, in order that priests from the East

Bank would not have to cross over to the Place of Truth on a regular basis.

The A10 hieroglyph after Neferabet's name identifies him as a deceased official. And according to the British Museum description of BM 305, which is in their possession, one title held by Neferabet was that of a scribe.

There is also a scribe glyph in the Rennes inscription, yet this follows the "true of voice" (or "deceased") sign. The scribe glyphs are therefore not part of Neferabet's title, but probably a phonetic value of the next word in the phrase following "true of voice". Yet this phrase is undecipherable.

Strictly speaking, the only official in the Place of Truth was the scribe of the tomb.

The Place of Truth

What do we know about the Place of Truth? It was intensely studied over several decades by the Czech Egyptologist, Jaroslav Černý, and a great deal has been written about the village and the workmen there.

In brief, the Place of Truth was a workmen's village that was set up in a narrow valley on the fringe of the western desert. It housed the community of skilled artisans, scribes, labourers, and other workmen who decorated the tombs of the royals and the nobles, and even decorated the tombs of some of their own community.

The workmen's village on the West Bank of Thebes was known in antiquity as *Set Ma'at* (the Place of Truth) or simply the *pa demey* (*p³ dmi*, the village). This was comfortably nestled in between the hills about three kilometres away from the river that separated it from the main city of Thebes on the eastern bank.

During the Ramessid period it occupied an area of around two hectares, with seventy dwellings or accommodation sites enclosed within the original walls and about fifty more outside. The workmen who lived there long-term were responsible for the tombs of the pharaoh and his family members.

The layout followed a more or less standard plan. However, there was increased accommodation space in the homes of the scribe and the two foremen.

In the typical dwelling for the tomb workmen, there was the first room, or reception room, an antechamber that contained an elevated structure identified by some scholars as a box bed. The present authors suggest that this structure would have more likely been utilised as an altar for ancestral worship.

The antechamber led to the main room that may have included a mud brick divan and to another two rooms, most likely a bedroom and a kitchen. The whitewashed walls were decorated with various scenes, and bands of various colours lined the lower parts above the floor. There were also two underground chambers, the first beneath the main room and the other beneath the kitchen. According to Friedman,[291] these rooms in the cellar would have served for the storage of household goods.

The workmen spent their days off work with their families here in the Place of Truth. However the greater part of their time was taken up in the Great Place.

The trail to the Valley of the Kings

It was a two-hour trek between the workmen's village and their settlement at the Valley of the Kings.[292] They collected their tools from the store rooms at the village every time before setting off to work in the Valley.

Their route started off in the slope of the hill from just behind the village cemetery. They pursued their march along the tortuous path at the top of the hill, enjoying a panoramic view to their right of Thebes across the Nile. The path eventually forked to the right that led to their settlement and the Great Place, the valley of the tombs of the pharaohs, whereas the left fork led to the Place of Beauties where the queens of Egypt were laid to rest[293].

The workers' settlement

The tomb craftsmen lived in a hut settlement during their eight day period of work at the Great Place. They shared these cabins with the other workmen of their gang.

Today the Valley of the Kings is punctuated with the remains of a number of these workmen's huts. Back in the early decades of the twentieth century, Howard Carter found a number of these above Tutankhamen's tomb. In recent years, Schaden found others above KV63, and even more recently Zahi Hawass has discovered a few more during his ongoing excavations in the Valley of the Kings.

The settlement was situated on the mountainside that faced the royal tombs at a distance of around 250 metres. It was made up of two groups of huts that were separated by a pathway. The settlement also commanded a view of the royal temples on the other side in the plains of Thebes.

This set-up ensured the workmen's constant proximity to their place of work during their work phase.[294] This work camp had been planned for the exclusive use of the workmen with no allowances or amenities for their families, though it seems that some of the officials did entertain visitors.

The huts had just two rooms each. The first was an antechamber furnished with stone seats against the walls; and the second, inner chamber served as sleeping quarters.

There was no need of a kitchen, for the food was brought over on a daily basis from the village. Instead of cooking, the workmen occupied their spare time in small workshops that they set up there for the creation of statuettes and ushabtis. Other workmen produced votive steles of stone.[295]

It is more than likely that this workmen's settlement was not always functional throughout the entire existence of the Place of Truth. The U-shaped stone seats of the foreman and scribe in the antechamber of two of the huts are inscribed with their names, and these tell us that this settlement was certainly in use during the second half of the reign of Rameses II.[296]

Ranks

The actual work-force at the Great Place included the stone-masons, draughtsmen, sculptors, and carpenters. These crafts were closely guarded secrets and were handed down the generations from father to son.

There were also the servants of the tomb, who acted as assistants for the workmen at the Place of Truth, and they included water-carriers, fishermen, gardeners, and potters.[297]

Other groups of young men from the workmen's village were assigned the duties of transporting the food supplies that were prepared by the women at the village for the artisans at work in the Great Place.[298]

The Place of Truth was a high-security zone, and the gates of it were the responsibility of the door-keepers of the tomb. These were assisted by the local police, the Medjay.[299] Together with the scribe, the door-keepers also supervised the activities of the servants of the tomb. The security personnel all worked on a roster basis so that the royal tomb in progress was closely guarded at all times.

Officials

The vizier in Thebes was responsible for the appointments of the three main officials at the Place of Truth. These were the scribe and the two foremen. The posts carried a number of potentially lucrative benefits that rendered them highly desirable. It is small wonder that sooner or later they degenerated into a family business affair where the position was inherited from father to son down the generations.

At the Great Place, the foremen and the scribe were known as the administrators or chiefs,[300] and they were also the wealthier individuals at the village. They were the persons who dealt with the vizier on matters regarding the workmen.

According to Lesko, the foreman was the official communicator, whereas the scribe was more probably involved in the authorship of the workmen's end of the correspondence.[301] The foreman even acted as an intermediary between the workmen and the higher authorities and also acted as magistrate in the local trials.

Some scholars, such as Černý, would rather attribute the task of receipt of deliveries of the raw materials to the tomb to the scribe. Thus the latter would first record the amounts of copper, tools, lamps, timber, and other materials received and he would then cause them to be stored in the designated rooms prior to their distribution, hence the secondary title of "Overseer of the Treasury in the Place of Truth".[302]

The foreman was responsible for the technical aspect of the work that was being carried out on the tomb; he controlled the material that was used for the tomb construction.

Yet while it was the foreman who controlled the work in the tomb, it was the scribe who prepared the official reports on the tomb's progress to the vizier.[303] The workmen's wages were in the form of rations, and it was the scribe who saw to these rations.

The vizier dealt only with the scribe, and he also made recommendations for replacements of workmen who had vacated their jobs for one reason or other.[304]

The foremen

There were two foremen at the Great Place, one for each of the two gangs, or crews, as they were also known. There was a right gang and a left one, and their accommodation in their settlement in the Valley of the Kings followed suit, for it was similarly split up into two sections. The reason for this was simple enough. It was easier to manage two small groups of workmen than a large one. Furthermore, if they all worked together in one group, they would not fit comfortably inside the cramped spaces of the tombs.

At the time of Neferabet's father the foreman for the left gang was a certain Kaha. However Neferabet's family members were associated with the notorious Paneb,[305] a foreman of the right gang, so it seems that Neferabet and his family members belonged to the right gang of workmen at the Place of Truth and the Great Place.

This position of foreman tended to be inherited from one generation to the other and thus remain in the family. At the time of Neferabet's father the foreman of the right gang was Neferhotep the elder; he had held this position since the time of Horemheb. Neferhotep's son, Nebnufer, succeeded him and retained this post for the next thirty years. It was Nebnufer's son, Neferhotep the Younger, who then took over the post of foreman of the right gang.[306]

Corruption[307]

The potential for bribery amongst the administrators was a real one. Corruption was certainly not unknown, and the workmen of the pharaoh's tomb were often diverted to work on the tombs of the foreman and the scribe. One of the most widely known episodes of bad behaviour concerned the foreman Paneb.

As a child he had been raised up by the above-cited foreman, Neferhotep the Younger, and his wife, Webket

199

who had no children of their own. The couple later adopted a second boy named Hesunehef.

Paneb was a workman at the Place of Truth from at least the year sixty-six of Rameses II. When his father was killed by partisans of the rebel pharaoh Amenmesse at the end of the civil war with Seti II, Paneb managed to bribe the vizier to have him appointed as foreman instead of his adopted brother Hesunehef.[308]

Paneb perpetrated his misdeeds during the reigns of Seti II and Siptah. Some of these are documented in the writings of the scribe Amennakht,[309] his adoptive father's brother.[310] In order to cover his tracks, Paneb even resorted to corrupting his colleague, the scribe Kenherkhopshef,[311] by having him turn a blind eye to his unorthodox activities. Other scribes such as Khaemope emulated Kenherkhopshef and similarly accepted bribes for cover-ups. Tomb robbing was one of the activities that were thus allowed to go on unchecked and unheeded.[312]

Though situated some distance away, the mortuary temples above the ground were also robbed. Two members of the work gang targeted the Ramesseum and removed worked stones from its superstructure, presumably for their own or their superior's private re-utilisation.[313]

Paneb was aggressive with the craftsmen at the Great Place in the Valley of the Kings. He plundered their tombs in the Place of Truth and then moved on to the funerary goods of the pharaoh, those of Seti II and Siptah.

He disturbed the peace of the village through his irregular sexual activities. Adultery seems to have been a relatively common affair in the village. One of the workmen, Userhat, indulged with married women quite often: with "Menat when she was with Qenna, Tayuenes when she was with Nakhtamen and Tawerethetepi when she was with Pentaweret".[314] However, it was not considered to be a criminal act, and the perpetrators were not even brought to trial; attempts to sort out the situation usually occurred at a local level within the village.

Paneb even managed to deceive the pharaoh Amenmesse with false reports and have the vizier, his direct superior, deposed and replaced by one who could be bribed.

Under these circumstances, labour conditions at the Place of Truth could not have been ideal. The very lives of the workmen at the Great Place were not secure. According to the scribe Amennakht, workmen who did not comply with their foreman Paneb's instructions were at times even eliminated by him.[315]

The personal property of the workmen and their wives and daughters were unsafe from the caprices of Paneb, who seemed to enjoy a substantial degree of immunity that permitted him to do as he pleased. Even the tombs of the workmen were not safe from plunder by Paneb. The need would certainly have been felt by Neferabet and his colleagues to double the security measures in their family vaults.

Paneb's highly irregular activities at the Great Place were the cause of his eventual downfall, and a fatal error on his part led to his being removed from his post, perhaps even executed. He was discovered with a stolen golden goose, "the sacred animal of the god Amen, from the tomb of a wife of Rameses II, a daughter of Seti I."[316]

The scribe of the tomb

There was only one scribe at the Place of Truth at any time. This was the case until the end of the Nineteenth Dynasty. From the Twentieth Dynasty onward, there was a scribe for each of the two gangs.

Although the draughtsmen and alphabetic workmen sometimes styled themselves as scribes and may even have fulfilled the roles of secondary scribes at some times, they were not *managing* scribes. There does not seem to be any evidence to confirm that there were any scribes living at the

Place of Truth. It was a craftsmen's community there rather than a scribal one.

The position of scribe of the tomb was a relatively comfortable one. Neferabet's father remembered the scribe Ramose, who had been involved in the project for the tomb of Rameses II since the fifth year of his reign.[317]

Thirty-five years later, the post was taken by the adopted son of Ramose, Kenherkhopshef, who in reality was the son of Panakht.[318] It was during the time that Neferabet was still in his early years as a workman at the Great Place that Neferhotep the Younger and Kenherkhopshef assumed their new positions as administrators of the workmen, the latter as scribe and the former as foreman of the right gang. Both of these officials held on to their posts for more or less the same period of time, approximately four decades.[319]

Kenherkhopshef developed a keen interest in the contemporary history of his native land. He was concerned with the lists of the pharaohs and particularly in the military encounters of Rameses the Great.[320] Kenherkhopshef even copied bits of the epic poem about the Battle of Kadesh onto papyrus roll and included it in his personal library.[321]

It was the scribe Kenherkhopshef, then the only scribe at the work camp,[322] to whom Neferabet made his request for leave of absence when his brother 'Anhotep (beloved of his father)[323] passed away. Although he was not particularly popular at the settlement, Kenherkhopshef continued in this post for a total of forty-three years, through the reigns of Rameses II, Merenptah, Amenmesse, and Seti II. The position was a very desirable one, for as we have seen, the scribes held on to their posts for as long as they could. His successor's period of duties was also long and extended over thirty-two years until the sixteenth year of Rameses III.[324]

It seems that like most other scribes in the Great Place, Kenherkhopshef abused the workmen and caused them to carry out work on his personal behalf. And it was not merely the quarrymen and the labourers who accused him of bribery on several occasions, but also skilled workmen such as the draughtsman Prahotep,[325] who launched his complaints of similar abuse to his immediate superior, the vizier in Thebes.[326]

Precious metals

One of the primary concerns of the scribe was the constant management of the group of coppersmiths in attendance for the supply, maintenance, and repair of the copper chisels that were required by both the quarrymen and the relief sculptors.[327]

Copper was a much sought-after commodity in ancient Egypt amongst the common people who could not afford gold or silver. Whether it was barley or a goat that was being valued, commodities were almost always measured against copper.

This was the Late Bronze Age, and bronze, as we all know, is an alloy largely made up of copper with smaller amounts of tin. Copper was essential for the economy.

The Valley of the Kings was difficult to guard against robbers. The storage of tools in the valley would have augmented the problem, and these implements were kept within the walled village at the Place of Truth when not in use.

The fine tools of the physician were made out of copper, and so were the chisels that were used by the workers in the Valley of the Kings. Precautions were taken to prevent their loss.

When the excavators and sculptors took their tools from the store-room, the scribe recorded the weight of each implement against that of a stone. This would then be marked with the name of the workman who borrowed it for the next eight working days. On its return, the scribe would monitor its weight against the stone with the workman's name on it to ensure that no copper had been shaved off.

When the chisels required sharpening, this was not done by the tomb workmen but by specifically designated individuals.

Security

Although they spent all their working period there, the workmen were not allowed free access to the Valley of the Kings. They could not just wander around according to their whims.

In order to go the valley, they would first have had to collect their tools and sign for them with the scribe of the tomb, their only administrator. They could then leave for the valley in gangs under the command of the foreman. Once the working week was over, the whole gang returned to the village, and the scribe collected each workman's tools and signed off the work attendance sheet, one instance of this being ostrakon 5634.

Security in the Valley of the Kings and the Valley of the Queens was considered to be of paramount importance. The members of the Medjay police force were the only ones who were allowed to walk around, as they were there in the valley on duty to guard the tombs. These were selected from the corps of men who policed the city of Thebes and were housed in a fortress that was situated along the workmen's path on the mountainside. There were also a number of guard huts from which the activities in the valley below could be constantly monitored.[328]

The choice of the person in charge of these police was a careful one. For a time during the reign of Rameses II, the chief of the Medjay police was a certain Ameneminet; he was the son of the High Priest of Amen, and his mother was the "Superior of Amen's Harem" in Thebes. Evidently a favourite with the royal family, several of Ameneminet's relatives were established in elite posts throughout the empire. Ameneminet had been the pharaoh's companion since childhood and was presumably more or less of the same age. He would thus more likely have functioned as chief of the Medjay during the earlier years of Rameses II's reign. His military roles saw him first as chief of the cavalry, then commander of the army. He was subsequently the royal commissioner for foreign lands and the superintendent of all his majesty's works, including the Ramesseum.[329]

The workers and the pharaoh

The pharaoh's legacy in monumental architecture was well known throughout the two lands of Egypt. His military prowess was not less known, and the nationwide publicity that had been created after his campaign against the Hittites in Kadesh had transformed Rameses II into a living legend. Scenes from this battle also abounded on the walls of his mortuary temple, the Ramesseum that was less than a kilometre away from the workers' settlement.

Though not constantly resident there on the East Bank, the pharaoh was not away from Thebes all of the time. In the winter months he would move to Thebes for its warmer climate, and during the summer months he would go to Memphis for a cooler one. His key courtiers, favourite wives and concubines, and children followed him around everywhere, even on his military ventures.

His representatives in the persons of the viziers were established both in Memphis and in Thebes. In fact it was the vizier of Thebes who effectively made all the important decisions on behalf of the pharaoh insofar as the workmen at the village were concerned. The vizier in Thebes was the official person responsible for the pharaoh's tomb, and in the pharaoh's name he was expected to inspect and review the tomb project from time to time, a task he carried out regularly and responsibly.[330]

The only opportunity that Neferabet would have had to see the pharaoh from afar, and never face to face, would have been during the religious festivals at Karnak when the pharaoh would go there with all his entourage to make offerings towards the prosperity of all of Egypt.

The pharaoh was known for his travels to all the corners of his kingdom, and every native Egyptian knew about the visit of Rameses II and Nefertari to Nubia in the twenty-fourth year of his reign in order to inaugurate the magnificent temples there at Abu Simbel.

Furthermore, the pharaoh travelled independently of the season for the two major festivals of the Theban year, when he would join the high priesthood in Thebes for a pompous visit to the West Bank.

In the second month of summer,[331] there was the Beautiful Feast Day of the Valley, when the cult statue of Amen travelled from its home at Karnak Ipet Isut across the river Nile to the Deir el-Bahri temple of Hatchepsut. There he was supposed to mate with Hathor, and nine months later Hathor would give birth to the god Nefertum.

There was also the Feast of Opet, when the shrine of Amen would be carried on the river from the temple of Karnak to the southern temple of Opet, the Luxor temple of today. The celebrations would have dragged on from mid-August to the first of September.

The royal retinue and the nobility were all in attendance during these festivals,[332] and the workmen on the West Bank would have been granted leave and given the opportunity to witness these festivities and even possibly catch sight of the pharaoh and his court.

The royal tombs

The landscape in the Valley of the Kings would have been different in the lifetime of Rameses II than it is today.

Natural phenomena have significantly altered the topography.

The royal tombs are scattered all over the Valley, yet the choicest site was right at its main entrance. Since this area was located in the lowermost parts of what had once been an ancient river bed, flooding episodes tended to be particularly likely to cause severe damage to the tomb. The steep decline of the corridors made these events even more likely to occur. In fact, they started to be cut in a straight plane during the later Ramessid period, possibly for this reason.

The pharaoh's agents would have taken all the necessary precautions to position the pharaoh's tomb in a location that was unlikely to suffer from flooding. Nevertheless, there were instances when the pharaoh's tomb was subjected to such natural catastrophes, and that of Rameses II suffered a series of flooding events that caused severe damage inside it.[333] And these episodes continued causing damage long after the king's burial.

In order to avert such disasters, the builders usually resorted to the construction of canals to divert the rain water; otherwise, alternative sites would have been sought for the pharaoh's tomb then under construction.

According to Bierbrier, the first tomb for Rameses had to be abandoned not long after it was begun due to the unsafe condition of the rock into which it was being excavated,[334] and a second one was started immediately afterwards. Already by the fifth year of Rameses II's rule, his second tomb had reached an advanced stage. The upper corridor had been finalised, its walls had been sculpted with the standard religious texts and imagery, and the quarrying of the lower sections of the tomb was under way. The architecture was immaculately executed and was precise to a hundredth of an inch.[335]

Once the bulk of the work on the tomb of Rameses II had been completed, the number of tomb workmen at the Great Place diminished steadily. This was just around the time that Neferabet started working at the Great Place. Once the cutting of the passage to the burial chambers was finished, the great stone sarcophagus that had been prepared in the royal workshops in Thebes would have been brought over for its placement inside the burial chamber.

Neferabet would have had the opportunity to examine the magnificence of the royal tomb while it was still in its pristine, though not completely finalised, state.

Right at the entrance gate, Neferabet would have been able to observe the beautifully decorated jambs and lintel, and on the inside surface of the gate, the delicate carvings of the goddess Ma'at, the goddess who traditionally greeted and welcomed the pharaoh to his tomb "with promises of endless life, power and magic gifts".[336] Beyond the entrance and the descending stairway, Neferabet would have started on his walk down the tomb and identified the first Litany of Ra on the walls of the first corridor. All along the walls there was the most beautiful and richly coloured decoration in raised relief, in paint and also in painted plaster.

Totally in keeping with the pharaoh's image in all its parameters, his tomb was one of the largest in the valley, at that time and forever after. It covered an area of 686 square metres altogether and extended for a distance of 168 metres into the rock of the large hillside. The opening of the tomb was situated very close to the entrance to the Great Place.

The right-angled tomb plan that had been adopted in the tombs of the Eighteenth Dynasty terminated with Akhenaten, and his was the first to be cut in a straight line. The others followed in the same style for a while, but there was a reversion to the right-angled layout with the tomb of Rameses II.

His father Seti I's tomb was renowned for its high-quality raised relief, a very laborious and time-consuming process. Although Rameses II imitated the decoration utilised by his father, he settled for the more rapidly produced low relief.[337]

The next major tomb project would be commissioned on the death of Rameses and the accession of his successor. The workmen at the Great Place would then utilise what they had learnt from the work of their predecessors on the tomb of Rameses that had been already carried out before they started to work there.

Besides the one under construction for pharaoh, there were also the tombs for his children that were accessed rather often. There were also the tombs of the queens and princesses in the Place of Beauties, today's Valley of the Queens.

Transferring the workers

The workmen would not normally have been unduly pressured for time.[338] Rameses II's tomb, KV7, was probably completed during his lifetime which was one of the longest amongst the pharaohs. Yet the workmen of the pharaoh's tomb had other jobs to carry out in the meantime.

When the work on the tombs was in a quiescent phase, some of the workmen at the Great Place were transferred to the Place of Beauties in order to prepare and decorate the tombs of the wives and daughters of the pharaoh, but particularly for that of his chief queen, Nefertari (QV66).[339] The tombs of the numerous wives of Rameses II also required decoration.

Since Nefertari died around the year twenty-five to thirty of the reign of Rameses II and Neferabet was not around before year forty-six, he would not have been involved in its decoration unless her tomb was decorated after her death. However, Neferabet's father, Neferrenpet, would definitely have been involved. There were also the tombs of Meritamen (QV68) and of Nebettawi (QV60), both daughters of Nefertari. They would presumably have passed away during the active painting years of Neferabet.

Rameses had also sired a considerable number of sons and daughters through a number of secondary wives and concubines. Halfway through his reign, several of the offspring had already predeceased him, and most if not all of these required a final resting place. So besides the main tomb for the pharaoh, the workmen would therefore also have been assigned the extra task of hewing out and decorating yet another major tomb across the valley floor on the opposite side. This extra tomb complex was meant for the sons of Rameses for so far, all bodily remains that have been found in this tomb are male. An estimate of the number interred there exceeds a hundred individuals.

This extra tomb is known today as KV5, and its extent has only been made known to scholars since 1987, when the Theban Mapping Project was set into operation. It is today the largest tomb known in the Valley of the Kings, with more than a hundred and thirty corridors and fifty side chambers that were set aside for the overgrown royal family of Rameses. For this reason, the tomb has a set-up and architecture of its own that is unique in the valley. [340]

From time to time one of the deceased children of Rameses would have been brought over in the manner deserving of a pharaoh's son to be interred in this tomb. Unlike that of their father, which would have been sealed permanently until the pharaoh's demise and burial, the tomb for the sons of pharaoh was opened up now and again whenever one of the many princes predeceased his father.

As a workman in the valley, Neferabet would have been acquainted with this tomb as well and would probably have contributed towards its decoration.

Neferabet would surely not have been able to visit KV5 on his own. The workmen were always in gangs, the right one and the left. So intricately complicated was its multi-levelled plan that some form of system must have been devised that enabled the workmen, inspectors, and visitors to return to the entrance. Because of the absence of adequate ventilation, the exposure to pollution and dust must have been enormous and the occupational health risks significant.

Besides the name of the pharaoh in its cartouche, Neferabet might also have painted the names and titles of his deceased sons and depicted them upon the walls of the tomb. There were other scenes, and these showed the pharaoh presenting his sons to the deities of the netherworld with texts extracted from chapter 125 of the Book of the Dead. As the years go by, the Theban Mapping Project continues to reveal more of KV5's secrets and makes us aware of what the tomb workmen were up to at the time of Neferabet's sojourn there.

Rameses II dies

The pharaoh Usermare Setepenre Rameses II eventually entered the Afterlife in the sixty-seventh year of his reign. When the time for burial came, the remains were escorted in a large procession of dignitaries and high priests that crossed the Nile from Thebes to the West Bank. The retinue then accompanied the dead pharaoh across the plains to the valley at the Great Place and to his tomb, where he was to be interred for eternity. The new pharaoh was there in the cortège, and it was part of his obligation before assuming the role of pharaoh to perform the opening of the mouth ceremony upon his predecessor, his father Rameses the Great.

News of the death of the pharaoh would have reached the settlement several weeks before. The process of mummification consumed seventy days, and during that time, the final touches to the tomb would have been feverishly under way. The furniture would also have been brought over from the workshops in Thebes and laid out deep in the mountainside, inside the funerary vaults of tomb KV7.[341]

As the final preparations proceeded at an accelerated rate, the scribe with the long name of Kenherkhopshef kept himself extremely busy with his usual log of all that was being utilised by way of tools, oil lamps, wicks, and other utensils on site. He also recorded the workmen's attendance and absences. But there was also the additional task of checking and auditing all that was being transferred in and out of the tomb. He was responsible for the whereabouts of the large quantity of furniture, statuettes, amulets, and all the other funerary equipment that had been prepared to accompany the pharaoh on his final journey.

Throughout his lifetime, Neferabet had only known Rameses II as king of Egypt. The pharaoh was truly an immortal god; his own sons were dying before him. Furthermore, Rameses II had significantly modified the political and military status of the two lands, particularly vis-à-vis the Asiatics to the East and the Nubians to the South. He had changed the landscape of Egypt with his massively larger-than-life monuments and statuary.

Neferabet would have been justified in asking himself what was going to happen next, and the answer was simple enough. Although an appreciable number of crown princes to the Egyptian throne had passed away before their father, there were many others who survived.[342] The eldest of these princes went by the name of Banenre Merenptah,[343] and he was in line to be the next king of Egypt. He was already advanced in years, and starting immediately on his tomb was considered to be a rather urgent business.

Although, this involved a heightened wave of activity for the workmen at the Place of Truth, there was no extra benefit for them for they received the same wages in the form of rations regardless of the amount of labour that they were contributing.

At the beckoning of the vizier in Thebes, the foremen and scribe at the Great Place were urged to start getting things moving. There was a recall to the Valley of the Kings of those workmen who might have been transferred to the

Valley of the Queens or who had been privately employed at the tombs of the nobles during the relatively quiet phase of tomb building towards the end of the pharaoh's reign.

The site for the new tomb was soon selected by a commission under the vizier, who would have visited the Valley of the Kings for this express purpose. In consultation with the new pharaoh, the royal architects then prepared the blueprints for the tomb that more or less followed a standard pattern apart from a few modifications.

The plans for beyond the main doorway were for an inclined stairway that led down to the first corridor, followed by a series of halls and other corridors. It was no longer the practice during the Nineteenth Dynasty to incorporate a pit and a false wall halfway along the tomb. Though it was believed for some time that this was an attempt to deceive would-be tomb robbers, several Egyptologists today are of the opinion that it was not a pit at all, but a well to catch rain water during those occasional storms in the Valley of the Kings.

The new tomb of pharaoh Merenptah was situated in the small side valley, practically next door to that of his father and running more or less parallel to its axis. The fears of cataclysmic floods had apparently not been ignored, for a deep trench was cut at the front of the tomb to prevent it from flooding.[344]

The project for the tomb of the new pharaoh was nearly as ambitious as that of his father and it is calculated that it occupied a total volume of 2,472 cubic metres. The entrance gates were very wide in comparison with the other tombs and measured 2.12 metres in width. The tomb extended for a distance of 135 metres in a straight line into the rock face of the hillside.[345] Nevertheless, it was still smaller than those of Rameses II and Seti I.[346]

For Neferabet, this was his first experience in building a tomb from square one. Once the plan of the tomb was finalised and approved, the quarrymen set to work on the rock face and started excavating the hillside. Armed either with a hoe-like pick-axe or a heavy wooden mallet and chisel, the team of tomb masons started breaking up the rock at the site of the selected entrance.

The quarry workmen were the first to be called in to work on the rock face, and once the main doorway was completed, they then started to carve out the first corridor in a series of steps that gradually descended to a lower level.

At this stage, the stone masons joined the work-force and set themselves to smooth the rough walls down to a flat surface. The plasterers followed upon their heels. After burning their gypsum and mixing it with water, they used the mixture to fill in the crevices left by the quarrymen and plaster the freshly excavated walls. They then whitewashed the walls in order to achieve a smooth, white surface.

The draughtsmen entered the tomb next, and these craftsmen sketched the texts and scenes in red ink upon the plastered walls. These religious texts and depictions related to the journey of the sun-god Re through the Underworld at sundown. The dead pharaoh was identified with Re, and his burial chamber with its sarcophagus marked the end of this journey. The pharaoh was thought to rise in the morning and make his journey with Re through the heavens and return once again to the Underworld at sunset.

The master draughtsman would then review his juniors' work for design proportions and correctness of wording and finally submit his corrections in black ink.

Next in line were the sculptors, who carved out the texts and designs with a bronze chisel to produce the depictions and texts in raised or low relief. Neferabet would have been able to follow all these steps that were carried out right before his eyes as he waited in line to come in and start painting the reliefs.

The decorators were next in line, and in addition to the sculptors of the depictions in relief, there were the painters who included Neferabet.

Neferabet would soon enough be busy in the tomb chambers. His brush and palette had to be prepared for the job ahead. There had to be adequate supplies of the basic minerals that he would need to create a new batch of paint once one was exhausted.

This time round, Neferabet and his fellow workmen were to be the ones to begin the decoration and, in all probability, see it right up to the very end.[347]

Some of the workmen were assigned the task of picking up the chippings and carrying them out of the tomb for dispersal on the floor of the valley next to the tomb. Some of these discarded slices of limestone ended up as *ostraca*, thin slabs of stone used as writing surfaces. A good example is the one we examined at the British Museum; as we have seen, it mentioned Neferabet taking leave in order to bury his brother.

The broad, pillared chamber used as the burial vault lay at the far end of the tomb, and that was where the sarcophagus was placed in readiness to receive the body of the deceased pharaoh. A number of side chambers served as store-rooms.

There as one particular incident that Neferabet would have certainly remembered for a long while. When the tomb was nearing completion, and in view of the pharaoh's advanced age, the vizier thought the time had come for the stone sarcophagus to be moved into the burial chamber. It needed to be lowered very slowly, held back by wooden beams stuck against the walls. The sarcophagus had to be positioned into the burial chamber before the painters started to work there, as otherwise it would scratch and damage the painted corridors.

Some Egyptologists are of the opinion that the sarcophagus was cut and sculpted in the quarry. However, others prefer to think that it was delivered to the tomb as a plain box and sculpted or engraved inside the tomb.

Just as the laborious process of sliding it down the tomb shaft was about to start, a major problem made its appearance. The calcite sarcophagus that was meant to be the fourth layer enveloping the pharaoh was a little bit too wide for the entrance. The gate was 2.12 metres wide, and the sarcophagus was 2.13 metres in width. The gates had already been decorated, but time was pressing, and the solution taken was rather a drastic one. Rather than have heads roll over the blunder committed by the architect and the quarrymen in not co-ordinating their projects,[348] it was decided to hack a passage through the gates by shaving the door jambs away and then repair them afterwards.[349]

The operation must have been a hurried process, for the chippings were left *in situ* on the floor and were not even removed and cleared away before the pharaoh's funeral.[350]

It might not have been an error in calculation after all. There are other options open for consideration. An extra sarcophagus might have been requested, either by the king himself or by his heir preparing for his funeral. As it would have been a last-minute delivery, they would have had to hack off the door jambs and would not have had time to sweep away the debris from the operation.

A flash flood hits the Great Place[351]

As already alluded to, the topography in the Valley of the Kings at the time was such as to permit the occasional occurrence of flooding catastrophes, and the workmen there ran the risk of being caught up in the valley below during one of these. John Romer describes one such occasion that he dated to the time of Rameses II. However recent excavations have shown that this dating could not have been a correct one, the end of the eighteenth dynasty during the reign of Aye being the most likely time frame.

Yet there were other flooding episodes and the closest to Rameses II in time of occurrence was dated to year 4 of Merenptah; a graffito in the Valley of the Kings documented this flood. This would have been during the time that Neferabet was one of the workmen there. A later one during the time of Rameses IV took place during the time that Neferabet's nephew Amennakht was performing the duties of scribe there[352].

According to Romer's account, it was at the end of a hot day in spring in the evening when the workmen were relaxing in their settlement as the heat of the day dissipated itself with the setting sun.

Dark rain clouds started gathering in the South. They were heavily saturated with water and were gradually moving towards them. Flashes of lightning suddenly started to spark between heaven and earth. This was an unusual phenomenon for the workmen to witness, yet what followed next was what took them totally by surprise and sent them reeling into a panic state.

A mighty roar caused them to turn round and focus all at once on the Mount of Meretseger. The Peak of the West suddenly became the centre of attraction and awe as it welled up with a massive amount of water that started bursting down its slope into the valley below, carrying with it tons of rock enveloped in a cloud of foam.

As the workmen raced inside their huts for cover, the storm clouds reached them overhead and provoked a major storm with heavy rain and incessant lightning. The electricity of the storm caused the ground to crunch and crackle, and this phenomenon startled the workmen to no end as they watched the cataclysm devastate the Great Place that they had been labouring on for so long. A few hours earlier and they would have all been caught and swallowed up in the devastation below.

The flash flood had wreaked havoc in the valley below as the massive amount of scattered debris that accumulated in the valley floor assumed a sludge-like appearance.

All was over in about twenty minutes, as the flood waters ceased to augment and spread themselves out all over the fields below and headed towards the Nile. It was an event that remained imprinted in the minds of all the workmen there.

For days on end the workmen were isolated in their settlement, ignorant as to the true extent of the damages wrought to the tombs that they had been working on for the previous years. The tomb of their pharaoh Rameses would have been closed at any time even if work was in progress. The question was whether the wooden door could have held up the water and debris out of the tomb; if not the corridors would definitely have been thoroughly flooded and filled up with rocky debris; unless of course diverting channels had been created at the start of the tomb excavations. Had the tomb been flooded, the decorations they had worked upon for so long a time would have suffered enormously.

This and other major floods would have covered over the low lying tombs that included those of Tutankhamen and of Rameses II. Tutankhamen's tomb could easily have got covered over and forgotten in this manner. The story is well known that Rameses VI/VII subsequently built his tomb [KV 9] on top of that of Tutankhamen and effectively delayed its discovery even further until 1922.

As they ventured down the valley when they thought it was safe to do so, the tomb workmen discovered that very large chunks of the cliff face had been swept away and carried along the prehistoric river bed in the form of boulders as high as twelve feet.

At the centre of the valley the storerooms and the old huts of the workmen had been shattered and lay buried under thick layers of sand and rock. More significantly however, the accumulation of boulders and wet debris had caused extensive damage to the tombs. Only a few withstood the brunt of the flood waters, and most had their corridors smashed and were flooded with water and debris that remained inside their labyrinth for centuries.

The tombs of the nobles at Abd el-Qurna and Dra abu Naga were dug into the hill; they had courtyards in front of their tombs enclosed by low walls. The flood waters would have flow down over them without wreaking too much damage. And in the Valley of the Kings only the early tombs were dug into the cliffs. The later tombs including those of Tutankhamen and Rameses II were dug at the bottom of the valley and were very prone to flooding. The workmen's primary concern was for the tomb they had been working on, for it had lain directly in the flood's path.

The tomb workmen could only wait until the valley floor dried up sufficiently for them to resume their work and start clearing away the accumulated debris and hoping to restore the damages incurred. In the heat of the Luxor sun the flooded valley would have most probably dried up in the course of a day or two.

As already indicated, The ancient Egyptians were certainly not unaware of these dangers and in fact there was a network of channels that they dug up in the Valley of the Kings in order to direct such accumulated water volumes away from the tombs. Even Zahi Hawass who is presently excavating there reported coming upon some of these ancient water channels in the Valley. There were also wells that were dug behind the tomb's entrance and behind its first chamber. These represented further efforts on the part of the workmen at minimising the danger of flood water entering the tombs.

Torrential floods continued to occur sporadically over the centuries so that the tomb of Rameses continued to suffer after his demise through the debris and water that entered its extensive labyrinth, and in modern times has constituted a major challenge to the archaeologist to excavate and document fully.

Illness and disease amongst the workmen

Natural catastrophes were not the only risks to health and life; illness was common amongst the workmen. Their most common of ailments were eye conditions and scorpion bites. Neferabet's grandfather was a scorpion charmer, but what

219

that actually entailed in the healing process is a moot point[353].

Remedies abounded for most conditions and ailments, but it is not probable that assistance was always available at the place of work. For instance, Paherpedjet, the acting physician at the work camp, was himself absent at one time tending to three other workmen at the village, Aapahte, Khons and Horemwia[354]. On another occasion the wife of the scribe at the camp was also ill and she too demanded the physician's attention at the village.[355]

Traditionally depicted as shaven dark skinned males dressed up in a simple loincloth, these workmen from the Place of Truth were in the shade for most of the daylight hours. They would have not been as tanned as their counterparts who toiled under the direct rays of the sun. However they were exposed instead to a number of detrimental environmental factors that affected their health to some degree or other.

The one, single task of the workmen at the Place of Truth was the creation of the pharaoh's tomb. According to Bierbrier, "all the phases of construction [of the tomb] – excavation, plastering, designing, carving and painting – would be going on at once in different rooms of the tomb"[356]. And according to Vernus[357] the working conditions for the workmen were at their worst for all the crafts involved in the tomb building process.

The diggers and excavators dug out the rock from the mountain face and had it removed manually. The artisans who worked closer to the entrance, in the rooms already excavated, would have been exposed to the dusty contamination that was constantly suspended in the air around them.

Their eyes would smart and their nostrils soon enough start to itch and annoy them. These minute particles formed a homogenous cloud that was unavoidably inhaled by the workmen as they walked down the tomb into its darker recesses. No doubt their breathing in of the polluted air later caused them to cough vigorously in order to remove the dust-impregnated catarrh. The catarrh was a good thing for it caused most of the air particles to stick to it, and thus prevent them from reaching down further into the lungs and causing severe illness. Over protracted periods of time however, such as when the workmen spent four-hour shifts at a time, the load of dust would have been too much for their lungs to cope with, and would inevitably have led to breathing problems.

Had there been any siliceous stone involved in the trenching operations and stone dressing procedures, this would have caused serious problems and prematurely fatal lung disease.

At the time that they were working at the entrance of the tomb, ventilation would not have been such a major problem, yet once the recesses of the crypt became darker and deeper inside the mountain, then breathing difficulties were inevitable.

Adequate illumination was obligatory if the job was to be carried out well, and the smoke emitted from oil lamps would have caused damage to both the health of the artisan and his art. However this problem had been catered for, and the traditional oil lamps had salt incorporated into the oil to minimize the smoke emitted by the linen wick[358].

The bones, joints and ligaments of the workmen were also affected in some way or other. Non exposure to the sun would have caused them to lack vitamin D and resultant liability to contracting rickets and problems with their bones if they drank insufficient amounts of milk or other Vitamin D containing foods to make up for this deficiency.

Restricted spaces in the tomb environment obliged them to assume unorthodox positions that would have strained their joints and their backs, caused them to kneel and assume the most awkward and cramped postures for most of the time and thus stress their joints further.

Their long exposure to conditions of attenuated illumination would not have rendered them more vulnerable to any particular problems with their eyesight. It would have been physical irritants in the air that would have had an effect upon their sensitive eye coverings, the conjunctivae, and caused repeated episodes of conjunctivitis. The involvement of the central part of the front of the eye at the cornea would have caused a keratitis that impaired vision, whilst foreign bodies that got lodged inside the coverings of the eyeball would have had a similarly irritating effect upon the eye surface. The particular nature of limestone in being especially irritating to the eyeball surface rendered it a chief culprit in causing much of the eye problems amongst these workmen.

Temporary blindness suffered by Neferabet

Our Neferabet seems to be a favourite prototype amongst authors dealing with temporary blindness amongst the workmen at the Place of Truth, and he is often quoted in the literature in this regard.

The European visitors to Egypt in the early nineteenth century remarked on the frequency of blindness amongst the population there. This was more frequently being reported in Lower Egypt and was more of a permanent problem.359 Neferabet lived and worked in Upper Egypt, and he suffered from a temporary form of blindness that eventually healed.

According to Heritage Malta, the Museum's research indicated that Neferabet suffered from an occupational loss of vision, 'through the terrible conditions of his job'. It would have been the excavators and sculptors who would have been most likely to suffer from injuries to their eyes from flying stone fragments. Those who smoothed the stone surfaces with abrasives would have been the ones most exposed to the irritants in the air around them that inflamed their fine and sensitive eye coverings, the conjunctivae. On the other hand the plasterers might have been blinded through their use of lime, and that would have been a permanent disability at the time when no corrective surgery for it was available. Yet the proximity of all and sundry of the other tomb workmen rendered them all vulnerable to the effects of the exposure, though to a varying degree.

The paints do not seem to have been the culprits. It seems that no solvents were used for their pigments. These were made up of a number of natural harmless ingredients – powdered malachite, ochre, coal, mixed with animal fats and eggs. The ochres and frits were ground or grated into fine powder and bound by medium such as plant gum or animal glue.[360] These ingredients do not produce eye infections or irritation. The malachite for example that was used for green paint was in fact also used by the physicians to treat eye infections[361]. Its low copper content permitted it to be used as a mild anti-inflammatory agent.[362]

Neferabet would have been blinded by some temporary inflammation of the eyes, for it is documented that he eventually recovered from it. He was apparently not aware of its cause for he tells us that his blindness had been caused by his sins. Hence an 'invisible agent' must have been assumed by him as the cause his illness. In one of his funerary steles Neferabet confessed that Ptah had caused his blindness because of a false oath that he had taken in the god's name.

Neferabet's 'angered god' would today translate into a viral agent or long standing inflammation of those parts of the eye known as the cornea or the iris. Respectively these would cause a keratitis and iritis that would have been responsible for his eye inflammation and temporary blindness.

The treatment for the condition would have been the responsibility of the village doctor, the *swnw*. At any one time there would have been only one *swnw* in the village and he catered for the needs of the entire community. Conveniently for Neferabet the *swnw* of his time was his father-in-law. Although we have the thanksgiving stele that was dedicated to the goddess Meretseger when his blindness was over, it would appear that his father-in-law must have also taken at least some of the credit for the cure.

Various medications for eye illnesses survive in the many medical papyri but in most we see superstitious and magical remedies rather than healing agents. Probably the most efficient treatment of an eye infection was honey and *kohl*. Pigments were also used as mild antiseptics; the cosmetic *kohl*, a black eye-paint, and the green paint malachite were examples of such. And honey was also known to have possessed a number of curative properties, as fungus and bacteria cannot survive in its substance.[363]

Other options as the cause of the blindness deserved some consideration. The prevalence of parasites such as *Entamoeba Histolytica* and *Bilharzia* in the Nile waters would be more likely responsible for infiltration of the corneal surface of the eye that would cause reduced vision. The traditional remedies for this condition that were available at the time would not have been very efficient at removing the parasite from the system and the blindness would have tended to be a permanent one. Furthermore the village was sufficiently far removed from the Nile to make bathing and washing in its waters most improbable, and therefore parasitic eye infections most unlikely. Furthermore the ancient Egyptians did not use the Nile water for bathing or drinking. They had wells from which they drew underground water. It seems that the Nile water was restricted to wash clothes, dishes, animals and for the drainage of sewage into it. Because of the presence of crocodiles, activities close to the river were a constant hazard to life. In fact the Bilharzia would have only affected the people who actually worked on the Nile waters: the washerwomen and men, the fishermen, sailors and also the farmers during the annual flood, when they would go bare foot in the fields.

Infectious diseases of the eyes would have been common in the workmen's village which was rather crowded in the accommodation provided, so that infectiousness and cross infection from one person to another was more likely. Outside their homes, the paths and dirt tracks that they utilised every day in their daily routines were, contrary to common belief, not significantly dusty and hence not a source of constant irritation to the eyes. In fact, the paving at the Place of Truth, as in the rest of the towns in ancient Egypt, was animal dung that was trodden down to a hard consistency. The roads were certainly smelly and also rather muddy after the occasional and rare rain shower.

However, once outside the town and the cultivated areas, especially in the open desert, wind borne sand and dust would have been a source of continuous irritation to their eyes.

Neferabet was certainly not the only workman at Deir el Medina who made mention of his temporary blindness that was healed through the intervention of a deity. We investigated the literature in order to get an overall view of the occurrence of blindness at the village and the frequency of cures. A number of funerary steles were available for this very purpose.

A diagnostic determinative?[364]

The hieroglyph that has been constantly used in these phrases relating to blindness was the determinative N46b. The use of it started during the New Kingdom and stood for 'night' or 'darkness'.

We looked for this reported 'blindness' in a number of artefacts. These included four steles from Turin and another two from the British Museum. These steles had been dedicated by specifically named workmen residing at Deir el Medina. The following translations were obtained for the phrases that incorporated the N46b determinative.

From the British Museum where it is preserved, Stele BM 589 concerned our Neferabet, with the text stating that 'he caused me to behold darkness by day.' The prayer is to Ptah, the god of the craftsmen and the hearer of prayers, and Neferabet seeks his eyesight back in order to see the god Amen. We had examined this stele at the British Museum when we visited the Department of Egypt and Sudan in 2008.

We had missed seeing the other stele at the British Museum that we were concerned with, BM 374. This depicted Amennakht, the scribe of Set-Ma'at, in a kneeling position facing the Mistress of the West, Meretseger, and the hieroglyphs translate into 'thou causest me to see darkness by day.' This was most probably referring to Amennakht the nephew of Neferabet. The name is his and so is the title, namely 'Scribe in the Place of Truth, Set Ma'at'. Amennakht was a trained painter like his uncle, and it seems that he too went through a transient phase of blindness. However, in his later position as scribe he would not have been exposed to the dust in the tombs or any ingredients in the paint.

I had also missed seeing Stele 50046 [318] when visiting the *Museo Egizio* in Turin. This shows the sculptor Neferrenpet[365] with his wife and daughter in front of Thoth, the hieroglyphs here translating into 'thou causest me to see a darkness of thy making.'[366] This was rather odd for Thoth was a patron of scribes rather than of sculptors.

The N46b determinative for the 'darkness' associated with blindness is also seen in the Turin stele 50050 that belonged to the woman Heria and was dedicated to Ahmose Nefertari.

Stele Turin 50051 [279] shows Nebtnuhet, the wife of the workman Wennefer, speaking out 'thou causest me to see a darkness of thy making', in front of a deity that has proved difficult to differentiate between Thoth and Soped.

Stele Turin 50052 belonged to the draughtsman Pai who faces Khonsu. Once again the hieroglyphs translate into 'thou causest me to see a darkness of thy making.'

There was yet another stele that included the determinative hieroglyph N46b, and this is known as Stele Bankes No. 6. It was dedicated to Iy-neferti, the wife of the workman Senedjem, and the text runs thus *'you have caused me to see darkness by day.'* The deity is not mentioned in the translation that was made available by David G. Smith.[367]

A number of scholars that include Galán and Manniche[368] argue that the darkness or blindness being referred to was not necessarily a physical one,[369] and this in view of the fact that the individuals referred to in the text as *'seeing the darkness by the day'* were all represented with perfectly normal eyes. Gunn studied a number of these texts and his translations are the ones being quoted here. He remarked that it was "very strange that this affliction should occur proportionally so often, and be at the same time the only one specified by the victims of divine retribution".[370]

It would seem that the temporary blindness suffered by Neferabet was either a very common one that afflicted the tomb workmen, or else was merely referring to some form of spiritual blindness commonly incorporated into these formulae inscribed on their funerary steles.

Yet if Neferabet was suffering from a spiritual blindness he would have consulted a priest, rather than, according to Bierbrier, his father-in-law, the village doctor or *swnw*[371]. It is far more likely that his blindness was a physical one. However this does not necessarily imply that the remainder of the villagers who mentioned blindness were constantly referring to physical eye illnesses. They might very well have been referring to a spiritual affliction.

A Polish study has been carried out that might shed some light on the complications on vision from working underground for long periods of time. A. Gosk and L. Borodulin-Nadzieja studied eighty-two copper mine workmen for field of vision and eye's resolving power. Their conclusions are summed up in the following.

"Preliminary examination was performed above ground before the miners started their work and later, after five hour's work under ground. During the follow-up examination the limitation of the field of vision was found in 64% of face foremen and in 13.6% of off-face miners. This limitation was observed in the lower temporal quadrants. The limitation is probably of central origin and is connected with the effects of occupational agents, e.g. noise. The eye's resolving power assessed underground was statistically remarkably lower than above ground. However, taking into consideration the inadequate lighting, one might expect more serious changes of this characteristic".[372]

John Romer offered a balanced view of the situation.[373] He proposes a significant incidence of infectious diseases of the eye in the crowded and dusty conditions of the workmen's job. The documented remedies in the form of tortoise brain and caustic soda would most probably not have been as effective as the normal nursing methods that are adopted today. On the other hand Romer's suggestions of the possibility of hysterical blindness or a temporary blood clot accounting for the temporary blindness do not appear convincing or likely to the present authors. In the days before antibiotics Neferabet's temporary blindness would certainly have been caused by infection.

More pharaohs to paint for

Other tombs followed the one for Merenptah and there was more hollowing out of the mountain side in the Valley of the Kings for the final resting places of the succeeding pharaohs, those for Seti II, Amenmesse, Siptah and Tawosret in the 19th dynasty. With the number of tombs in the Valley increasing in number, it became quite common for tomb shafts to be aborted when they ran into a previous one.

The first pharaoh of the 20th dynasty was Userkhaure Sethnakht. Just as soon as his tomb site was identified, the workmen started immediately on their project at hand. Progress on the quarrying was steadily being maintained and the decorators had already set to work on the entrance and first corridor when a major problem erupted. The corridor that was being quarried broke into the corridor of another tomb and the project had to be abandoned.

Sethnakht was not unduly bothered and ordered his vizier to see that the tomb of Sitre Tawosret who had ruled before him be requisitioned and taken over for his own use[374]. Sethnakht ruled for only two years, though according to the recent discovery of a stele at Karnak his maximum regnal year was 4. He died before his tomb was completed and his heir had him placed him as best he could, together with Tawosret in the latter's tomb.

But then two years later the same thing happened again with the succeeding pharaoh, Rameses III when his tomb shaft had to be abandoned because of the nature of the rock into which it was being excavated. This time the solution was to utilise the shaft that had been started for his father and have it re-directed in order to avoid the adjoining tomb.[375]

The trail back to the village

John Romer provides us with a good description of the route back home from the Great Place to the Place of Truth. A path led up from the valley towards the top of the hill where the horizon of Thebes could be viewed in all of its glory. Halfway up, the police officials who were stationed in the Medjay's fortress would have monitored the workers and given them clearance before they continued their climb upward along the path.

The route then followed the sinuous trail in a northerly direction along the path on the top of the hills that led to the workmen's village at the Place of Truth.[376]

It would have been shortly before sundown that the tomb workmen started marching on their journey home. There were the excavators, stone masons, plasterers, draughtsmen, painters, the scribe, and the two foremen.[377] This was the day when the workmen at the Great Place would leave the work camp and walk back along the two-kilometre stretch of land that separated them from their family homes.[378]

The long stretch of eight working days had gone by, and the eagerly anticipated rest period had finally arrived; there were two days of weekend that Neferabet and his father could spend with their families.[379]

Together with the other artisans and labourers, Neferabet and his father, Neferrenpet, marched up along the path that led from the valley of the pharaoh's tombs. Each workman carried his toolkit with him in order to return it to the storerooms in the village.

It had been a sojourn of hard work for the fifty-odd "servants at the Place of Truth", as the artisans and other workmen there were known. The two gangs of tomb builders normally worked an eight-hour day that was split up into two four-hour shifts. However, there were a number of festivals throughout the year that gave them more days off, amounting to 125 days off annually.[380]

Once they reached the Place of Truth, Neferabet would have needed a shave of his face and scalp. His body required bathing, for the rations of water they were allotted during the work phase would not have permitted such a luxury. The priorities there were the quenching of thirst and hunger. Once back in the village, the availability of water was not a problem. Servants were assigned to transport all the necessary water supplies from the Nile to the village on the backs of asses.

Promotions in the family

Towards the end of his life, Neferabet was privileged to become a village elder. He was also fortunate enough to witness a number of promotions within his family circle.

Two of Neferabet's brothers were Amenemopet[381] and Ipuy.[382] Both were selected as foremen of the workmen's gangs.

According to Bierbrier, Ipuy's eldest son, Amennakht, was a painter for a time and sometime later became a draughtsman.[383] When Ipuy died in office as foreman of one of the gangs, Amennakht was only twenty-five years old and was considered too young for a foreman's job. Although the position of foreman at the Place of Truth tended to be an inherited one, he was not elected into his father's place, and another family took this position over.

However, Neferabet's nephew persisted in his attempts to get a promotion. With the termination of employment of the foreman Paneb, a certain Anakht assumed the duties of foreman for a short while, but it was Neferabet's other brother, Amenemopet, who eventually replaced him.[384] He was later upgraded to guardian of the tomb.[385] This title should not be confused with that of a doorkeeper; rather, it was the title of the person who controlled the royal storehouses where the tools and other paraphernalia required for the tomb construction were amassed.[386]

Besides being a trained painter like his father and uncle, Amennakht was apparently also very skilled in the art of writing, because just five years following his father's death he was appointed to the post of Scribe of the Royal Tomb.[387] This position was the highest administrative post in the village. The inscriptions to this effect were engraved in both of the royal valleys, in the Great Place and the Place of Beauties.[388] They read thus: "Year sixteen [of Rameses III], the third month, the Overseer of the City, Vizier To, came to appoint scribe Amennakht, son of Ipuy, as scribe of the tomb".[389]

Strike action

Thirteen years after the date of his new appointment, Amennakht was faced with a crisis in the valley. In year twenty-nine of Rameses III, the tomb of Rameses II was broken into and robbed.[390] Enquiries, trials, and punishment of the culprits would have been the inevitable outcome of such a serious development in the royal valley.

Amennakht maintained his position as scribe of the tomb until the reign of Rameses IV,[391] when his responsibilities rose sharply as the work-force at the Place of Truth suddenly increased to include 120 workers.[392]

He had the opportunity to prove himself a very capable official when dealing with extremely volatile situations. One of these was the apparently unprecedented state of affairs when the workmen at the Place of Truth suddenly went out on strike and this without any previous notice of any kind.

In the second month of year twenty-nine of the pharaoh Rameses III, Amennakht was still in office, and this was the time of the well-known workmen's strikes in response to delayed rations. Whether the workmen at the Place of Truth struck regularly for better conditions is uncertain; the historical record is blank on this apart from the singular papyrus that has been given the name of the "Turin Strike Papyrus" by Egyptologists. It was one of the papyri that I had the opportunity to see during my tour of the *Museo Egizio* in Turin. The episode outlined below must have been special in some way or other, and might even have been the first of its kind in ancient Egypt, for the cited papyrus manuscript by Amennakht attests to it in some extra detail.

The workmen at the village had not received their wages for about three weeks and had initially manifested their discontent by visiting a royal funerary temple, that of Horemheb.

The problem with the supply of rations was not a one-time episode but a recurring one. Eventually, the workmen were forced to abandon their place of work and move out of the village. They headed towards the mortuary temples on the plains in the West Bank and engaged themselves in noisy protests to their supervisors.

They subsequently entered the precincts of the Ramesseum and manifested their grievances there in a more determined manner.

Although their demands were eventually met, the problem came up again in the following months, and this time the workmen involved their families in the evacuation process from the village and the protests in front of the mortuary temples.

When their protests once again fell upon deaf ears, the workmen threatened to violate the tombs. At this stage, the vizier provided them with half their rations under the pretext that the granaries were empty.

Amennakht intervened at this point. He assumed a key and decisive role, one that involved a modicum of courage when dealing with an angry mob of disgruntled workmen. His friendly, persuasive manner proved to be an effective tool in pacifying the workmen and getting them to return to their place of work. After distributing a part of the rations to the workmen, he led them over to the riverbank and urged them to return to their village.

But four days later, the workmen were incited to protest once again over their half wages in rations. Yet once again a very diplomatic Amennakht managed to tide them over during the crisis and stabilise the situation.[393]

Strike action against unjust conditions of work had taken root and became entrenched in the system as a means of protesting against the authorities; strikes continued to be common under succeeding pharaohs. However by this time Neferabet had long passed away.

Life after death

The ancient Egyptian's preoccupation with the Afterlife and the body's final resting place was not the sole concern of the pharaoh. This was a universal phenomenon that was spread out across the human spectrum of society, from royalty right down through the nobility, the upper and middle echelons, and even the working classes.

It must have been another sad day for Neferabet when his father, Neferrenpet, passed away.[394] He had sired a large family. Mahi had borne him several children of both sexes, sixteen in all. Neferabet had nine brothers, 'Anhotep, Ipuy, Amenemopet, Meryma'a, Merysakhme, I, Nebenter, Houi, and Pay; there were also six sisters, Taese, Moutnofre, Esetnofre, Tenamente, Tenthay and Taysenofre.

Neferabet carried on in the same tradition of his father when it came to siring children. He had six sons, Meron, Nedjemger, Neferrenpet, Pashed, Lot, and Ramose; there were also nine daughters, Iy, Mahi, Moutemope, Henttou, Hentta, Hetepi, Esetnofre, Tenthay, and Hentone. Neferabet deeply missed his deceased sons, and especially Meron, who died at a relatively young age. There was one granddaughter documented at the time of Neferabet's demise. This was Ra'meret, and she was most probably the daughter of Nedjemger. She too had pre-deceased her grandfather.[395]

When children died at a very tender age in ancient Egypt they would be buried under the floor of the family residence[396] rather than in the cemetery. This was done in the hope that the spirit of the dead child might be reborn to the grieving mother. Neferabet's brothers Ipuy and Amenemopet started off as painters at the Place of Truth, but their next brother Houi did not make it for he passed away before he was old enough to join the work force.[397] Houi would probably have died young for he is not listed as occupied at the time of his death.[398]

The infant mortality rate was high at the time, and Neferabet lost a number of his own children prematurely. These young deaths must have further prompted him to start the work of preparing his own tomb earlier rather than later. This was probably standard procedure for all the workmen at the Place of Truth.

Although most of his children survived into adulthood, all his sons pre-deceased him and these included Neferrenpet, whom he had named after his father, Nedjemger, Ramose, Lot and his 'beloved' Meron; out of seven daughters he lost six, Tenthay, Esetnofre, Hetepi, Moutemope, Mahi and Hentone. His wife Taese also passed away before him. Neferabet was apparently survived by just one daughter, Hentta.[399]

Neferabet's burial

Neferabet had survived a succession of pharaohs, from Rameses the Great right up to Rameses III. He had outlived most if not all of his contemporaries. His longevity earned him a rare privilege, according to Romer, that of being elevated to the status of a village elder.

During Neferabet's modest burial procedures, his surviving children would first have delivered his cadaver to the embalming workshop. After mummification and wrapping, the eldest son would have carried out the "opening of the mouth" ceremony. His son would also make funerary offerings whilst Neferabet's mummy was being deposited inside the tomb where his wife and many of his children had already been laid to rest for eternity.

The full mummification procedure as we know it was affordable only to royalty and the nobility. It was beyond the reach of the workmen.

The process for royalty and the nobility was rather a lengthy one. After a period of dehydration, the internal organs were removed and preserved in special containers known as canopic jars. The brain was disposed of, but the heart was returned to the chest. The body was then packed in order to approximate it as nearly as possible to its form in life.

It was then immersed in natron for forty days to desiccate it. Natron was a natural preservative and dehydrating agent. After wrapping the body in a shroud, a *cartonnage* mask was applied over the head and upper shoulder and the body was placed in its coffin or sarcophagus.[400]

However, the common people were mummified through a technique that was much less costly. The body was desiccated in the same manner, by immersion in natron. The internal organs were not removed by dissection through an abdominal incision. Instead, the dead body was injected with palm wine and the anus plugged. After some time, the body was unplugged and the dissolved internal organs were flushed out.

The tomb workmen would hardly have afforded a wooden coffin and definitely not a stone sarcophagus. A *cartonnage* cover over the bandaged mummy was the most that the craftsmen could afford.

Once again, stele BM 305 helps to provide us with a glimpse of some of the processes entailed in Neferabet's funerary ceremonies.

The opening of the mouth ceremony is at the top. The four mummies on the left of the scene are those of Neferabet; his wife, Taese; his mother, Mahi; and probably his father, Neferrenpet. Two male and two female mourners stand around them, and in front stand four individuals. The eldest surviving son holds up the adze and performs the ritual on the mummies. The scribe Ma'atnakhtef reads from a papyrus, and two women stand behind him. (Fig. 34)

Courtesy of the French Institute of Archaeology in Cairo

Figure 34. Some of the details of Neferabet's funerary
ceremonies can be seen on BM 305.

In the second scene, a functionary with a jackal mask leans forward over the mummy. This was a way of representing the embalmment of the deceased. The jackal-figure is attended by four sons and two women. The mummy shown here is that of Neferrenpet, Neferabet's father.

Chapels

If the religious inclinations of the workmen's community can be measured by the number of chapels that were dedicated to the gods, then these were truly remarkable. There were sixteen to eighteen chapels at the Place of Truth and a total of fifty shrines at the work camp in the Great Place.

At the northern end of the village there was the chapel of Hathor and Rameses II, whilst another to Ptah lay along the south-western path that led to the Place of Beauties. Offerings would have been placed inside these chapels to the various deities, and these included the local goddess Meretseger, the "lady of the western mountain", a deity that was considered as worthy of honour amongst the village community as Osiris himself.[401]

These chapels would also have served as depositories for the busts of deceased forebears that made up the visible elements of the ancestor cult. The head and upper torso of a dead ancestor was typically carved out of limestone and given a tripartite wig. Family members made offerings to this image in exchange for intercession with the gods.

The ancestor bust phenomenon is not yet satisfactorily explained. The ones at the Place of Truth would have been placed inside niches in the bedrooms of private houses. These busts consisted only of a rounded pedestal decorated with a large flower necklace, which represented a human head with a long wig and the upper part of a torso. These are similar to the Amarna style with large lips. The ancestor bust most likely represented the spirit of a dead ancestor.

These particular statues in the home of Deir el-Medina would most likely have played a funerary function, and this is demonstrated by a vignette on one of these busts. The text derives from the chapter for the formulae of the mysterious head in the Book of Dead[402]. The famous Book of the Dead was known as "The Book of Coming Forth by Day" to the ancient Egyptians. It is a collection of religious spells deriving from the Old Kingdom pyramid texts and Middle Kingdom coffin texts.

The French excavator at Deir el-Medina, Bernard Bruyère, excavated a number of these busts during the 1930s and 1940s, and a few have reached the museums of Europe. One of these artefacts reached the Maltese islands, and I was allowed to see it privately one afternoon by arrangement with the staff of the Museum of Archaeology in Valletta.

A visitor from the United States had been to the vaults of the museum and was permitted to examine a number of objects that were related to Egyptology. There was one artefact that was unusual, and the kindly curator on duty at the time volunteered to show it to me whilst it was out of its normal storage container. We started off from the foyer close to the ticket office on the ground floor and then went down the stairs together to the lower story. The artefact was standing erect on a wooden table in the first room that we entered. I had been asked not to take photographs, and I therefore brought some drawing paper and a sharpened B3 pencil. I also brought along a measuring tape in order to get some statistics.

It measured 50 centimetres in height and had a chest circumference of 83 centimetres. The shoulders spanned a distance of 34 centimetres. The statuette was wearing the typical tripartite wig, with the two tresses at the front framing the face and the one behind reaching as far down as the middle of the back.

Somehow it looked familiar. I must have seen it before, but I certainly had not. This *déjà vu* solved itself immediately when I recalled seeing it in a small photograph that was published early in the twentieth century by a German scholar, Albert Mayr. That was good news, for I had this early photograph that was probably far more valuable than a recent one. I also had this notion that there was a lateral view of this artefact somewhere on one of my external hard disks.[403]

The lower parts of the bust were considerably deteriorated, but it was still possible to identify a few features from what remained. It had been carved out of yellow limestone, and chemical tests had been carried out upon the stone in order to elucidate its source. The bust was originally assumed to have been found in the Delta near Naucratis, and to have been brought by the Greek merchants there over to Malta during their trading activities. But the results of the chemical tests proved a more southerly source. The limestone had been mined in Wadi Gharbah, a site in the eastern desert of Egypt near Helwan.[404] This was still quite some way off the Place of Truth.

The destiny of the Place of Truth

By the end of the twentieth dynasty the village at the Place of Truth had come to an end. This was due to the fact that the very last 20th dynasty king Rameses XI preferred to be buried in the North, perhaps at Tanis, where the royal tombs were located in front of the first pylon of the Amen temple there. His tomb KV4 was started in the Valley of the Kings but was left unfinished, abandoned, and unused.

At first the tomb seemed to have been taken over by the High Priest of Amen, Pinudjem I, who later became pharaoh in Thebes alongside the post-Ramessid pharaohs ruling from Tanis in the North, but he too abandoned the project. The Valley of the Kings was no longer favoured as the most sought-after site for the royal burials.

The craftsmen of the Place of Truth were not completely disbanded. The High Priests of Amen of the 21st dynasty were assuming pharaonic prerogatives that included having their tombs decorated; the workmen at the Place of Truth were still in demand, and they were relocated to the village that had since grown around the mortuary temple of Rameses III at Medinet Habu.

The old village at the Place of Truth was inexorably claimed by the desert sands and it then lay buried and hidden from the public eye for centuries[405].

However, during the time of the Ptolemies several of the tombs there were re-utilised. And once again, during the time of the Copts, the tombs seem to have been re-occupied and used as living quarters, with damage to the walls and some defacement of the decorations resulting as a consequence of this.

The Place of Truth remained buried beneath the sands and remarkably intact until the beginning of the nineteenth century when it shared the fate of other ancient sites that were systematically plundered, and numerous artefacts were transferred to the various museums of Europe. With the political takeover of the Muslim world, the site became known as Deir el Medina.

In the early eighteenth century the site of Abd el-Qurna some distance away was identified as Gournei by F. L. Norden and R. Pococke, two European travellers who described the village there. The British traveller Edward Lane described a 'ruined' village in the area in 1826.[406] And a map by the British Museum of 1832 outlined the Ptolemaic temple of Hathor but did not mark the site of the ancient workmen's village immediately to its South.[407]

The chapels of the workmen's tombs were amongst the first to lose their artefacts to the treasure hunters who followed in Napoleon's wake. The votive steles and statuettes that had been placed by the workmen in the various chapels and shrines at the Place of Truth and at their village settlement at the Great Place were picked up in the early decades of the nineteenth century and built up the repertoire of Egyptian artefacts in the museums of Europe.

Amongst the steles and other artefacts that were removed from the site, a significant number had not derived from the actual tombs of these workmen but from small temples where the workmen had deposited them as votive offerings.

In sharp contrast to the ancient religious inscriptions found elsewhere in Egypt, the steles from the Place of Truth were characteristically linked with themes of crime and punishment, contrition, forgiveness and humility.[408]

Egyptologists like Breasted interpret these hymns as a new development of the Ramessid period, whereas others like Gunn[409] refer to them in terms of 'religion of the poor people'. Lichtheim sees the emergence of the 'self-awareness of the individual person', where there is a merging together of the hymn with their prayers.

Illnesses were interpreted by the workmen as the just punishment for their crimes or indiscretions, and the recovery from the malady was attributed to their contrition and subsequent intervention of a deity who had to be thanked for his or her divine mercy in a visible manner, such as through a votive offering.[410]

Thus the draughtsman Nebre and his son, the scribe Khay, offered a stele[411] to Amen-Re *'who gives breath to him who is wretched'*. Nebre's father was Pay, another draughtsman at the Place of Truth, in keeping with the tradition for several members of the same family to be involved as workmen there.[412]

The tombs were discovered and excavated later, towards the turn of the twentieth century. That of Neferabet was photographed and excavated by Ernesto Schiaparelli in 1908[413], and several of the artefacts inside the tomb were carried away to the *Museo Egizio* in Turin where I had seen and photographed them just a few years earlier.

But other artefacts from Neferabet's tomb and chapel had already been carried away before this time and ended up in other museums, in the British Museum, the Cairo museum, and that of Rennes, to mention a few. If our research has shown that the proper context of this Neferabet's statuette was in the island of Gozo, then this artefact would have reached the islands before 1713.

We had considered most of the artefacts that were in some way associated with our Neferabet. It was time to study our statuette in Malta in more detail.

PART THREE

AN ANALYSIS

Investigating the statuette

The original artefact that was at the root of our investigation was a sculpture in white limestone. The statuette portrayed a dedicatee in the act of presentation of a triad of ancient Egyptian gods; it was originally dated to the Nineteenth Dynasty.[414]

The front of the artefact presented the three deities upon a throne with a back rest, and behind them stood the larger dedicatee, the individual who was presenting the triad.

This type of Egyptian artefact was not a very common one. There were various other examples of similar artefacts with a dedicatee presenting a triad of gods that varied according to the area in which the ancient Egyptian lived.[415]

Several groups of these triple deities or triads existed at certain major cult centres in ancient Egypt. The trio was usually composed of father, mother, and son. It is possible that the concept of the triad developed as a suitable theological solution for bringing together deities of an area that were previously separate. Osiris, Isis, and Horus were also venerated individually in the major shrines of Abydos, Philae, and Edfu respectively.

Deities of the triad

The pantheon of gods in ancient Egypt was a varied one that catered for practically every need both of the living and the dead. Which three of these divinities had Neferabet selected for his statuette?

A variety of deities has been proposed since the time of Sonnini. Sonnini identified the rearing cobra as a "serpent's head" without naming the divinity that it might have represented; he interpreted the solar disc above the cobra as a "lunar orb". He got the two seated deities wrong, identifying them as "Osiris with the head of a hawk and Isis with a human head". Surprisingly, Sonnini even mistook the gender and role of the dedicatee, identifying him as a priest*ess* "who carried the images of the gods at the Isiac processions, and who were called by the Greeks *pastophores*".[416] At the time of Sonnini, however, hieroglyphs had not yet been deciphered, and he might perhaps be excused for his incorrect attempt.

Next in line was the Maltese curator Dr Cesare Vassallo. He labelled the dedicatee as a 'Talamifera'; the deity on the right was interpreted as Osiris with the head of an Ibis, the female on the left as Isis, and "Horus in the middle with the large disc on his falcon's head".[417]

The British author William Tallack was in contact with Vassallo, and he merely repeated the latter's assertions, identifying Osiris and Isis as two of the deities of the triad.[418]

Dr Vassallo's successor to the curatorship of the Bibliotheca was Dr Annetto A. Caruana. A copy of his 1882 publication was fortunately at hand, and on locating his description of the statuette, we saw that Caruana had merely repeated his predecessor's identification of the dedicatee as a 'Talamifera', the deity on the right as Osiris bearing an "Ibis head", the one on the left as Isis, and the "falcon's head in the middle" as Horus.[419] Yet the deity on the proper right of the statuette's pedestal bore the head of a falcon rather than that of an Ibis, and the frontal photograph of the statuette in his publication of 1882 clearly indicates a cobra as the central deity rather than a hawk.

Then in his Museum Guide of 1919, Zammit suggested other deities for the triad. Instead of Osiris, Isis, and Horus, he identified the divinities as "Horus and Meat, goddess of Truth, one on each side of the Moon disc." The "moon disc" was clearly reminiscent of Sonnini's lunar orb, and Zammit also utilised Sonnini's *pastophores* analogy.

The dedicatee is described by Zammit as a "standing priest" with the name of Nefertanpet.[420] Where had Zammit obtained this information from? Our guess for his source was the Austrian Egyptologist Professor F. W. von Bissing, who examined the statuette in 1907. Zammit's Museum Guide for 1931 is similar to the previous one of 1919 in its attribution of the three deities.[421]

In Rosalind Moss's description of the statuette in 1949, the dedicatee is referred to as a "standing man in a long pleated skirt", and the gods are identified as "Re-Harakhti and Maet with a uraeus between them".[422] The central serpent or "uraeus" is not identified as a deity.

Finally, on the basis of Meza's research study, the gods on the triad were identified by Heritage Malta as Re-Horakhti, Ma'at, and Wadjet.

Other statuettes with triads of gods

The other ancient Egyptian statuettes presenting triads that we were acquainted with were of high officials in the pharaoh's service. Marta and I had earlier separately seen two other very similar ancient Egyptian statuettes presenting Theban triads of gods, one in the Museum of Egyptian Antiquities in Cairo and the other in the Luxor Museum of Ancient Egyptian Art.[423]

Forty centimetres in height, the statuette now in Cairo was discovered in 1905 at Karnak, in the Courtyard of the Cachette in the Temple of Amen-Re.

Upon a pedestal on a pilaster that is engraved with three vertical registers of hieroglyphs, the triad of gods includes Khonsu, Amen-Re, and Mut[424]. The dedicatee is Ramesses-Nakht, the high priest of Amen, and it is dated to the beginning of the reign of Rameses IV. This was the period immediately following Neferabet's and was similar to it in several ways.

Ramesses-Nakht was the son of a high official in the pharaoh's service named Meribast. Promoted to the post of high priest of Amen by Rameses IV, Ramesses-Nakht served for approximately twenty-seven years under six pharaohs.

249

His statue holding a triad of Theban gods had found its place in the temple of Karnak itself.[425]

In some ways, this statuette is similar to that of our Neferabet. The wig style is composite, and the carving of the facial features of both men indicates they are from the same period, though the status of the two individuals differed widely.

The main difference is the elegance of carving of Ramesses-Nakht's statuette when compared to the relatively clumsy workmanship of Neferabet's. The postures also vary; Rameses is kneeling whilst Neferabet stands.

Ramesses-Nakht has a garment on his upper body; the elbow length sleeves are visible. Neferabet appears to be bare-chested. Ramesses-Nakht's triad is the Theban one made up of Amen, Mut, and their son Khonsu, whereas Neferabet's is different as discussed above.

A strikingly similar statuette is preserved on the first floor of the Museum of Ancient Egyptian Art in Luxor. The triad of gods is identical, the dedicatee is similarly attired and in a kneeling position, and Amen-Re is the central deity between Khonsu and Mut. The dedicatee of the triad is Qenu, the head of the storehouse of Amen, and its dating is also assigned to the Twentieth Dynasty. The context of its discovery is not given.

Late in 2009, Marta and I saw another example of a larger statue of a dedicatee presenting a triad of gods at the British Museum. It was dedicated by the royal scribe Panhesy, and he too held a triad of gods. The cartouche of Rameses II on his shoulder made him contemporary with Neferabet, and the fashion of the wig and clothing confirmed this further.[426]

Yet there were differences between the two statues. The main ones are, firstly, that Neferabet is standing while Panhesy is kneeling. Secondly, Neferabet holds an offering tray with the triad, whereas Panhesy holds a *naos* with the triad inside. Thirdly, since the deities on Panhesy's triad are of a holy family (Osiris, Isis, and Horus) that is different from the Theban one, it would seem that its place of origin might be Abydos rather than Thebes.

Workers at the Place of Truth other than Neferabet dedicated statuettes to gods, but these were not triads. Two near-contemporary workers were the scribe Ramose[427] and the worker Penchenabu.[428] However, Ramose presented a pair, Osiris and Nephthys, whilst Penchenabu's deity was a single one, that of Amen.

Identification of the deities

Our Neferabet presented three deities. Who were they? We were not happy with any of the identifications offered so far.

We started with the deity on the proper right of the statuette. Did the falcon's head in Neferabet's triad represent Osiris, Re-Horakhti, Horus, or another deity? Whilst in the process of researching this, the temple of Khonsu in Karnak came to our rescue and provided us with some very useful clues.

In this sanctuary of the temple of Khonsu, Rameses IV offers to Khonsu in one relief and to the Theban triad in another. Both these reliefs proved crucial in solving the mystery of the identification of the deities in Neferabet's triad.

The first relief depicts Rameses IV offering to Khonsu, who has a falcon's head. Marta commented firstly on the headdress surmounting the falcon head, which is a disk upon a crescent moon, and secondly on the absence of a uraeus. (Fig. 35) The crescent indicated a moon deity, so that meant either Khonsu or Thoth; and in fact the same temple of Khonsu in Karnak has a baboon statue that represents Thoth.

The second relief scene at the sanctuary of Khonsu at Karnak depicts Rameses IV before the Theban triad. Re-Horakhti wears a uraeus. (Fig. 36) On Neferabet's right

251

FC

Figure 35. Khonsu with the moon and crescent but no uraeus.

Courtesy of the Supreme Council of Antiquities, Cairo   *FC*

Figure 36. Re-Horakhti with the uraeus on his forehead.

shoulder, there is a small sunken relief of Re-Horakhti wearing a disk and a uraeus, but the falcon on the proper right of the pedestal wears no uraeus. The one orifice lies on the top of his head; the absence of an orifice on the forehead argues in favour of the identification of the falcon in Neferabet's statuette as Khonsu and against it being Re-Horakhti.

By the end of the New Kingdom, Khonsu was a healing deity,[429] and Neferabet underwent a period of temporary blindness for which he resorted to Ptah and Meretseger, but Khonsu could have been particularly important for him to include in his votive or funerary pantheon as well. Rather than Re-Horakhti, Khonsu was therefore the most likely candidate for the falcon in Neferabet's triad of gods.

The seated goddess

These two reliefs in the sanctuary of the temple of Khonsu in Karnak were also valuable in solving the identity of the female deity on the proper left of Neferabet's triad. Was it Ma'at as proposed in the Museum exhibitions of 2003 and 2005, or was it Mut as we were hypothesising?[430]

In the triad held by Neferabet, the seated goddess has an orifice on the top of her head where a headdress was once attached but is now lost.[431] And on the forehead there are the remains of a uraeus. Would these features make her more likely to be Ma'at or Mut? We were uncertain at the time as to whether Ma'at wore a uraeus or not, so we looked out for her depictions in the archaeological record.

Fortunately for us, Ma'at was depicted in the same sanctuary of the temple of Khonsu in Karnak, and it was Marta who picked her out. The goddess is wearing a headband in the first relief with Rameses IV before Khonsu, and she could therefore not have had a uraeus on her forehead like the goddess on the pedestal of Neferabet.

Figure 37. Neferabet's statuette. The seated goddess on the right has an orifice on the top of her head and the remains of a uraeus on the forehead.

AM

Figure 38. Southern wall of Hypostyle hall at Karnak.
(Rameses II); Mut stands behind Amen-Re, and she wears
the double crown and a uraeus.

Figure 39. Stele from Horemheb's tomb at the British Museum. Ma'at wears a headband and has a feather at the top of her head but no uraeus on the forehead.

We found another relief that depicted Ma'at in the kiosk scene of TT55 where the deity is seated behind the enthroned king identified with Amenhotep III.[432] Ma'at wears a hair band and no uraeus.

The opportunity to confirm this further came during our visit to the Nebamun exhibition at the British Museum. Marta identified a stele amongst the three large artefacts there that had been lifted from Horemheb's tomb. The central stele had a depiction of three deities at the top, above the hieroglyphic registers. The goddess to the observer's left was Ma'at, again with headband that did not permit her to wear a uraeus on her forehead. (Fig. 39)

What about Mut? At Karnak she is represented with her double crown and uraeus on the southern wall of the Hypostyle hall, (Fig. 38) and also in the second relief of Rameses IV before the Theban triad.

Besides Mut, there are a number of other ancient Egyptian goddesses with a headdress and a uraeus. The identification of the goddess should therefore be determined by the Theban[433] nature of the triad, by the associated male deity, and by the hieroglyphic inscriptions on the statuette.

The logical conclusion was that the female deity on the proper left of the triad held by Neferabet was Mut with her uraeus and crown, rather than Ma'at with her feather.[434]

Ma'at is seen on Neferabet's left shoulder in sunken relief; she wears a feather but no uraeus.[435]

The serpent deity

The rearing cobra situated between the two seated deities in Neferabet's triad represents a third deity.

Oddly enough, this snake divinity was identified as Wadjet at both the Valletta exhibition of 2003 and the repeat in Gozo two years later. This is a most improbable identification in the opinion of the present authors. The goddess Wadjet[436] was associated with protection, and she was a patroness of the Delta. What possible connection could there have been between a goddess of Lower Egypt and Deir el-Medina in Upper Egypt?

Right from the very start, even before the visits to Turin and the British Museum, Marta suggested that this central deity could not be any other than the snake goddess Meretseger, [437] the patroness of the Valley of the Kings – the so-called silent one, venerated at Deir el-Medina and represented by a cobra. (Figs. 26, 27 & 29)

As the Turin stele confirmed to us, Meretseger was the goddess of *Upper* Egypt who had helped heal Neferabet of his blindness. [438] And as the artefacts dedicated to Meretseger at the *Museo Egizio* showed, the goddess was constantly represented by a serpent or a number of them.

The cobra was associated with sun worship, and the round disc therefore indicated a solar deity. After discussion of the several points that were raised by Marta about this issue, she and I eventually concluded that the cobra and sun disc most probably represent the goddess Meretseger, "She Loves Silence". [439] Furthermore, silence is a typical feature of cemeteries. She was the guardian of the royal necropolis.

Meretseger was also referred to as the cobra goddess of the peak, a so-called natural pyramid that towers over the Valley of the Kings. The peak was called *Ta Dehent* in ancient Egyptian, which simply meant "the peak". (Fig. 28)

If we are correct in our identification of the cobra as Meretseger, then Neferabet's statuette is unique in this respect, namely that it is the only one known that incorporates the Goddess of the Peak in its triad of divinities.

Unlike other triads, such as Ramesses-Nakht's statuette discussed above, Neferabet's choice of gods was not that of a holy family. The three Theban deities were made up instead of a mother, her son, and an unrelated female deity – respectively Mut, Khonsu, and Meretseger.

Whereas Mut wears the double crown of Upper and Lower Egypt on Ramesses-Nakht's statuette, she could have been wearing a modius on Neferabet's. On Ramesses-Nakht's statuette, Mut embraces her husband, Amen, but on Neferabet's, she embraces her son, Khonsu. On Ramesses-Nakht's statuette, Amen holds the *ankh* and Khonsu the crook and flail of kingship, but on Neferabet's, Khonsu holds the *ankh* and there are no regal paraphernalia.

Dating the statuette

Once we were satisfied with our identification of the deities, other points needed to be tackled, and one in particular related to the dating of the statuette. The information panels at the exhibition of 2003 in Valletta stated that "the person making the votive offering was a certain craftsman named Neferabet who lived during the time of the Nineteenth Egyptian Dynasty". Yet according to the same Morris Bierbrier who was acknowledged in the exhibition as a contributor, the dating should have covered part of the Twentieth Dynasty as well. A good case has also been put forward by yet another Egyptologist, John Romer that our Neferabet lived in the Twentieth Dynasty during the reign of Rameses III.[440]
    The position held by the present authors takes into account the fact that Romer's main concern in his publication *Ancient Lives* was not with the specific dating of Neferabet. He was dealing in more or less a general way with the various craftsmen at the Place of Truth throughout the entire history of the site.
    Marta dated Neferabet to the Twentieth Dynasty on the basis of Romer's chart, in which Ipuy, Neferabet's brother, appears as foreman. She adopted the assumption that Neferabet would have lived for at least as long as his brother, who died in year eleven of Rameses III. Neferabet would have been an active painter during the Nineteenth Dynasty. With the onset of the Twentieth Dynasty, he was

probably retired if our hypothesis about his longevity is correct.

Presumably those like Bierbrier and Meza who date Neferabet to the Nineteenth Dynasty are doing so on the basis of the *ostrakon* BM 5634, dated to year forty-six of Rameses II. Meza quotes Themistocles Zammit's dating of the statuette to the Nineteenth Dynasty as correct.

As Marta summarised, "once we accept that the *ostrakon* dated to the forty-sixth year of Rameses II refers to our Neferabet, then he clearly spanned both the Nineteenth and Twentieth Dynasties, and he should not be dated to either of them singularly. Neferabet started his professional carrier under Rameses II in the Nineteenth Dynasty and presumably lived into the second half of the reign of Rameses III in the Twentieth Dynasty. He can thus be dated to the Nineteenth/Twentieth Dynasty".

Comparing images

The restoration processes upon the statuette deserved a detailed analysis; we hoped to achieve this through a study of the available depictions of the statuette.

The images we were comparing were spread out in time over more than a century, from 1882 to 2003, and there were a few others in between. We had in the meantime also acquired copies of the four photographs published in 1949 by Rosalind Moss in *The Journal of Egyptian Archaeology*.[441]

We thought that we would start with comparative visual scans of the grosser features of the statuette. We started off with the oldest photographs that were available to us, the frontal and left side views of 1882.[442]

A slanting crack was an immediately evident feature in the head of the statuette. In 1882 there was a small gap between the two split surfaces, and this was particularly evident in the front view. This fracture was also clearly

Figure 40. The crack in the head in 1882 is visible in both front and side views.

AM

Figure 41. The crack in the head in 2003. Several superficial scratch marks are also visible.

AM

visible in the photographs of the statuette on exhibition in 2003.

But then we had a look at the 1931 photograph that was published in the Malta Museum Guide of that year. We were both surprised to observe that this gap was not visible.

The Museum Curator at the time, Sir Themistocles Zammit, had evidently been able to carry out a remarkable repair job on the statuette, one that left no indication at a distance of the fracture to the head. (Fig. 42)

The repair had been carried out through a simple and perfect apposition of the surfaces and had resulted in a straight linear deformity with no gaps. So what had transpired to cause the gap to open up again?

A closer look at the crack in the head on our enlarged exhibition photographs from 2003 revealed a number of small rounded bodies between the surfaces of the fracture. (Fig. 41, front view) This feature certainly seemed rather odd. How and why had these particles been inserted into a perfectly repaired fracture?

In 2003 the statuette was definitely more similar to the 1882 photograph than to that of 1931. Yet on the exhibition panels it was indirectly being stated that the contributors were ignorant of the 1882 photograph and were only aware of the one of 1931. How was this incongruity to be explained? There was no satisfactory solution that we could offer at the time.

We moved on to another part of the statuette, its base. Starting once again with our scanned images of the 1882 photograph, we focussed on the proper left of its lower parts until we came upon a rectangular defect in the base. Oddly enough, this defect was only visible in the frontal view and not in the side one. (Fig. 43)

This absence of the defect in the side view was initially problematic. The options available were either that the damage had occurred after this photograph was taken or else that the repair had already been carried out between the photographing of the frontal and side views. In the latter

Figure 42. The crack in the head immaculately restored in 1931.

case, which seemed to us to be the more likely in view of the small linear mark at the site in the side view, this defect would have been filled in accordance with the standards of the day, though not according to the standards of today. [443]

When we looked for the defect in the later photographs of Bedford's publication, there it was. The photograph he had used was practically identical to the frontal one utilised by Caruana in 1882.

But when we moved forward to the 1931 photograph, the defect in question was no longer visible. Together with the crack in the head, it had been repaired extremely well by that time, also probably through the intervention of Zammit. (Fig. 44)

Yet another query presented itself to us. What had happened to this defect in the base? Our scanned image of the 1931 photograph was not sufficiently focussed to permit us to identify a fracture line. So we resorted to our own repertoire of photographs taken in 2003. Was there a visible fracture line on these, and was the repaired segment clearly indicated through a different coloration? Modern protocol in the restoration of archaeological artefacts dictates that the repaired area should be identifiable through the use of a different colour tone in the restoration material.

I had fortunately taken a few photographs of the base of the statuette from all its angles, and so we fished these out and enlarged them with Adobe Photoshop. The way we were seeing things was that if the repair job by Zammit in 1931 had been disassembled – as was evident by the head fracture – then this repair in the base would also have been disassembled. If this had been repaired, it would have had to be carried out according to the standards and requirements of today, in accordance with the modern methods of conservation and preservation. The repair of the base should show today through a difference in coloration at the site of the repair.

We scanned all the photographs that were available for the spot in question. Maximum feasible magnification was adopted. There was no difference in coloration at the site of the defect in the base. There was not even the slightest indication that there had ever been a defect at that spot. (Fig. 46) So what had happened to the basal fracture on today's statuette?

When we had a look at the 1949 photographs published by Rosalind Moss, we confirmed that the restoration work on both these areas of the statuette, the head and the base, was still intact. (Fig. 45) The reappearance of the head fracture must have occurred after this time.

The exercise was becoming an exciting one. We were getting very clear signals that the statuette that was photographed in 1882 was not identical to the one that had been on exhibition.

Furthermore, in 2003 the statuette was no longer in the condition that it had been in 1931 and 1949, but for some reason it seemed to be in practically the same condition as it had been half a century earlier in 1882. So what had happened to it in the interval between 1949 and 2003? [444]

We stopped in our tracks for a while and wondered what ramifications and implications these findings of ours might entail. Confronting us was a panel of renowned international experts, and insofar as everybody was concerned, they were the designated interpreters of the Egyptian statuette. Marta and I were simply two amateurs who should really be minding children rather than Egyptian statuettes. As Marta pointed out, we required even more evidence in order to sustain the contention that something was amiss. It had become more a question of proving the irregularities in the statuette to others than of merely convincing ourselves.

Within the image: *Discovered at Gozo.*   C.L.FORMOSA PHOT

Figure 43. Rectangular defect in the base in 1882 (arrowed).

Figure 44. No visible crack in the base in 1931.

Courtesy of Captain Charles Zammit

Figure 45. No visible crack in the base in 1949.

AM

Figure 46. In 2003 the repair site at the base of the statuette is invisible.

AM

Analysing the hieroglyphs on the statuette

We still needed to use the photographs for the hieroglyphs. The exercise had been done earlier of comparing the morphological features on the statuette on display in 2003 with those in Sonnini's published engraving of it in 1798. The outcome of this exercise conducted at an early stage of our investigation had been a rewarding one. Significant differences had been picked up that cast some doubt upon the identity of the two entities.

The photographs had also been utilised for the identification of the sequence of the restoration attempts that had been carried out upon the statuette, principally upon its head and base.

Our target this time was to carry out a comparative analysis and identify any significant discrepancies between the hieroglyphs on our 2003 photographs and those on the various other depictions of the statuette.

By way of a recapitulation of what was available we made up a list of the sources available.

The earliest known repertoire of hieroglyphs was published by Sonnini in 1798. There had been a drawing of something very similar to our statuette and this was allegedly executed in 1778.

The first unquestioned documentation of the statuette in Malta was that done by Carl Lepsius in 1842. This consisted of a description of the statuette, a short history of its discovery and a drawing from the front and the proper left. He transcribed the hieroglyphs on the front of the pedestal, the pilaster and the base and also those on the proper left side of the pilaster. Lepsius also made casts in red wax of all the hieroglyphs that covered the statuette, and these we were planning to examine at some point in time. We had to find out first where they were being preserved.

The crucial 1882 photographs of the statuette came next. These were published by the librarian and director of antiquities, Dr Annetto A. Caruana. There were two views of the statuette, one from the front and the other from the proper left side.

In 1949 the British Egyptologist Rosalind Moss published all four vertical views of the statuette together with the transliterated repertoire of the hieroglyphs and their translation into English.

Finally there were the photographs of 2003 from a number of sources.

Examining the hieroglyphs

James P. Allen had not seen or examined the Maltese statuette, but had carried out his translation from the hieroglyphs that appeared on Sonnini's engraving supported by a few digital photographs of the statuette that had been on display.[445] Allen would first have assumed that the engraving and the statuette were one and the same artefact, and secondly, that Sonnini had executed his copy of the hieroglyphs most diligently and correctly. We have seen that Sonnini exercised a certain amount of artistic license in his copy of the statuette, adding arm bands and missing out on *ankh*s. The translation of the hieroglyphs for the exhibitions of 2003 and 2005 was therefore not strictly legitimate.

Was there a need for the translation after all? A genuine translation was already available. The entire repertoire of hieroglyphs upon the statuette's surfaces had already been transcribed by the Danish Egyptologist, Dr Erik Iversen, and then translated and published by the British Egyptologist Rosalind Moss in 1949 in an official journal of Egyptology.

We compared the hieroglyphs as they appeared in the three 'complete' sets, namely the repertoire furnished by Sonnini in 1798, the one by Moss in 1949 and finally that presented at the Valletta exhibition in 2003[446]. The exhibition was assuming that all three were one and the same thing.

The outcome of this short exercise was immediately evident and the results rather disappointing. The translation of the hieroglyphs at the exhibition was practically identical to the one published by Moss in 1949. In addition the poorly defined hieroglyphs that Moss had not been able to identify[447] were replaced at the exhibition by those deriving from Sonnini's engraving.

It had therefore basically been an exercise where the hieroglyphic texts from two sources, Sonnini and Moss, were patched up together into one whole. Once again it was being assumed that Sonnini's engraving was faithfully reproducing the Egyptian statuette on display.

What if the statuette on display was a copy? Can it be assumed that the hieroglyphs were faithfully reproduced? There was a significant vacuum that could not be filled in by assumptions.

We attempted to identify the original hieroglyphs through an analysis of the early photographs. The earliest available to us were those of 1882.

The scanned photographs had resulted in a massive 165megabyte file that was saved in 'Tiff' format. Opening the files from the hard disk took a very long time indeed, and playing about with the magnification took even longer, but the effort was worth the while.

Marta started off with the uppermost register, that on the proper left face of the pedestal holding the triad, and she read the hieroglyphs thus, "funerary offerings of the great Mut; may she give life, stability and health to the *ka* of his father Neferrenpet justified". The part of the inscription that was situated towards the end of it was all squashed up but it was all there.

Next in line was the part I was really interested in, that on the proper left face of the pilaster[448]. There was a problem in the middle of the inscription; this related to the name of Neferabet's brother. In the 2003 translation given by Allen, that name was 'Anhotep, but he had placed a question mark on the 'eye' hieroglyph. [449] Likewise Moss before him had her reservations on the translation 'his beloved brother 'Anhotpe, well justified in peace.'[450]

The 'An' was being represented by what appeared to be a 'mouth' on top of an 'eye' sign. This feature was also evident on the 1882 photograph and in Lepsius' drawing, where however the hieroglyphs of the name were slightly different. It seemed to me that there was no 'water line' glyph above the 'eye' sign in the name, but rather a straight horizontal line above two 'R' glyphs.[451] (Figs. 47 & 48)

So what was the real name of Neferabet's brother 'A - n - r - ir – hotep??[452]

We considered some other options. Were we seeing a double 'R'? If we were, then the name should not be read as 'Anhotep, but rather as Rere-hotep (or with another variant of the vowels). If there were 'mouths', then it was 'RaRaHotep' – 'man of good speech'. Was it an 'eye with a brow' plus a 'hotep'?

Marta had a go at the name from the exhibition photographs. (Fig. 49) These were unclearly defined but there seemed to be an 'eye' sign between the 'An' and 'hotep' signs. Marta's comment on this was that "the hieroglyph of mouth reads 'ra', though this was not the same as the god's name 'Ra' or 'Re'. The mouth 'ra' may be translated as 'speech' or 'man'. Thus *An ReReHotep* for us could be *'An-'man of satisfying speech'*, that is, a wise man".

Next we took up Sonnini's engraving. The hieroglyphs on the left side of the pilaster were actually different from the ones on the statuette. And in fact, there were no ''Anhotep' hieroglyphs on Sonnini's engraving but what looked like a three-coiled spring instead. (Fig 50)

At the end of the exercise we were still in Limbo insofar as 'Anhotep was concerned. We therefore postponed dealing with the problem and waited as we searched for a similar composite hieroglyph that would perhaps settle the question for us.

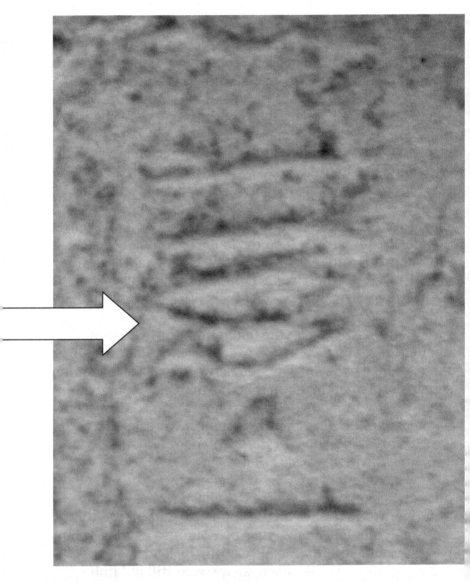

Figure 47. The hieroglyphic signs for ''Anhotep' on the left
face of the pilaster in 1882 (arrowed).

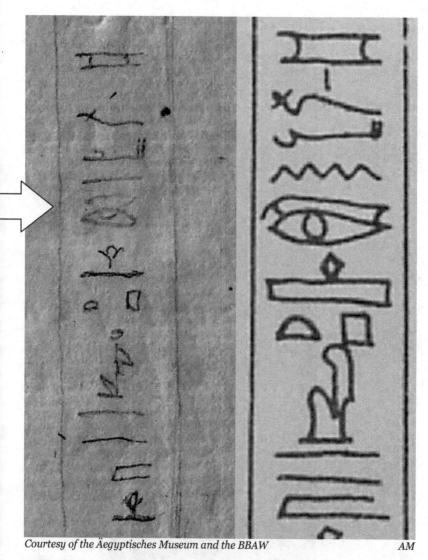

AM

Figure 48. The left face of the pilaster in Lepsius's cast of 1842, and in the edited version of 1913. 'Anhotep arrowed.

AM

Figure 49. The left face of the pilaster in 2003.

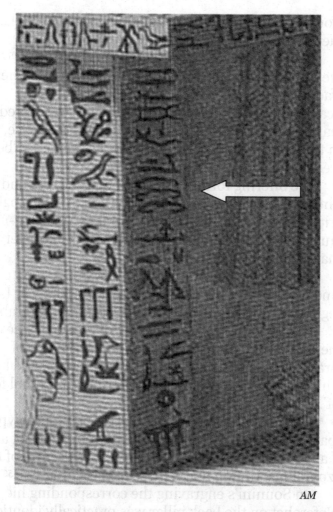

AM

Figure 50. Sonnini's left face of the pilaster, (shaded).

The back pillar

We found the main offering formula on the back pillar of the statuette; this was addressed to Amen-Re and Mut.

This vertical strip of hieroglyphs at the back[453] of the statuette was really the most important portion of the artefact for it was clearly indicating the name of the dedicatee. Although the name of Neferabet was stated to appear three times upon the surfaces of the statuette, it was upon this back strip that the hieroglyphs seemed to be the clearest.

The offering formula started off at the top, and ran in a right to left direction in a single column. The hieroglyphic inscription commenced with the standard '*hotep-di-nesu.t*' formula, and ended at the very bottom of the register with the name of the dedicatee.

The strip of hieroglyphs was reading 'A royal offering of Amen Re, king of the gods and great Mut, lady of Isheru, giving everything good and pure for the *ka* of Neferabet'.

The hieroglyphs for the name of the dedicatee of the statuette were the phonetic signs giving the name of Neferabet. The name of the dedicatee was indicated by the 'nfr' hieroglyph followed by the quadriliteral symbol for 'aAbt'.[454]

Right below this long vertical strip of hieroglyphs on the back pillar, there was a different combination of an 'nfr' with an 'aAbt' sign. This was situated in the centre of the horizontal inscription on the *base* of the statuette. [455]

On Sonnini's engraving the corresponding hieroglyph for Neferabet on the back pillar was practically identical to that on the statuette, except that there were three triangles rather than two in the 'aAbt' multiple hieroglyph. However this quadrilateral glyph was a very rare hieroglyphic sign, and there was no other sign that was so similar to it that it could cause difficulty in interpretation. In Marta's opinion my triangles were more like zigzag lines that in antiquity may have represented a pleated cloth.

AM

Figure 51. The hieroglyphs for Neferabet on the back pillar
are not identical with those on the base.

We next moved on to examine the close up images of the corresponding 'Neferabet' hieroglyph on the back pillar, and it was abundantly clear to us both that the 'aAbt' part of the quadriliteral hieroglyph was not a proper 'aAbt' hieroglyph after all. The upper part of the supposedly rectilinear side of the upper triangle was rounded, and its lower side was serrated – it seemed that a 'T' and an 'N' had been joined together into a deformed triangle. (Fig. 51)

Furthermore, the 'feather' and 'club' signs on either side of the zigzag were not there. At least they were certainly not engraved to the same depth as the other elements of the compound hieroglyph were. They seemed to be more like later additions, and, coupled with the situation at the top of the 'aAbt' hieroglyph as a whole, this was strongly suggesting that this quadriliteral hieroglyph that was denoting the 'aAbt' portion of Neferabet might have been touched up. Was this the original statuette?

Moving on next to the pedestal, once again the offering formulae were addressed to Amen-Re and Mut', the left half for 'Neferabu', the right for his father 'Neferrenpet'.

We had already explored the proper left side of the pilaster for 'Anhotep. So we moved on to its two other faces.

There were two columns of hieroglyphs on the front of the pilaster supporting the pedestal. This face of the pilaster contained respectively the epithets of Re-Horakhti and Ma'at in two vertical columns that are damaged. These hieroglyphs corresponded to the deities above them on the pedestal.

Shifting to the proper right side of the pilaster we came to the dedication meant for his son, 'making his name to live, Neferrenpet justified'.

The hieroglyphs for this are a combination of the usual 'nfr' sign together with the 'rnpt' sign - this is denoted by a hieroglyph in the form of the stick of Moses with a bump in mid-shaft on the outer border. In antiquity this was a palm frond or branch.

When we examined this register on the statuette, the 'duck' hieroglyph for 'son' was too smudged to be identifiable on the statuette. Marta could not see anything like a duck to read 'sa' for a son. The viper snake sign 'f' for 'his son' was not there either. When she reviewed the exhibition photos for a second time at a later date, she could still not identify any sign for 'son', the 'sa', the hieroglyph for which is a 'duck'. The sign for brother 'sw' was not there either. This was similar to the word *swnw*, a physician, indicated by an arrow pointing downwards.

Next to tackle was the base of the statuette. This comprised a double formula that corresponded to the deities sitting on the pedestal above. The left half was addressed to 'Re-Harakhti, Great God, King of the Ennaead', and the right half 'to Ma'at, daughter of Re, Lady of Heaven, Mistress of all the gods, in favour of Neferabu'.

Nefertanpet

We still needed to clarify the name of the dedicatee as first suggested in the first known 'translation' of the inscriptions. The Austrian Egyptologist from Munich, Professor F. W. von Bissing was responsible for this. He provided the translation after examining the statuette in Malta in 1907.

At that time, these hieroglyphs were interpreted as a prayer to Amen-Re Saker (Sokar), and Ma'at, the great goddess of Thebes. Ma'at was invoking the spirit of *Nefertanpet*, the dedicatee of the triad of gods, and a prayer to Re Horakhti, and Ma'at, the lady of the skies and mistress to the gods.[456] The dating was assigned to the 19th or 20th dynasties.[457]

So had the name of Nefertanpet been mistakenly translated instead of Neferrenpet?[458] The name of Neferrenpet was being presented on the information panels at the Exhibition as the name of both the father and the son of Neferabet.

The hieroglyph for 't' is not very different from that for 'r'. If not carved or written properly, the former hieroglyph, the 't' resembles a flat dome, and this is a type of bread used in temple offering; the latter hieroglyph for the 'r' takes the shape of a bi-convex lens, or a mouth.

Yet Zammit's rendering of 'Nefer-Tanpet' from von Bissing's translation was for the dedicatee, and not for his father or the son. Still, was this new name 'Nefer-Tanpet' that Zammit was quoting in 1919 a misreading of the hieroglyphs on the part of his source, the Egyptologist Professor von Bissing, or was there something amiss with the translations that were made since? Once again the question crept up, was it the same statuette?

Original or copy?

The possibility constantly loomed over our heads that for some reason the original statuette could actually have been replaced with another. It would have been very possible for a perfect copy of the statuette to have been manufactured, and the machines to do this have been available in the Maltese islands for at least the past thirty years.

We were practically convinced at this stage that a copy of the statuette had been made at some time after 1919 and that the copy had been exhibited since that time.

The possibility of finding further evidence to corroborate our hypothesis urged us forward to search for more clues that would conclusively show beyond any doubt that a copy of the original statuette had been created.

Making a copy might not have been such a bad idea after all, if the main concern that motivated the procedure was to protect the statuette, and if it was being stated that a copy was being exhibited, and that it was a true copy. However, if the copy was in any way different from the original, then the task incumbent upon us was to demonstrate an obvious difference between the original and the copy. Naturally, allowances had to be made for any possible deterioration that might have occurred between the time of the original's photograph and today.

Neferabet re-exhibited

The Maltese statuette saw the light of day once again after the lapse of two years. The Museum of Archaeology decided to set up the exhibition one more time, using precisely the same materials and without any modification of any sort, for the sister island of Gozo, where it was reliably documented to have been discovered.

This time around we were advised well in advance. At the beginning of July 2005, the *Kultura* insert in the local newspaper, *The Sunday Times of Malta,* announced the repeat exhibition between 5 and 30 September 2005. This time it was to be set up at the office of Heritage Malta in Victoria, the capital of Gozo, otherwise known as the Citadel.

The caption gave a few more details about the presentation: "Shedding new light on the Egyptian Statue of Neferabet, exhibition of an imported ancient Egyptian statue, currently forming part of the archaeology reserve collection in Valletta".

The museum authorities had apparently ignored all the problems that were associated with the hypothesis they had proposed in the 2003 exhibition, and simply decided to repeat the exhibition in Gozo.

We had photographed the statuette quite thoroughly during its exhibition in Malta. But soon enough we were reconsidering. In the end we decided to avail ourselves of this opportunity and make an outing of it for the Egyptology Society of Malta. We would test our hypothesis with the other members over the authenticity of the statuette.

We could also attempt an actual measurement of the statuette's vital statistics in order to confirm its authenticity.

If we managed these, we would be able to compare them with those given for the statuette by Cesare Vassallo in 1851. If the measurements of 1851 differed from those of today, the two artefacts could not be one and the same.

Vital statistics

Our point of reference was a description of the statuette from the mid-nineteenth century. William Tallack's description of the Egyptian statuette in his 1861 publication made reference to a previous publication by the curator Cesare Vassallo.

This could only have been Vassallo's first publication, the *Cenni Storici* of 1851. There must have been some measurements of the statuette there that were not to be found in his Museum Guide of 1871 that I had in photocopy.

Although I had already scanned the *Cenni Storici* of 1851 from selected photocopies at the very beginning of the investigation, I had not taken any notes on measurements at the time. I had then been mainly concerned with deriving the archaeological context of the statuette and the number of publications that mentioned it before Caruana in 1882.

In retrospect I should have photocopied it in its entirety back then, I thought. We suddenly required it urgently for the statuette's earliest recorded measurements. These had been taken a century and a half previously and were thus extremely crucial to our comparative study.

There was a choice of public libraries to visit between the one on mainland Malta or else the one in Gozo, a smaller institution but certainly more user friendly.

Going to Valletta for the Bibliotheca in Malta would have taken me a mere fifteen minutes, but I preferred not to take my chances with the difficulty of finding parking nearby and the elaborate protocol involved in conducting the type of research that I wanted to carry out. This was basically photocopying the relevant parts of the publication and getting them back home that day.

Going to the library in Gozo with its fantastic atmosphere was worth all the travelling and time expended, and the coffee with herbs prepared by George in the side room of the main hall of the library was a fantastic overhead benefit. Besides, it was great to see old friends once again.

So early on the Monday morning, at 7.30 am, I phoned up my great friend George Borg whom I knew very well since my younger days in Gozo. He was already at work at the National Library in the capital of the sister island, Victoria. George was assistant librarian way back in the seventies, but he was then in full charge as chief librarian. I asked George whether they had a copy of Cesare Vassallo in the library there that was dated to before 1861.

When he came back to me a few minutes later he said that there were four dates that were available for Cesare Vassallo – these were 1876, 1872, 1871, and ... the pause was forever ... 1851. 'George! I need to see it today!' upon which he answered that I would have to make it before 13.30.

'George? Will the photocopies be ready by the time I reach there?' I did not even await his answer, but simply hung up and took off without further delay. George was used to these egoistic requests of mine.

Getting over to Gozo from St Julians in Malta involves a number of stages. There is first a 45-minute drive towards the Northwest, to the Ferry quay at Cirkewwa, and then another average 45-minute wait in the queue for the ferry. The ferry trip to Mgarr in Gozo takes 25 minutes and another 20 minutes are needed to reach and park close to the library in Vajringa Street in Victoria.

There were three home visits to my paediatric patients that had to be done in the morning, and these were seen to first of all. I then sent a text message to another patient in order to inform her that I would be visiting after five in the afternoon, and I took off for Gozo.

At 10.00 I was on my way to the ferry in anxious anticipation. I took along with me the 1871 edition in Italian of the Museum Guide by Vassallo, together with the readings that I had just copied from it on a piece of notepaper. I was hoping to be able to compare it with the measurements in the earlier publication of Vassallo at the Gozo library.

I was at the Gozo library just before noon. Traffic had been extremely light that morning, and parking was readily available just outside the library in the shade under the cover of the few trees that lined the street. It seemed to me that Gozo had already entered into siesta mode. I thus had ninety minutes at my disposal, and that included the fifteen-minute herbal coffee break with George.

The library was on the first floor of the building that also housed a government primary school. I was up the stairs in no time, and George was as usual engrossed in dealing with sundry matters over the telephone. I actually counted the minutes – there were seven of these anxious moments, after which George came over to me with a large A4 envelope.

His predictable smile invited me to his lair at the very back of the library towards the left wing. George dropped a small quantity of his favourite liqueur 'Southern Comfort' into the herbalised coffee in the pot on the boil, and he then prepared two cups. I just added three sweetener tablets to mine and we set off in discussion.

Although I was anxious to get to work on the photocopies, it felt good to speak to a sincere and genuine friend, and so I made the most of it.

It was not long before one of the library staff intervened in order to tell George about a call from the Malta offices, and he excused himself with me as he rushed off. I thanked him as I assured him that he would soon be seeing me there once again in the not too distant future. I asked him for a snapshot together and he smiled as he acquiesced. I paid the assistant librarian for the photocopies and rushed down the stairs and out of the building. I finally got the opportunity to have a look at the photocopies once I reached my car.

It was still thirty minutes past noon, and I had a few minutes to browse rapidly through the photocopies before I took off for the ferry queue at Mgarr. I opened the envelope and started scanning the pages. It was written in Italian, dated to 1851, and was in fact the first edition of the '*Cenni Storici*'.[459]

As I read some of the paragraphs, I confess to feeling a deep sense of frustration, as nothing seemed to be making sense any more. The urgency of getting back to Malta in order to see to my medical visits did not make matters any better. I decided to drive down to Mgarr and start off once again from there, first in the queue and then during the trip. I thought I would be more relaxed once I was at Mgarr in the car queue. I would just make it to the 1:00 p.m. boat if I rushed a bit.

Fifteen minutes later I was in line two as the ferry came in from Malta. Once again I went through the paragraphs that dealt with the Egyptian statuette. The more I read the more confused things seemed to be getting. I had not solved my problem at all by coming over to Gozo. Rather, the dilemma seemed to have been augmented by what I was reading, and I began to have heart palpitations that were probably accentuated by the several espressos that I had drunk that morning on top of George's coffee. As I boarded the ferry, I kept on reassuring myself that this anxious state was totally uncalled for.

Only the day before, I had been reading Vassallo's Museum Guide of 1871, and the only measurements that I recalled from that text concerned the height of the stand and the width of its base. These readings I readily recalled as 5½ and 6½ inches.[460] But in the copy that I had just acquired from the Gozo Library, Vassallo stated that the *piedestallo* was only half an inch thick.

No matter how hard I tried to reconcile the readings, I could not make any sense out of the seemingly conflicting measurements of the statuette from the two publications by the same author. Had I copied the readings from the 1971 publication correctly?

The 1871 edition of the Museum Guide was packed somewhere in the car booth. The car was parked, so I searched this out and found it immediately. Back in my car seat and under the glare of the early afternoon sun, I scanned the photocopied pages of both volumes with some impatience.

I was half excited and half frustrated. I tried to keep calm and collected. I remained seated in the car after boarding, and my mobile remained silent once it was shielded all around by the metal body of the ferry.

I started off with the recently acquired copies of the 1851 edition of *Cenni Storici*. I felt a hint of frustration and the taste of disappointment as to I confirmed my dismay that there were no measurements of 6½ and 5½ inches mentioned there. It was only the half-inch thickness of the pedestal, the *piedestallo* that was referred to. So I turned to the 1871 guide and the measurements of 6½ and 5½ inches. What were these readings referring to?

It was some time before I finally realised to my immense relief that the 6½ inch reading was referring to the width of the base, the *predella*, and the 5½ inch measurement to the height of the *cattedra* or stand (our pedestal and pilaster) upon which the deities stood. The Italian terminology, or rather my ignorance of it, had been the cause of my confusion.

Suddenly everything seemed to make sense as the pieces dove-tailed together in perfect unison. Between the editions of 1851 and 1871 of Vassallo's publications, I had the full range of measurements of the statuette as they had existed at the time of Vassallo. The earliest readings of the thickness of the pedestal, the height of the stand, and the width of the base were known. The one common measurement was the height of the statuette that was given as 14 inches in both publications.

Once I sorted this out, I felt relaxed in the assurance that I was in an ideal position to compare these measurements with those of the statuette to be displayed.

Getting the statuette's measurements.

Once the statuette was lined up for another exhibition there was that golden opportunity to measure it and then compare figures with those of Cesare Vassallo's.

The next part of the exercise was not going to be easy by any means. There was no way that the authorities would let me examine the statuette outside its case in order to measure it. I needed to devise a procedure that allowed me to get these readings from *outside the glass case*.

The major problem that impeded me from taking a direct measurement of the statuette was its case of transparent Perspex material. It could not be measured by an ordinary tape measure. Nor could I measure it in any other way I then thought. Well before the exhibition I had been tackling the problem so that when the exhibition in Gozo was on, the appropriate machinery and technology to measure the statuette from outside its case was ready for it.

Several options presented themselves initially, such as using right-angled view-finders that could be placed on the case and moved into position until aligned at the desired spot. But this was not a feasible proposition – unless, I finally realised, I could use a visible marker that could penetrate the case. Finally the answer came up – I would use a laser light on a right-angled base and would be able to take the measurements in parallel. The laser light would guide me as to the start and end of the reading.

Naturally there were a few obligatory specifications. The apparatus had to be small, light, portable and sufficiently smooth so as not to cause any friction at all on the display case. I hunted for small laser lights, and these came in all sizes and price tags, but I finally managed a small one that measured about 15 centimetres in length, three in breadth and two in width.

There was a problem with the difficulty that would be encountered with using a very small surface area to get a flawless ninety degree apposition. The light had to be positioned on the case with its three by two centimetre surface whence the laser beam emerged flat upon it. This surface was too small for precision. However a method was soon devised whereby the breadth of the instrument was extended by another five centimetres. The gadget was attached through mini clamps to a smooth right-angled base that basically extended across this length. The resulting eight centimetres of smooth surface were precisely at right angles to the laser beam, and the device could be very easily slid along the outside surface of the statuette's case.

Precision of readings was considerably enhanced in this manner for the points to be measured from inside the case were being directly projected to the surface outside the case where a direct measurement could then be accurately carried out with a standard measuring ruler.

I carried out a few experiments with the assembly at home and compared them with the actual readings. After half an hour of practice measurements, the method I had devised was giving me readings that varied by less than three millimetres from the actual ones taken on direct measurement. I was ready to go.

Back in 2003 Alicia Meza had been allowed to measure the statuette and she published these readings in her *JARCE* article of the same year. Although this initially seemed to have rendered futile the process of measuring it with laser in Gozo, I decided to go ahead and confirm that Alicia Meza had examined the same statuette that was on exhibition in Gozo two years later. Meza's measurements would also confirm or refute that the technique that I employed for measuring the statuette inside its case was a very reliable one. Meza's measurements in the metric system yielded the following readings – total height 41.5 cm, base 4.5 cm high, 13 cm wide and 16.7 cm deep[461].

The trip to Gozo for the measurements was planned for the first boat on the first Saturday of the exhibition. I could have an early start, well before the tourists started to flood the exhibition hall. Parking was easy enough right in the centre of the city of Victoria itself, at a distance of thirty metres from the Cathedral at the top of the Citadel. It was a continuous uphill along the steps by the walls of the bastions until the offices of *Heritage Malta* were reached, and it was still early on in the day when I reached the exhibition hall, but this was still closed – opening time was scheduled in fifteen minutes.

As I awaited the curator I sat on one of the low steps there, and the equipment was gradually assembled – the batteries for the Olympus, the clamps for the laser light with its ninety degrees angle, and the notebook.

The curator Mario Galea soon appeared as he was climbing up the steps of the ancient Citadel towards his office. I recognised him just as he took off his sunglasses to salute me. The sun was not significantly up yet, and I hoped to get things done as early as possible so as not to become drenched in sweat with the humidity that prevailed during that month of the year.

I rose and went down the steps to follow Mario into the Gozitan offices of Heritage Malta and into the Exhibition Hall. After the usual salutations and queries about family health, Mario entered his office next to the exhibition hall and he left me to my own devices. So I set up the tripod with the Olympus and managed to get several close up shots of a number of details on the statuette. I was itching to start with the laser-guided measurements, and so I unpacked the necessary gear that I had prepared for the occasion.

The measurements of the sides of the base were the crucial ones, and so I started off with these. I mounted up the laser gadget secured to its right-angled corner brace with four spring micro-clamps. As I carried out a preliminary test, I was elated to confirm that the laser beam shone directly at a right angle to the surface that it was being applied to, in that instance the Perspex housing of the statuette.

Getting a point using the laser light as a guide was child's play. The first point I went for was the junction between the front and the proper left side of the base. This I identified with a liquid black micro-line applied by a *Stabilo* point 88 fine 0.4 pen. Moving to the junction between the left and back sides of the statuette's base, the second point was obtained in the same manner. The first measurement between these points was then read off a grey aluminium *Cox* CB-300 ruler. The statuette's proper left side of the base measured precisely 17 cm. On repeating the exercise on the right side of the base, the measurement was slightly larger by 2 mm. [17.2cm].

These readings tallied comfortably with the measurements that Meza had obtained and published in 2003. It was justifiable to assume that we had measured the same statuette.

I could not resist a quick conversion of the figures that I had just obtained into inches in order to compare them with those taken by Cesare Vassallo in 1851[462]. I used the pocket electronic calculator that I had brought along with me for this occasion. Vassallo had naturally taken his measurements in inches, and his reading had been 6½ inches, and my reading of 17 cm converted into 6⅝ inches. The error was precisely as large as the width of my laser beam, one eighth of an inch.[463]

All that I had managed to demonstrate and confirm that far, through these laser-assisted readings, was that Cesare Vassallo had actually measured the statuette accurately. This was hardly a notable achievement, hardly an exercise that was worth the while.

I was obliged to carry out a fast mental recapitulation in order to ascertain the significance of my readings. In my first of the series of measurements, the proper left and proper right sides of the base had measured respectively 17.0 and 17.2 cm, an average of 17.1 cm. But then with the second series of readings, the front side was measuring 13.9 cm, and the back was 13.2 cm.

After measuring the thickness of the base at 4.2 cm, I moved on to take another series of readings. I then opted to measure the length of the pedestal upon which the deities were placed. My reading was 9.6cm, which is equivalent to 3⅝ inches.

The thickness of the pedestal measured 1.9 cm, and this was equivalent to ⅝ of an inch. Vassallo had read it as half an inch, and so there once again was a variance of an eighth of an inch with Vassallo's measurements.[464] I also measured the width of the two sides of the pedestal, and these were found to be unequal, the left side measuring 7.4 cm and the right was 8.1 cm.

The measurement of the pilaster supporting the pedestal also required a comparison with that reached by Vassallo. The width of the pilaster at the top measured 4.6 cm and 4.7 cm at its base. The pedestal itself measured 13.8 cm in length, and this was equivalent to 5⅜ inches – Vassallo's reading for it was 5½ inches. The precision to one eighth of an inch was once again remarkable.

When the measurements that were obtainable that morning were compared with those taken by Cesare Vassallo and Carl Lepsius over a hundred and thirty years previously, the proximity of the readings was remarkably constant to within an eighth of an inch.

Before leaving the hall, a few other measurements were taken for posterity. The length of the wig was 8.4 cm and that of ribbon 28.4 cm. [465]

The height of the statuette together with the base varied from one part of it to the other, but it averaged 41.7cm, and this translated into 16⅜ inches. Vassallo had given this measurement as fourteen inches, the difference being equivalent to approximately seven centimetres *shorter*. According to the measurements that had been taken by Heritage Malta in 2003, the statuette measured 41.5 cm in height.[466] This height was identical to that documented by Rosalind Moss in 1949.

In fact, when Moss published her *JEA* article, she provided two measurements of the statuette that conflicted with one another. From her own observations the height of the statuette was "16½ inches", yet when she quoted the measurement of the statuette as published in 1882, the height then was fourteen inches.

Thus the major discrepancy between the statuette described by Cesare Vassallo and that on exhibition was its length; Vassallo's measurement was equivalent to 35.56cm and the other readings were all approximately 41.5 cm. This difference of around seven centimetres could not be regarded as an insignificant minor error in measurement.

When Sonnini attempted to give an indication of the height of the statuette that he saw and drew in Cairo, his measurement was an extremely gross one – 'more than a foot'.[467] Lepsius gave an approximate measurement for the total height at approximately a foot and a half.[468]

A few days later the society visited the exhibition as a group. This was very appropriate for it had been the statuette that had triggered off its founding. The excursion of the two-year old Egyptological Society to Gozo was organized for the 7th of September 2005.

I acted as guide for the group and at the same time tested my hypothesis with the other members by pointing out the discrepancies between the statuette on display and a number of photographs that I had brought along with me. There seemed to be no major objections to what my investigations had led me to conclude about the statuette on display. I had learnt this ruse from the British archaeologist Professor David Trump who conducted several archaeological tours around the Maltese islands and who volunteered to share this strategy of his freely with all of us who participated.

Once the visit to the Heritage Malta offices and the statuette was over, we proceeded as a group to the Museum of Archaeology less than a hundred metres away. Stephen was the assistant curator there and has constantly been a very good friend. He took us round the artefacts and these included the Egyptian ones that mostly comprised a number of amulets in the standard ancient Egyptian canon that had been picked up from a number of Phoenician tombs on the island, and already hinted at above[469].

On my part I had another look at the Phoenician artefact that was also being displayed there alongside the Egyptian artefacts. It had been discovered in the Neolithic temple of Ggantija in Gozo, and just like the statuette had been replaced with a copy. Could the motives for these substitutions have in any way been similar?

There was another possibility to consider. Could the Ggantija temple have also been the archaeological site in Gozo where the statuette was discovered? The Neolithic temples in the Maltese islands were often re-utilised as sacred sites by succeeding cultures, typically by the Phoenicians and the Romans. Classic examples include the site at Tas-Silg in the south-eastern part of mainland Malta and the extinct temple of Juno in the Grand Harbour area. Egyptian artefacts were commonly incorporated into these adapted sanctuaries by both Phoenicians and Romans. If it had not been the Ggantija, another megalithic temple site in Gozo was the most likely context for the statuette.

Then something unexpected came up.

Casts in red wax

One afternoon there was an attachment with one of the e-mails from my son-in-law Guillaume. On opening it up I saw an unusual photograph of a number of wax casts in red. These were supposed to be of the hieroglyphs on the statuette. There were no clues in this first e-mail as to who had produced them.

Since the writing was in German, the options were either Carl Lepsius (1842) or Albert Mayr (1901). The next e-mail from Guillaume contained the URL of the attachment, and it was an overwhelmingly pleasant surprise to discover that the casts of the hieroglyphs were the ones taken by Carl Lepsius himself in Malta in 1842. This particular website, by a Herr Stefan Grunert, had been open since 2001 and should have been available to anybody who was researching the statuette.

The words of the mid-nineteenth century librarian Dr Cesare Vassallo immediately came to my mind, for he had declared that Carl Lepsius had taken a record of the hieroglyphs on the statuette during his visit to Malta in 1842. This was a veritable goldmine, a godsend!

The writing was entirely in old German manuscript, but the helpful website manager had included a translation of some extracts. One of these was the earliest evidence yet for the documentation of the provenance of the Maltese statuette. According to Carl Lepsius's own personal notebook, it had been discovered in Malta before 1800. He had seen and examined the Maltese Egyptian statuette in the Bibliotheca of La Valletta and had also described the statuette on several of the pages of his notebook on 14 September 1842.[470]

There were other links on this website, and on clicking on one of these, I was rewarded with a familiar sight. The Maltese statuette crystallized before my eyes. Lepsius had drawn this unique artefact to scale from the front and the left side.

There were also his transliterations of some of the registers of hieroglyphs – those on the back strip, the pedestal, pilaster and the base. But what was particularly rewarding was the set of casts of four of these registers of hieroglyphs. Judging from the reddish colour of the casts, it seemed that these had been produced through the application of red sealing wax. The hieroglyphs on the cast were evidently visible in *bas relief* and were also inverted horizontally.

There was more to be gleaned from the notes of Lepsius. In the folio extract on the page next to the drawing of the statuette, there were notes below the transliterations of the inscriptions. Lepsius's scribble was confirming the provenance of the statuette as deriving from Malta before forty years previously, or even longer than this. As that was in 1842, Lepsius was effectively being informed, presumably from the curator Cesare Vassallo that the statuette had been discovered in Malta[471] in the 18th century, sometime in the 1700s, during the time of the Knights.[472]

According to the official sources of nineteenth century Malta, the statuette was reported as having been found in an archaeological site in the sister island of Gozo.

The archaeological site *par excellance* at the time in Gozo was the Giants' Tower, the Ggantja, a megalithic temple that was erected a thousand years before the Step Pyramid at Saqqara. There was a Phoenician inscription that was also found there[473] that indicated that the sanctuary had been re-utilised by succeeding cultures.

And discovered at around the same time as the Egyptian statuette, a golden calf was also found on a hill near the capital city in Gozo.[474]

There was some more information relating to the Egyptian statuette. Three scholars had taken up the *Notizbuchs* of Lepsius. Eduard Naville, Walter Wreszinski and Hermann Grapow published his visit to Malta's antiquities between the 12th and 14th September 1842[475]. It was printed in Leipzig in 1913[476] and a copy was available at the *Brandenburgisches Akademie der Wissenschaften*[477].

The attachment to Guillaume's e-mail had led me straight to Lepsius and the repository of several of his works and publications. The *BBAW* in Berlin had to be the next establishment to visit if I wanted to examine the journals and casts of Carl Lepsius that were preserved there.

Although I already had access to four of the casts that were taken by Lepsius, there were at least five others that I had not seen. I asked myself, would it be worth the while of going there to have a look at all of them, if they were still available? There was also the bonus of other material that would certainly be interesting to see in the journal entries of Lepsius's visit to Malta.

Furthermore there was the strong possibility that additional information could be gleaned that would cast further light on the Maltese Egyptian Statuette. I had to go to Berlin and scan these *Notizbuchs* of Lepsius.

Initially it started to feel as if all the staff at the *BBAW* was on vacation leave, for my queries by phone and e-mail remained unanswered. It later transpired that they had actually been in receipt of them, but as they explained, for some reason or other, there must have been some form of unimaginable and unidentifiable incompatibility between our electronic mail servers.

I purchased my usual 'Lonely Planet' guide book of Berlin and eventually managed to book a hotel there for three days just a few blocks away from the *BBAW*. I asked my archaeologist friend, Professor Anthony Frendo for a letter of recommendation to the director of the *BBAW*.

The name I identified as the key person to speak to for me to have a look at the documentation by Lepsius was the director of the *BBAW*, a certain Professor Stephan Seidlmayer. His name was familiar from a chapter he wrote for the well-known coffee table publication in Egyptology - *Egypt, the World of the Pharaohs*.[478] So I read that chapter once again just in case I needed something special to break the ice on my first interview with him.

His office was on the second floor of the *BBAW*. All I had to do was to go there, introduce myself to him and ask for permission to view the casts and the diaries. It all seemed so simple.

My travel agent got me a booking for the 25th of September, with a return flight on the 28th. Four days in Berlin would be sufficient to trace the notebook and copy what I required. I would also be able to visit some of the excellent museums in the German capital city.

I did not sleep much on the 25th, barely half an hour. There were papers that I still needed to include in my bag, including a reminder to measure the casts. There was the constant worry at the back of my mind as to whether I would be able to locate the *Lepsius Archiv* and be permitted to view parts of it.

I needed the complete address of the BBAW to show to the taxi drivers who would take me there - *Altagyptisches Worterbuch*, number 8, the *Unter den Linden* Avenue, D-10117 in Berlin. I also included the telephone number in my notebook. I had been trying to get in touch with this number from Malta but never managed.

There was also an *Archiv der BBAW* at the *Jagerstrasse* 22-23 10117 Berlin, and this was noted as well, together with the telephone number there.

To Berlin

The airport at Luqa was packed with travellers in long queues to Munich, Manchester, Heathrow, Dusseldorf and other destinations. A hot chocolate did the trick and set me in a very good mood for the day. We left at 07.40. It was an unusual experience for me to be completely surrounded by Germans on the Air Malta flight KM 376 to Berlin.

301

The flight was over in 2 hours 35 minutes – during this time photography was possible of the Grand Harbour of Malta, and then the mountainous, soil-brown coloured North-Western corner of Sicily at Trapani.

The weather was fantastic and the sky cloudless as we were about to land in Berlin at 10.25. There was a slight mist at ground level, the Rhine meandered along its course, and the home chimneys were smoking despite the fact that it was still the end of September.

The industrial zone lay to our right. The *Vodafone* signal showed a T-Mobile D and I sent a few text messages to Malta to announce my safe landing.

The taxi driver was extremely helpful – Dilo (or was it Ghilo?) pointed out on his map the route we would be obliged to take to the hotel because of the international marathon taking place just then. However, it did not take us that long to drive there, and we were at the *Hotel Gendarm* in no time at all. I gave Dilo 22 Euros for the 18.50 he asked me for and alighted on to the pavement opposite the hotel. This was strategically situated on the *Charlotten Strasse*, number 61, right in front of the Berlin Hilton, and barely two hundred metres away from the *Unter den Linden* Avenue where the *BBAW* was situated. The kind receptionist at the concierge gave me a fantastic room at number 10.

It was still early and time wise possible for me to go to the *Altes Museum* and see some of the Egyptian antiquities there; I was obliged to cross the line of marathon runners at one point on my way there.

After standing for an hour in the sunshine it transpired that I was in the wrong queue – the very long one I was in was for the Goya exhibition.

There were no queues at the *Altes Museum* just a few corners away, and for an entrance fee of eight Euros I managed to scan the entire collection and take excellent photographs – Nefertiti was there on the first floor, beautiful and radiant as ever – small wonder Zahi Hawass wants her back in Egypt. Her exportation out of Egypt a century earlier had been rather unorthodox. For some reason she reminded me of Helen of Troy, with a long cold war between Cairo and Berlin in the background instead of the one we all know about. Does Hawass have a Trojan horse, I wondered?

At the bookshop I looked for a catalogue of the collection, but only managed a limited selection. Whilst I was speaking to the person in charge there about the notebook of Lepsius, he gave me what I then imagined to be bad news. The journals of Lepsius were only available at the *BBAW* – that I knew, but the other bit of news that he gave me was that the director there was a certain Herr Schultze and he was rarely around. The prospects of seeing the journals of Lepsius and his casts suddenly turned extremely gloomy.

I had never heard the name of Herr Schultze before. The man I was supposed to meet was Seidlmayer; my letter of recommendation from Malta had in fact been addressed expressly to him and to nobody else.

There was nothing for me to do at that late hour. How could I have got the name of the director wrong? Was it the case that there had been a new director installed over the previous weeks? Was that the reason for my not receiving anything back from the *BBAW*? It seemed to be the only option at the time, and it was not good for me at all.

It was also becoming too hot inside the museum. On the outside everybody seemed to have taken to sun-worshipping. I thought I would visit the coffee shop. I first asked for water – this was provided free of charge. I then had a coffee and lamented my bad fortune. I had come to Berlin for nothing, I suspected. I was not going to be able to see the *Notizbuch* of Lepsius after all.

I spent the late afternoon and evening walking along the *Charlotten Strasse*. I had identified the *BBAW* earlier when on my way to the *Altes Museum* at noon. I was

303

impatient for the morrow's outcome – there just had to be a way for me to see the *Notizbuch*.

Everybody in Berlin was so gentle and courteous. The locals were even trying to muster their best English in order to answer my queries. It would be nice if the staff at the *BBAW* were equally helpful I thought.

The sky remained cloudless. I stayed for an hour on a table at another café, the *Dom Terrasse Café* and had a *Cappuccino* and a sandwich under a massive white umbrella.

Meeting the director at the BBAW

It was a very early night for me at 20.00. I was awake in the early hours of the next morning and was soon down for breakfast. My mood was better, I was optimistic. I was still hoping to get in touch with Professor Stephan Seidlmayer. The letter from Professor Frendo would hopefully get me an introduction to him. I would enhance the importance of having a look at the earliest drawing of the Egyptian statuette in the hope of rescuing some of the hieroglyphs that had since been eroded away. This I hoped would lead on to a favourable discussion and an equally favourable outcome.

I was at the *BBAW* within ten minutes of leaving the hotel. I entered the square courtyard and went through the main door on the right. There was an exhibition on Albert Einstein at the time – I had seen a number of large photographs of him in the *Unter den Linden*, and a number of photographs and memorabilia were distributed in cabinets on the ground floor and along the hallway.

I went up two floors with a total of 78 steps and I reached the administrative section of the building. Whilst I was still on the first floor I hesitantly asked the first person I saw there for Seidlmayer, half expecting an answer to the effect that he was no longer the director there. But to my complete and pleasant surprise the kind lady diverted herself from the task at hand and asked me to follow her up to the second floor to his office.

So I had not been wrong after all in seeking out Seidlmayer, I told myself, as I released a weighty sigh of relief. My mood swung full circle in the right direction. I hoped Seidlmayer's humour was equally good that morning.

The obliging lady knocked lightly upon his door and went inside. She was only in for a few seconds and when she came out again it was with an invitation for me to go in. He was not seeing anyone at the time, and was free to talk to me. It all seemed to be dove-tailing in perfect unison.

The next stage was crucial and I put on my best smile as I entered the office. Everything was in the neatest order and in its proper place. The director was on his chair at his mahogany desk and he instantly greeted me with a sincere smile.

He seemed to be an extremely pleasant person and seemed to be in a receptive mood. He invited me to take a chair that faced his desk and I sat there. Encouraged by the way things were going, I maintained the confident smiling face and introduced myself, handed Seidlmayer the envelope with Anthony Frendo's recommendation and embarked upon my mission without further ado. I was as brief as possible, but at the same time I concentrated upon emphasising the importance of Carl Lepsius' Egyptology and of the *BBAW*'s crucial role in preserving his documentation and that of several others.

Seidlmayer scanned the letter; he smiled as he looked up and assured me that he would comply as best he could. I was staggered at this immediate acquiescence on his part. Seemingly not wishing to waste another second of my time he immediately stood up from his chair and led me out of his office on to one of the two *Altagyptisches Worterbuch* rooms across the corridor. There and then he introduced me to Stefan Grunert and Angela Böhme with a strong recommendation for their assistance in my regard. I was visibly stunned at the outcome of that morning's proceedings and remained speechless. Things were definitely working out in my favour far better than I ever expected in my wildest dreams.

That gesture from the director was extremely kind, generous and crucial for it sealed the success of my mission there. The director's blessing would surely ensure the best possible outcome for the task ahead of me, and this sudden twist of good fortune was immediately reflected in my internal mood. It had been barely ten minutes earlier that I had practically accepted my visit to Berlin as a total failure.

Seidlmayer shook my hand and went away and back to his office across the corridor. I was left with Stefan Grunert, and his associate Angela. Another colleague Ingeldore Hafeman was away from the office on vacation, and so was Frank Feder in the office next door. Stefan and Angela were managing the *Altagyptisches Worterbuch* section of the *BBAW* on their own and from their manner they seemed to be coping very well.

There were several long tables in their office and also two large computer desks. Atlas-size volumes were neatly stacked in tiers one above the other, and a wall-to-wall mahogany brown unit decorated the wall opposite the entrance. A number of metal cupboards held publications that were relevant to that section of the *BBAW*.

The Altagyptisches Worterbuch

Stefan was in his early forties, had a clean-shaven head and sported a small blonde goatie. Angela maintained a perpetual smile. She took me aside at one time and pointing to Stefan remarked silently that 'he is your man.'

After scanning his website, I had tried to make contact with Stefan Grunert through e-mail during the few weeks prior to going over to Berlin. Although I received no answer from him, he was fully aware of what I required. He had in fact already located the Lepsius notebooks – there were two of them rather than one – and he led me to the office next door and Doris Topman. She was a tall woman with beautiful long white hair and a gentle smile. She brought the *Notizbuchs* out of a metal cupboard and placed them on a metal desk in front of me for inspection. Within a few minutes of my arrival at the *BBAW* I had achieved my mission to Berlin.

I sat down on the desk and browsed awhile, starting off with *Notizbuch I*. This was as small as my own notebook, measuring six by four inches, and dated to the 25th October 1841. Though there were another two persons in the same room all was exceptionally quiet. There was a student in the office, a certain Gerzen who was doing some research of his own. And Doris continued with her own work on the computer.

Ten minutes down the line I casually asked Doris if I could take a snapshot of some of the pages, and after a mini-interval of wild tachycardia within my chest she nodded and smiled. So I got my Fuji out and started to take a few photographs of the material that was relevant to my research.

The entire scanning and photography of the two notebooks took me barely twenty minutes. The crucial pages were then all preserved in digital format.

The Verzeichniss

There was another manuscript available inside the office and this was entitled the *Verzeichniss* 1842-1845. Its A4 size folios were much larger than the *Notizbuchs*. There was one interesting page with the name of 'Malta' upon it and 'Monumente'. This too was an important document and therefore I started to photograph it for later translation and decipherment.

The card on my Fuji camera ran out of memory. I asked Doris if it were possible for me to get another camera from the hotel and she gave me the go-ahead right away.

I was back at the *BBAW* in twenty minutes and continued with the exercise, even repeating the photography on the *Notizbuchs* with my Sony and its much greater resolution capacity. I was done within thirty minutes.

I thanked them all very profusely for their kindness and generosity and left them to their lunch break. I went off to the corner chocolate shop at the *Charlotten Strasse*, the *Fassbender and Rauch – Chocolatiers am Gendarmenmarkt*, and got the members of the staff at the *BBAW* a box of pralines for the females, and red wine for the males. They all richly deserved even more than this.

Whilst there was still time, I headed once again to the *Altes* in order to view the Greek section of the museum that I had missed the day before. As I walked along the avenues, I recall reminding myself that this was the land of the Mercedes, BMWs and Volkswagens – the cream coloured Mercedes taxis especially were everywhere.

I viewed and studied a great deal from the Greek section, though my mind was still focussed on what I had achieved that day at the *BBAW*. Everything I needed from there was documented on the memory cards of my Sony and Fuji, and there was a lot of study to be done once I returned to Malta.

It was worth a celebration, and I selected the *Maredo* restaurant on the *Charlotten Strasse* on one of the tables on the pavement, *al fresco* under a massive umbrella. I got my jacket for the evening chill. It was 200 grams of grilled salmon with sauce, and wild rice. It had been a fantastic day – most museums were not open on Mondays, and I had been so fortunate in getting the *BBAW* done on a Monday. It was the Pergamon museum on the morrow, after a brief walk to the *Brandenburgh Tor* at the other end of the *Unter den Linden*.

Back in my room at the *Gendarm*, I downloaded all the photographs that I had taken at the *BBAW* and the *Altes*. As I was browsing through some of the images, I translated the page from the *Verzeichniss* volume, and it transpired that whilst in Malta, Carl Lepsius had purchased five Egyptian statuettes. These had been found in Malta, in graves that were situated close to the ancient capital of Malta, Civita Vecchia, and the Mdina of today.

That made a lot of sense, for the Phoenicians in Malta frequently included Egyptian and Egyptianising artefacts inside their graves. This circumstance provided another option for the discovery context of our statuette. If it had not been a megalithic temple site, then a Phoenician rock cut tomb in Gozo was another likely spot where the statuette would have been placed as part of the funerary furniture.

There was also the possibility, as Marta later pointed out to me, that these statuettes mentioned by Lepsius were similar to some of the Phoenician 'ushabtis' that were preserved at St Agatha museum and that we had visited as a group two years earlier.

My mood was the best ever possible as I turned in. It was then that I realised that I had completely forgotten about the second part of my mission to Berlin. I had been so completely overwhelmed by my access to the journals that the other task of seeking out the casts had completely slipped out of my mind.

A change of plan was evidently necessary for the morrow. The casts had to be seen to while I was still in Berlin and so close to the *BBAW*. I had to go back there and ask Grunert to have a look at the squeezes that Lepsius had taken of the hieroglyphs on the statuette in 1842. I still did not know then whether and how many of them were still available.

Seeking out the wax squeezes

After an early breakfast the next morning I was off to the offices of the *Altagyptisches Worterbuch* once again. Grunert was there alone on his desk, busy as usual on his computer. He greeted me cordially. I told that I had not thanked him enough the previous day.

He thanked me for the wine and asked me whether there was anything else that he could oblige me with. I mentioned the squeezes – how many of them were there, and had they all survived?

"Ah, yes!" His response was immediate. He switched his computer off and took some keys out of a drawer. He asked me whether I would like to go with him down to the vaults.

"Definitely, yes!" I answered him with a visibly grateful smile. That was another big bonus for me. I just love visiting underground vaults loaded with ancient archives.

We walked out of his office together and he led me to a lift that took us down to the *Abklats Archiv* in Room 7; this was where all the casts of the establishment were stored.

Stefan had initially told me that when he examined these casts some months earlier he discovered that numbers 2 and 9 were missing. Even if these were missing, there were still some casts that I had not seen, and, hardly believing my good fortune that far, I looked forward to see the ones remaining.

Stefan moved the sliding archive holders around. These were extremely tall and all in white. The setup reminded me of the basement vaults at the Natural History Museum in London.

He opened one of the drawers and extracted two archaic A3 paper folios. There were seven strips in between the folio sheets. These were what had remained of the initial nine casts. He positioned the folios under his shoulder, closed the drawers and led me out of the room.

We retraced our short journey and returned to Stefan's office on the top floor, and on the way there I asked him whether he would oblige me with scans of the casts. He volunteered to copy them for me on disk. "That was just perfect", I assured him.

But there were a few problems. First of all, the number one cast had gone astray since 2001, the date that the website was started. And secondly, the scanner was a new one and was not being recognized by the computer. The software for it needed to be installed, and there was no CD available to do it.

Stefan then remembered that the computer next door had already been installed with the software. So he transferred the scanner there, set it up and started copying the casts for me. The problem was solved, or so I thought.

Once he was finished I took a number of photographs of the casts from both of their faces. Stefan too had scanned the casts from both surfaces and at that stage they were stored on his hard disk.

The final stage was getting the images from his hard drive on to the compact disk, and this procedure was meeting up with some problems. Finally, after a number of failed attempts we managed – the compact disk was burnt and was there finally in my hands. I was elated!

My *Toshiba Portégé* laptop was not equipped with a compact disk drive. I could not copy the files on to the hard disk when in Berlin. I would have to do this once back in Malta. I treated the compact disk with great care, protecting it from any possible harm like I would have done with a premature baby.

I had eight casts in all, but one of these was a 'double' or a 'two-in-one' that included two adjacent sides of the base. I would have to elucidate which sides these were after comparison of the hieroglyphs back home. The double cast would definitely prove useful to compare the original measurements of the base with those of the statuette. Would these measurements tally? This query would have to be sorted out back at home.

I had all the casts from Lepsius's number two to nine. I also had the missing number one back home in Malta though this had been a downloaded image and was not of the same high resolution as the ones I had just acquired.

"What about image one?" I asked Stefan. He would search it out, it had to be somewhere in the vaults of the *Abklats Archiv*. Once he found it he would scan it for me at 300 dpi and send it by e-mail.[479] That seemed like the perfect arrangement. I assured Stefan that I was indeed extremely grateful for all the favours that he done for me, and I truly was.

Just before leaving I mentioned Alicia Meza to him, and he volunteered the information that he had already provided her with copies of the casts that Lepsius had taken of the statuette.

For some reason it seemed from his expression that her mention reminded him of something else. He signalled me to wait for a bit as he then brought over to the table a large A2 size book that he said should provide more information for me. The title read *Topographical Bibliography of ancient Egyptian Hieroglyphic texts, reliefs, and paintings*. VII. Nubia, the deserts, and outside Egypt. The two authors were Rosalind Moss and Bertha Porter. It had been published at the Clarendon press in Oxford in 1951. This was a very welcome surprise for me for I had only known about it through the references.

I scanned through the pages and searched out the reference to the Maltese statuette. There was the crucial information that the authors' attribution of the statuette in question was the 'Island of Gozo ... found in 1713'.[480] Rosalind Moss and Bertha Porter found no reason whatsoever to doubt the integrity and validity of the statements made by the first series of Maltese curators of archaeology on the context of the statuette.

Figure 52. One of the present authors with Stefan Grunert (on right) at the *BBAW* in Berlin, where the casts of the statuette (below) are preserved.

The organizers of the Museum exhibitions in 2003 and 2005 must therefore not have been aware of the contents of this publication for they made no mention of this attribution of Porter and Moss to Gozo in 1713.

The two British authors in question had mentioned Sonnini's publication, but the only comment they made about it was a bracketed note, namely 'seen in Cairo, and said to come from Thebes'.

Porter and Moss were apparently not sufficiently impressed by Sonnini's context for they listed the statuette in question with the artefacts that were discovered *outside* of Egypt. It was published specifically in the section dealing with Cyprus, Rhodes, Crete and Malta.

Their attribution of the statuette to Neferabet was based on the hieroglyphs in Sonnini's engraving. What Moss and Porter were basically saying was that the statuette was found in the island of Gozo in 1713, but was reported as having been *seen* in Cairo in 1778 in the hands of an Italian priest of the *Propaganda Fide*.

It seemed that Heritage Malta had relied way too much trust on what Sonnini had to say about the statuette, and had ignored the dubious nature of the third hand information about its context. On the other hand Moss and Porter simply treated this declaration by Sonnini as a statement and mentioned it as such without attaching any particular significance to it – their message was clear enough.

There were other Egyptian artefacts in this same publication that were reported by Moss and Porter as having been discovered in Malta, such as the steles discovered at Bighi in 1829. Moss and Porter were also giving the references to these.

The way I saw it was that by 1951 this fully referenced publication by Porter and Moss had clearly defined the provenance of a number of Egyptian artefacts *on Malta*, and these included the statuette with the triad of gods.

314

Moss had also consulted Wilkinson's notes that are preserved at the Bodleian Library in Oxford, for she quoted from them for the Bighi steles. But she did not quote anything about the statuette from Wilkinson's sources. It seemed most likely that there was nothing by Wilkinson at the Bodleian on the statuette, and so a visit there would not have been fruitful insofar as Neferabet was concerned.

After sorting out the copyright and reproduction credits with Stefan – the owner of the Lepsius diaries was the *Äegyptisches Museum*, and the director was Dietrich Wildung – Stefan came up with another pleasant surprise. He laid out on the large table of his office a manuscript of 1893 that had transcribed the *Notizbuchs* and drawings of Lepsius. In this manuscript these same hieroglyphs that Lepsius had scribbled upon his notebooks had been transcribed into a 'neater' format.

Stefan provided me with photocopies of the relevant pages and I took some photographs as well for later comparisons at home.

All the tasks that I had set out to accomplish at the *BBAW* had been terminated. All that was left was for Stefan to e-mail me the material that had not been seen, especially image one of the casts.

It was time to bid Stefan farewell and he was probably extremely relieved that I was finally content with my achievements there.

I made the Pergamon in the afternoon. Blocks of entire buildings had been transported over from Turkey and reassembled in the museum. I would be visiting Turkey in the coming year, and there in Berlin were most of its Classical period remains.

Assessing the BBAW information

I returned to Malta and started working first of all on the hieroglyphs in the 1893 publication that had been provided by Stefan Grunert. I went straight for the proper left side of the stand - this hieroglyphic register had not been satisfactorily dealt with yet. The segment dealing with the name of "Anhotep' showed an 'eye' sign with an extra border on the upper eyelid. This was a peculiar hieroglyph that required further elucidation. As already mentioned above, the validity of this hieroglyphic strip had been questioned in 1949 by Rosalind Moss and once again by James Allen in 2003.

Clarification of this issue was finally achieved a few months later in Malta. Through a stroke of good fortune, Marta was going through one of the latest publications by Zahi Hawass.[481] In the photograph of the painted wooden door from the intact tomb of Senedjem (TT1) there was a familiar group of hieroglyphs. The name they were referring to started with the sign of the outstretched arm – 'a' or 'an'. The 'eye' with the upper lid inverted was next; had the iris not been included, it would have resembled 'two eyes', or 'two mouths'. However the iris gives it away as an 'eye' with the upper lid turned upwards. The 'htp' follows together with the determinative of a seated male and 'true of voice'. We had finally found a parallel that could be read as 'Anhotep. The name of Neferabet's brother was confirmed.

Senedjem's burial chamber had been closed by a wooden door that was plastered and painted. It was most likely that the same situation prevailed in the tomb of Neferabet prior to it being robbed and vandalized.

In Senedjem's tomb there were twenty mummies in all, nine were coffined mummies and the remainder were not. The coffined mummies survived their removal from the tomb and are today dispersed around the world museums. Ideally they should all be put together as they were originally planned to be, for eternity – at least in one museum, and preferably in Luxor or Cairo.

The uncoffined mummies had certainly not been properly desiccated, and had gone through the most economical form of mummification; they disintegrated soon after their removal from the tomb. The workers at the Place of Truth folk could not afford the more costly mummification ritual of the elite. They were obliged to cut corners.

Despite the water that continually dripped upon them, the skeletal remains would have survived for more than three millennia had the mummification been appropriate. Well mummified bodies like KV55 survived these adverse conditions.

And if such a wealthy artist as Senedjem had twenty mummies in his luxurious tomb, presumably all members of his family, a poorer Neferabet would have had even more. In fact it can be justifiably postulated that those individuals pictured on Neferabet's tomb walls as 'true of voice' were all buried in his family mausoleum, TT 5. The stele with four mummies, BM 693 [305] certainly suggests that Neferabet and Taese were buried together with Neferabet's parents, though evidently not necessarily at the same time.

The undocumented evacuation of TT5 leaves this query unanswered.

Analyzing the casts

I had been back in Malta for a week when Stefan e-mailed to inform me that he had found the 'missing squeeze', and that he was attaching it there and then.

I was now equipped with all the casts that Lepsius had taken of the Egyptian statuette during his Malta sojourn in 1842. A detailed comparison was possible between the images on these casts and those on the statuette of today.

I started with the strips for the pedestal; these were clearly the narrowest ones, and the side ones ended in a 45 degree angle. I studied these for the name of Neferabet, but at the very end of the inscription the characters on the cast were far too squeezed for a reliable transliteration.

Next in line were the casts for the front and sides of the stand. Damage to the statuette had already been sustained by the time that Lepsius examined it, and the dented areas on the cast tallied with those on the statuette, though more wear and tear had evidently taken its toll on the engraved surfaces since the time of Lepsius.

A surprise was in store in the 'two-in-one' cast that Lepsius had taken of the base.[482] As I scanned the hieroglyphs, I came across the "aAbt" sign that was clearly part of our Neferabet's name. So this was the back side of the base. As I followed the signs on the cast, they merged into those of the proper left of the base. Although there were signs of damage to the base at this site, the "aAbt" hieroglyph was clearly visible next to the upper part of the "nfr" sign. So it seemed abundantly clear that the name of the dedicatee of the statuette was Neferabet after all.

Did the measurements tally with those I had read with the laser? The casts that Grunert had sent me had fortunately been scanned alongside a scale. On measuring the 'two-in-one' cast, I discovered that the reading for the back side was around 13 cm, whereas that for the proper left side read 17 cm. These measurements tallied comfortably with those of the corresponding parts on the statuette. The statuette was apparently the same one studied by Lepsius in 1842.

Next I searched for the photograph that I had taken of the back side of the base during the exhibition and found that it was providing us with additional, comparative and crucial information. (Fig 51)

Two of the mentions of the name of Neferabet were situated one above the other, one on the lowermost end of the back pillar and the other in the centre of the back side of the base. Yet whilst the latter rendering of the name was clearly Neferabet, containing both the M35 and the M19 signs, the hieroglyphs at the bottom end of the back pillar were clearly dissimilar. There was no convincing "nfr" sign, M35, and the supposed "aAbt" hieroglyph, M19, had no lines enclosing the pseudo-zigzag sign; it was definitely different from the one just below it in the centre of the base. It seemed that the name on the lowermost end of the back pillar was not Neferabet.

The two options we considered were either that the statuette had been carved for somebody else or that it was custom made and remained unfinished.

The third mention of Neferabet's name was situated in the end hieroglyph on the statuette's proper right pedestal. But this was too squashed up for recognition. There was thus only one unambiguous and incontestable mention of the name of Neferabet on the statuette. Even this was damaged in the lower end of the "nfr", M35, but the assumption was a fair one.

The engraved surface of the statuette that had sustained the least damage was the long strip of hieroglyphs at the back. I considered it worthwhile to investigate this surface in more detail to carry out comparative studies.

Hard copies

At the time in question, digital photography was a relatively new medium for Malta. I considered it to be an extraordinary technique for the sheer numbers of images possible, for economy, for rapidity of access, and for the various modes of presentation. And there was nobody that I was aware of then who knew more about digital imaging than a very good friend of mine, John Baldacchino. A trip I made frequently in the extremely hot afternoons of August was to the town of Qormi during the peak traffic hour – time consuming but well worth it.

Viewing images on the laptop screen and comparing them with one another was not sufficient when fine comparisons and measurements were necessary. There was nothing like a hard copy for the purpose of comparing details. When I took my images to John on a CD or a memory pen, I could know from the very start that I would end up with fantastic photographs of A4 size. The clarity of his images would then permit me to carry out the kind of examination that I wanted.

The task at hand seemed simple enough. I would take the photograph of a cast that had been procured from the BBAW in Berlin and the photograph of the corresponding part from the statuette that had been placed on exhibition. The exercise which I planned to carry out was simply to confirm that the hieroglyphic strips matched one another in form and alignment. If there was any discrepancy to be picked up, this long strip was the ideal one to examine.

At first glance, it seemed that there was a perfect match between the two strips on the laptop screen. Of course I could have done the Adobe Photoshop drill myself at home on the two images and compared them on the screen. But I decided that this had to be done properly, the scales had to be maintained at all times, and above all, the performance by an unbiased operator such as John ensured complete neutrality of interpretation.

He was always busy when I visited him, usually bent over his console in the inner room of his photography establishment and sandwiched between the two large machines that whirled constantly away. On that particular occasion, John was checking and setting images from a negative reel before dispatching the next part of the developing and printing process to the computerized mechanisms.

Always ready for me with a smile in anticipation of carrying out something very different from his usual daily routine, John was ready in less than a minute and asked me what we were doing that afternoon. I took my time to explain my intentions, and he had no difficulty in complying immediately.

We opted to begin by carrying out the procedure with one cast, and I started off with the hieroglyphs at the very front of the statuette, those on the front of the pilaster just beneath the pedestal that supported the deities. Once they were scaled down to the same size and reproduced on photographic paper, I started to compare the two images whilst still in John's studio.

I was on the constant lookout for minor deviations; however, I was obliged to conclude that they matched one another nearly perfectly, though not quite so perfectly. If there was a stonemason copyist involved, he had done a very good job of it. He would of course have concentrated on precision particularly on the front of the statuette, the part that was more frequently in full view during exhibition.

Nonetheless, I could observe that the angles of some of the hieroglyphs were not quite identical on the two images. And what was even more significant was that, from the viewer's point of view, the damage along the right border of the pilaster that was evident on the cast was not visible on the statuette. Artefacts do not improve naturally with time, and if repair had actually been carried out as part of the preservation program, then it would have been carried out in a manner that clearly indicated the precise extent of the repair job. No such patch of repair was evident on the statuette, and that was sufficient to raise an iota of suspicion that the statuette on display might not be the original one, certainly not the same one examined by Carl Lepsius in 1842.

I felt that I required even more evidence to back me up. And so for the second set of comparisons I decided to go straight to the site that was normally the least exposed. This was the rear of the statuette, specifically the back strip of hieroglyphs that extended from the dedicatee's neck down to his heel. Once again I provided John with a photograph of the back strip from the back of the statuette and a photograph of the corresponding cast.

This time around, there was an image of the cast and an image of the back pillar of the statuette. They both had a resolution of 300 dpi, but I required his expertise to match them in size and then position them next to one another for comparative purposes. The actual colours were not as important as the details of the hieroglyphs. And furthermore, an adjustment had to be made to make up for the process of the making of the cast – not only was this rotated horizontally, but the bas relief had to be converted to an inscription. Adobe Photoshop served very well for this. The image on the cast had to be rotated horizontally and then inverted in order to make it perfect for comparison with the hieroglyphs on the statuette.

Accustomed to this as to the palm of his hand, John made light work of the process that eventually resulted in two vertical and neatly apposed images. He then adjusted the contrast, brightness levels, curves, and several other features that I was not fully acquainted with, and I was spellbound by the result.

"Shall we print this?" he asked.

"Wow! Definitely."

"What size? Will an A4 size do?"

"Definitely!" So John buttoned the finalized image into the workout program, checked that it had started off, and then turned his attention to a few medical queries he had for me about his children's health. The sounds from the machines surrounded us as we spoke, but they also reassured me that there was an entertaining and interesting session ahead for us with the photograph that was being processed.

Once the photograph was ready, he placed it inside a large envelope for me and wished me a good evening. The two images of the back pillar hieroglyphs stood side by side, ready for a detailed comparison.

John had work to do, so I took my leave to continue the exercise at home. So I left him to it and drove off, totally oblivious of the traffic congestion that slowed my return back home.

Comparing hieroglyphs

I felt that I should involve Marta in the next phase of the comparative study, that is, if she had the time for it. So I called her, and she was as anxious as I was to have a go at comparing the images. Fifteen minutes later, I was persuading her two-year-old son Gabriel to let us work on the photographs while he handled an auroscope from my medical bag that had reached the end of its serviceable life, and Gabriel hastened the process.

In a previous exercise, Marta and I had already scanned a series of photographs and drawings of the statuette in order to see whether they tallied well with one another. We had managed to pick up a number of differences in outward appearance between the statuette of today and the engraving depicted by Sonnini. These discrepancies had led us to believe that the two artefacts were not one and the same. Features like armbands and the ankh were only present on one artefact and not the other, whilst the restoration processes that had been carried out on the statuette between 1882 and 1931 were no longer visible in the statuette exhibited in 2003 and 2005.

I was holding the photograph in my hand as we sat down at the table of Marta's spotless kitchen, rapidly making comparisons for any gross differences as we initially scanned the juxtaposed images on the print. We were using the magnifying glass that I had inherited from my father which was ideal for our purpose.

It soon became apparent that the two images were not a perfect match. My eyes were drawn to the letters on the right-hand side at the very top of the inscriptions. I pointed out this part of the photograph to Marta, and she too then focussed on it. These hieroglyphs represented the "[r]sw" sign, M23/24. But the impressions on the cast and the statuette were definitely not a match, and in fact whilst the one on the cast was totally correct in form, the one on

323

the statuette was arching up, minimally but definitely, the wrong way towards the right.

I asked myself and Marta why the copyist had blundered so stupidly with such an error. This hieroglyph simply did not exist in the way it had been depicted on the statuette. The copyist certainly had no idea of hieroglyphs, for otherwise he would not have committed this foolish error.

But this was not all. We moved our eyes over to the hieroglyph to the left of the "[r]sw", and this was "spd", M44. Here again there was no match in the hieroglyphs between the cast and statuette. This time, instead of an isosceles triangle, the shape of the "spd" on the statuette looked like a right-angled triangle with the right angle on the left.

Furthermore, the left side of this triangle was deeply indented when there was no indentation on the cast, and the other side of the triangle was clumsily curved to a point towards the base. This contrasted strongly with its counterpart on the cast, where the line was perfectly straight. The circular defect at the side of this line was also different – it was integrated into the line in the cast but had somehow disentangled itself from the line on the statuette. The exercise was starting to be an exciting one. We had identified our first discrepancies for that day. (Fig. 53)

As we continued making further comparisons between casts and photographs, we focussed all our concentration on the hieroglyphs in an attempt to identify the dedicatee. Although the hieroglyphs on the pedestal had not been helpful for Neferabet's identification, the inscription on the back side of the base included the two component hieroglyphs of his name, the "aAbt", M19, and the "nfr", M35. We decided to follow the third mention of his name on the back pillar.

The representation of the name on the exhibition panels was somewhat different, but the general outline of the hieroglyph on Sonnini's engraving was sufficiently close

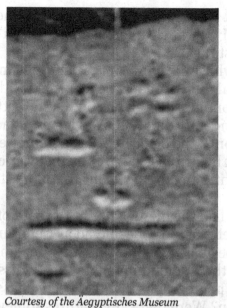

Figure 53. Lepsius's cast of the uppermost hieroglyphs on the back pillar (above) and the corresponding area on the statuette on display (below). The forms of the hieroglyphs are clearly not identical.

to this. All it lacked was an extra zigzag on the "aAbt", M19. The "nfr", M35, was clear enough on Sonnini's engraving and on the statuette.

Yet whilst the name of the dedicatee in Sonnini's engraving might reasonably be identified with Neferabet, the corresponding hieroglyphs on the statuette and on the cast were evidently different. And it was in fact the identification of the dedicatee of the statuette as Nefertanpet by von Bissing in 1907 that was casting doubt on the identification of the dedicatee of the statuette in question.

Why had the hieroglyphs at the base of the back pillar of the statuette of today been read as Nefertanpet in 1907? Would we be able to answer this sometime in the future?

Was there something that we had missed in the large numbers of photographs that had been amassed during our investigation? Were there any features somewhere that would settle the issue once and for all?

We had already gone through a comparison between the hieroglyphs on the back pillar of the statuette and those preserved in Lepsius's cast. We had picked out a few dissimilarities between the two, but otherwise they could still have matched each other if we stretched our imaginations.

But then we noticed a fundamental anomaly that had not been picked up earlier, and this was certainly indicative of dissimilarity between the hieroglyphic strip on the cast and that on the statuette. As Marta ran her index fingers down the two parallel columns of hieroglyphic script, it was possible to observe throughout the extent of the entire columns that there was a variation in the spacing between the individual glyphs on the statuette and the cast. Although they started at the top and ended at the bottom at the same levels, their alignment to one other fluctuated down the line. Halfway down the columns, they started to drift apart. Further down, the copyist must have attempted to remedy this by making the remaining signs closer to one another.

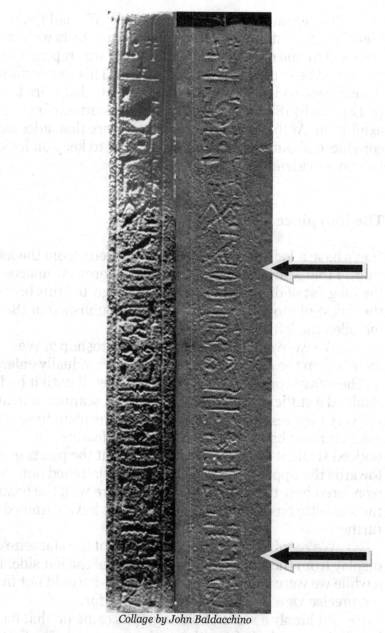

Collage by John Baldacchino

Figure 54. The back pillar, on the statuette (left) and on the cast (right). The arrows indicate the extent of the asymmetry in spacing between the individual glyphs.

327

The asymmetry was incontestable. We had finally identified irrefutable proof that the two artefacts were not identical to one another. The experiment was repeatable and could be confirmed by third parties. This was certainly the clearest evidence thus far that the casts that were taken by Lepsius in 1842 did not belong to the statuette on exhibition. At that stage we were both more than adequately convinced about this, and yet we decided to keep on looking for more evidence.

The hairpiece

"Let's have a look at the head of the statuette from the left side", I told Marta as I went through the preview images on the long list of digital photographs. I suggested this because the oldest photographs available, those published in 1882, included the left side view.

We were still using the Adobe Photoshop 7. We focussed on the head of the statuette and gradually enlarged it. The image continued to maintain its detail until it had attained a sufficiently large size, for I had scanned it in at the very high resolution of 1200 dpi. It was plain to see that wear and tear had taken their toll on the features. We noticed straight away the obvious fact that the pleats of hair towards the upper part of the head were flattened out. We wondered how this feature would compare with the head of the statuette on display. Would the pleats have flattened further?

We required a recent photograph of the statuette on display from the same angle, a side view of the left side. For a while we were actually concerned that we would not find the precise view of what we were looking for.

Suddenly a score of photographs came up that had been taken precisely from the angle we wanted. The first three were immaculate, all crystal clear. We zoomed in on one of these, enlarged it, and moved to the top of the head.

Figure 55. The hairpiece of the statuette in 1882 (above) shows signs of wear and tear with flattening of the pleats at the top of the head.
In 2003 the statuette on exhibition (below) sports what seems to be a newly engraved hairpiece with the pleats in near pristine condition.

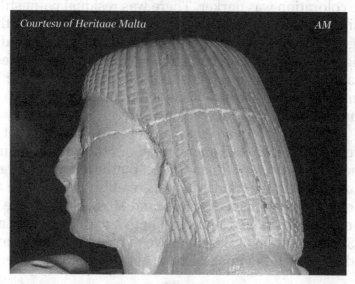

AM

Our efforts were immediately rewarded by the image that stood there before us in perfect focus and flawless clarity. This straight view from the left side of the statuette at the exhibition was practically limited to the hairpiece of the dedicatee. Throughout the entire surface of the head of the dedicatee and right to the top of the head, the hair pleats of the dedicatee were near pristine. It was as if they had just been carved out there and then. This was in stark contrast to their flattened appearance in the 1882 photograph. (Fig. 55) Once again, we had stumbled upon irrefutable evidence that excluded the identification of the original statuette with that on display.

This was a perfect example of reverse deterioration with time. After a hundred and twenty-one years, the flattened hair pleats on the dedicatee's head had been restored. I felt so good about this second major breakthrough that I just had to make a joke about it. "This should go very well with an agency that promotes hair restoration", I remarked to Marta.

As we scrutinised the photographs further, Marta picked up a very significant detail. She pointed out two areas on the enlarged 1882 photograph on the laptop where the coloration was darker. There was residual paint still visible on the altar and also in some of the grooves in the wig. At one time the statuette would have been painted with bright colours, and we had already come across a perfect analogy of this in an artefact that was preserved at the *Museo Egizio* in Turin. This was the statuette of Penchenabu already described above.

Marta was in an especially observant mood that afternoon. Hardly had she pointed out the paint remains when she indicated a linear defect on the left arm of the figure holding the triad. This was readily visible in the 1949 photographs published by Rosalind Moss. (Fig.56) We immediately shifted our attention to have a close look at the 1882 photograph of Caruana. We moved towards the arm and magnified the image. There was definitely no defect on

Figure 56. The left side view of the statuette published by Ross in 1949 shows a defect in the left lower arm.

Figure 57. The defect in the left arm is not present in the
1882 photograph.

AM

Figure 58. The left arm defect is not visible in 2003.

the left arm in 1882. (Fig. 57) This injury must have been sustained in the period between 1882 and 1949.

We looked at the photographs we had taken of the statuette at the 2003 exhibition next. There were numbers of these, and we scanned them one at a time until we came upon a perfect view of the left arm. (Fig. 58)

"There's no defect on the left arm," whispered Marta. "And there is certainly no sign of one ever having been repaired either!"

"It is definitely not the same statuette!" I insisted. "All the evidence is converging towards this one conclusion!"

It was no longer simply a question of comparing the statuette of today with the engraving by Sonnini. Apart from the dissimilarities between the two, there was now the issue of the authenticity of the statuette. The artefact on display was a copy and visibly different from the one that was photographed in 1882.

"But is it possible to create a counterfeit statuette so closely?" asked Marta.

"Certainly!" I replied. "The gadget they use is called a pantograph, and I know somebody who was using the machine fifteen years ago for making identical balustrades in stone from the original model."

I had in fact been trying to get a look at these machines, which measured between nine and thirteen feet in length, and there were quite a few specimens around on the island. These contrivances are armed with very fine cutters, and they can make very good and precise copies of a master model. They are principally used to make replicas of originals in stone, and they can produce detail down to a millimetre and can copy engravings even down to the width of a hair. Electric motors work the machine. In the same manner that a key is copied, the operator goes over the original, the master, and the machine cuts up a copy of it. The *materia prima* can be wood, limestone, marble, granite, or even glass. A pantograph could easily have been used in Malta to make a replica of the limestone statuette.

We then started to make some sense of the superficial scratch marks that we had observed earlier on the enlarged images of the face. (Figs. 41 & 59) These could be readily explained as the grinding effects of the copying procedure. And the varying length of the statuette as measured by different scholars could also be possibly explained through this process.

These features were further confirming to us that what was being exhibited at the museums of archaeology in Valletta and in Gozo was a copy of the Egyptian statuette rather than the original one.

Conclusion

The statuette under investigation was but a minor constituent of the Egyptian cultural heritage. It was far more likely that it had been found for the first time in Thebes, yet could it have been exported from Egypt and found in Malta the second time around?

The ancient Egyptians were not interested in sailing across the Mediterranean. Apart from isolated long voyages like the one to Punt, they only hugged the coast when they sailed. It is unlikely that they ever reached Malta.

However, this situation would have changed from the Late Period onwards, at a time when the seafaring Greeks were established in towns like Naucratis in the Delta; the Egyptianised Greeks could readily have sailed to Malta. During the time of the Ptolemies they confidently sailed up to Rome, and Egyptian ships would very likely have stopped over in Malta for fresh water supplies and food provisions. These sailors would not have been native Egyptians but rather made up of diverse nationalities of immigrants.

There is no doubt that the unique and remarkable culture of the ancient Egyptians that furnished the framework for their brilliant civilization also exerted a strong influence upon all the major subsequent civilizations that followed it, including the Greek, the Roman, and the Christian.

Invasion of foreign lands and their colonisation was a feature of the ancient Egyptians during the New Kingdom. They utilised significant numbers of foreign mercenaries for their military operations, and territorial expansion by the military pharaohs was not limited to the contiguous land that later acted as a buffer zone between their homeland and their perennial enemies.[483] Tuthmosis III even went up to the Euphrates in Mittani and occupied Kadesh on the Orontes.[484] Palestine and Syria could almost be described as forming part of the ancient Egyptian Empire.[485]

337

The ancient Egyptians utilised no native missionaries to spread their culture outside their borders. This diffusion of Egyptian culture was accomplished by other peoples with whom they had had significant contact, such as the Phoenicians, who also disseminated Egyptian wares outside the shores of Egypt. After the Phoenicians, there were the Romans, who exported ancient Egyptian antiquities.

Several of these ancient Egyptian artefacts were discovered at various locations outside Egypt. A number of Egyptian obelisks are still spread around the piazzas of Rome, whilst other obelisks and sphinxes have turned up in other sites, such as Istanbul and Cagliari. Excellent Egyptian statuary is still to be found in the Vatican museum, with the prized artefact of Mut-Tuya, the mother of Rameses II, taking pride of place – this was transported to Rome at the request of the emperor Caligula.

And last and certainly not least, during the early nineteenth century, Egypt was severely despoiled of its archaeological treasures by booty hunters and European governments alike.

So theoretically any of the above three groups – the Phoenicians, the Romans, or nineteenth-century travellers in Egypt – could have imported the statuette to Malta or Gozo.

What was the reason for this widespread exportation of objects from ancient Egypt to other areas? For the Phoenicians, it was religious attraction. For the Romans, there was the added fever for collecting antiquities. And for the nineteenth-century travelling folk, it was simply a matter of trading in antiquities.

The main controversy over our statuette thus had to do with its precise context. Was it present on the Maltese islands in antiquity, or was it brought over to Malta in modern times? The statuette with the triad might well have been one of those artefacts brought over to the island by one of the several travellers who used Malta as a bridge between Europe and Egypt. The hoard of Egyptian artefacts that was brought over to the islands by Lord Grenfell in 1903 is a later example of such traffic.

What about our dedicatee? As a workman in the Valleys of the Kings and Queens, Neferabet's means were necessarily modest. He had been born into a family of tomb painters, and as the eldest son he would have been expected to follow in his father's footsteps, and he did so.

His family was a numerous one, and he carried on this family tradition as well. Infant and child mortality were high by modern standards, and Neferabet survived a significant number of his own children and even one granddaughter.

Occupational hazards were conspicuous, and illness was a frequent occurrence. Several of the workmen suffered from a form of temporary blindness, and this malady seems to have been particularly severe for Neferabet. Although his wife was the daughter of the village physician, it seems that the latter's efforts did not suffice for his cure, and Neferabet resorted to the gods to heal him. His prayers took some time to be heard, and Neferabet attributed his cure to the goddess of the peak, Meretseger. In fact, if our hypothesis is correct, he dedicated the statuette of Malta to her and had it placed in the cave sanctuary of Ptah along the path from the village to the Valley of the Queens.

Neferabet's experience in tomb painting placed him in a favourable position to furnish his own tomb.

He lived to a ripe old age and was probably fortunate enough to see his nephew Amennakht appointed to the enviable position of a village scribe. Neferabet earned the respect of the community, which elevated him to a village elder.

Like so many of the tombs of the ancient Egyptians, Neferabet's final resting place was looted. This probably occurred at the turn of the twentieth century, and his remains and artefacts are today scattered in various institutions. His mummy has not yet been identified.

The cave sanctuary of Ptah was also looted in antiquity, and later cultures considered Neferabet's statuette a suitable object to be placed in one of their own sanctuaries that they had established in a remote island in the central Mediterranean.

What had started as an enquiry into the real identity of the dedicatee of the statuette resulted in the identification of a probably substituted statuette that had replaced the original one. What was being exhibited at the National Museum of Archaeology in Malta was possibly only a copy! The question of where the original one lies now remains unanswered.

If the statuette in question is a copy, then the original is probably still around, most likely in some private collection. The copy might be identical to the original, but then it might not be, and a different individual might have been responsible for dedicating it.

Our investigation has considered the tomb painter Neferabet. But what if the original belonged to somebody else? The only certain hieroglyph that we have of the original is the one appearing on the back pillar from the cast taken by Lepsius in 1842. By way of an interpretation, we have the translation of the Austrian Egyptologist von Bissing in 1907. The name he suggests is NFRTNPT. But the hieroglyphs for the T and the R are easily transposed in translation, and the individual represented on the statuette might even have been Neferabet's father or brother, Neferrenpet. An examination of the original statuette would solve this question.

The original statuette was last exhibited in the early years of the twentieth century and has since disappeared from the public eye. The original statuette rightfully should be preserved at the Museum of Archaeology in Gozo, the island where it was discovered in 1713 in unrecorded circumstances.

The precise motive for this substitution still escapes us. Could there have been a number of reasons or motives?

AM

Figure 59. The abundance of superficial scratch marks on the statuette of today further suggests that a copy has been manufactured in modern times.

AM

We have not revealed the full mystery of Neferabet's statuette. Admittedly, we proved that the artefact in the exhibition was a far from perfect copy. But what has happened to the original? Was it damaged at some time in the museum store rooms and a replacement copy executed?

Whatever the reason and no matter how good the copy, this move has limited research into the investigation, including making it impossible to confirm the provenance of the stone through geological analysis. Where was this quarried, in Malta or in Egypt? The first persons who described the statuette described it as having been created out of the normal Maltese sandstone.[486]

Another major query should be addressed towards the manner in which the statuette ended up in Gozo. There is some mystery as to how the statuette of Neferabet reached the central Mediterranean, and even more so as to when this occurred. It is highly unlikely that any ancient Egyptian before the Ptolemies ever set foot upon the Maltese islands.

Our provisional hypothesis attributes the relocation of the statuette to the Phoenicians or the Romans. Both were constantly exporting ancient Egyptian antiquities to other shores, including the Maltese.

The establishment of both the Phoenicians and Romans on the Maltese islands is well attested in both the literary and archaeological records, and there is in fact an abundance of Phoenician and Roman remains on both Maltese islands. On the sister island of Gozo, there are also two Roman villas, one at Ramla and the other at Xewkija. Roman architecture also lies beneath the modern capital of Victoria. The scenario is not at all impossible.

The Phoenicians probably did not reach Upper Egypt, but the Romans did so, as we have seen. After Caligula, in a mission to identify the sources of the Nile, the emperor Nero dispatched two centurions and their men up the river with orders to travel its course southward until the sources were reached. The river is over 4,000 miles in length, and Nero's mission was not accomplished. They did, however, reach a very southern latitude, well beyond Thebes and Abu Simbel. They reached into the Sudan beyond the junction of the Blue and White Niles at Khartoum. They were eventually stopped by the notorious Sudd, an extensive stretch of mud and water that impeded all sorts of ancient navigation.

And yet the Phoenicians could also have been possible candidates for the transport of Egyptian artefacts to the islands in antiquity. In Malta they adorned their own tombs with ancient Egyptian artefacts, and like the Romans after them, they also re-utilised the same megalithic temple structures on Malta and Gozo for religious purposes. The two options that spring to mind for the placement of the statuette are a re-utilised megalithic sanctuary or a rock-cut tomb.

Extensive looting of archaeological artefacts in modern times could also have been responsible. The trade in antiquities remains an active one, and the lucrative nature of this commerce perpetuates it despite the strict measures that are enforced to discourage it.

The placement of the statuette in the Maltese context also needs to be addressed. As already hinted above, one option that presents itself is a funerary context in a Punic tomb. The numerous ancient Egyptian or 'Egyptian-influenced' artefacts that were included amongst the other funerary objects in Maltese Punic tombs did not merely include amulets but also statues. [487]

There is also compelling evidence for the inclusion of the statuette inside a megalithic sanctuary, almost certainly the Ggantija complex in the village of Xaghjra in Gozo. This megalithic temple was adapted for religious usage by subsequent cultures, including the Phoenicians and Romans. Other archaeological artefacts of succeeding cultures were discovered inside the Ggantija temple. These include a remarkably large Phoenician inscription, the Melitensia Quinta, and cult objects, such as a bust statue that is somewhat larger than our statuette. In other megalithic temples on the mainland, such as the Temple of Juno, these introduced cult objects include alabaster sphinxes that recall those transferred to Diocletian's palace in Split. In the temple at Tas-Silg in South-eastern Malta, succeeding cultures' architectural adaptations to the original Neolithic temple are still visible today.

And as Marta pointed out when she came across the Dalmatian Palace of the emperor Diocletian in Split, Croatia, all sorts of ancient Egyptian artefacts were carried away from Egypt to adorn his residence. These include granite columns and the large sphinxes of Amenhotep III and Seti I.

Statues were also seized and transported to adorn private villas, such as that of Hadrian. The Romans did exactly the same thing in Malta. They adorned the now-lost Roman temple of Juno in the Grand Harbour area with, amongst other artefacts, alabaster Egyptian sphinxes that were still in place when the site was visited in the early sixteenth century. Four funerary steles of the Middle and New Kingdom were discovered just across the bay on the other peninsula jutting out into the Grand Harbour of Valletta.

Several questions still remain unanswered. The mystery of Neferabet endures. Whatever the circumstances that led to the statuette of Neferabet finding its final resting place on the Maltese islands and whatever motives might have led to its substitution, the artefact has now been placed in its proper context among the few similar statuettes that are now spread around in museums worldwide.

Neferabet's tomb remains relatively well preserved on the West Bank. It received brief mention by Zahi Hawass in his recent treatment *The Lost Tombs of Thebes*, where he refers to it along with three others as an interesting tomb. A large colour photograph of its inner chamber and another of one of its vignettes were also included in the publication. Its modest decoration presents a stark contrast to those of the nobles on the same West Bank.

Neferabet still remains mostly unknown, a modest tomb painter in the Valley of the Kings. Through this equally modest publication, a glimpse has been offered of this painter of the pharaoh's tomb who made it to the reputable standing of village elder at the Place of Truth.

Was the statuette of Neferabet simply taken off the shelves of the Museum of Archaeology in Valletta and sold to a collector of antiquities? The trail ended at the home of the chevalier just prior to his demise, and I had been one of the two persons who had seen it there.

My attempt to follow it through a possible outlet was fruitless, and the only hope of regaining sight of it is either a chance spotting in a private home or an auction sale sometime in the future. Should this come about, further investigations would be possible on the hieroglyphs and on the stone itself. Its source could also be elucidated.

The Maltese statuette with the triad is the only one of its kind deriving from the workmen's village at present day Deir el-Medina. In the meantime, we have the earliest photographs of it taken by Dr Caruana in 1882 and a drawing and the casts of its hieroglyphs taken by the German Egyptologist Carl Lepsius forty years earlier in 1842.

If this investigation results in the unearthing of the original statuette, it will have achieved its main purpose.

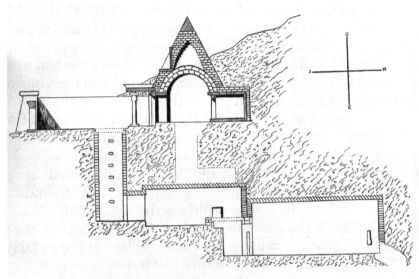

Courtesy of the French Institute of Archaeology in Cairo

Figure 60. Plan of Neferabet's tomb
(from Vandier 1935)

APPENDIX

The documentation of TT 5

In 1935, Jacques Vandier published *La Tombe de Nefer-Abou*; his wife Jeanne produced the drawings.[488]

Apart from a very thorough documentation of all the elements that made up the tomb of Neferabet through photography, diagrams, illustrations, and a translation of all the hieroglyphic inscriptions, the Vandiers also included a chapter on the other sources for Neferabet and the artefacts contained therein.

The following is a summary of their findings at the time. The architecture is tackled first of all.

The style of Neferabet's tomb at Deir el Medina is also found in several of the other burial vaults; these were very probably the work of the same artist. Amongst these feature the tombs numbered 211 of the foreman Paneb, 219 of Nebenmaat, 323 of Pashedu, 335 of Nakhtamen, 336 of yet another Neferrenpet, and 356 of Amenenwia.

The shaft that led into Neferabet's tomb is situated in the courtyard, approximately two metres in front of the chapel. This is dug out vertically into the ground, and measures 750 by 140 centimetres at the surface; this is just enough to permit a person to go down its depth through the extent of four metres. The surfaces of the baked bricks are coated over with a white layer of plaster.

The descent into the tomb is facilitated by a line of grooves dug into the wall of the shaft at intervals of approximately 60 centimetres. Out of the five steps that lead into the first chamber only the last one is original, whilst the other four are modern editions to facilitate access.

The first chamber of the tomb

The first hall is of modest dimensions. It measures two by just over five metres and is made up of a long room that is orientated along a North to South axis. The ceiling is vaulted in a low arch and made up of an assembly of oblique blocks in baked brick. The walls are entirely covered over with paintings over a coat of plaster.

The vault is split open more or less at the centre of the chamber and it permits a view of the ancient construction of bricks that belongs to the shaft of an earlier tomb[489]. This is a clear indication that Neferabet had utilised a more ancient tomb to fit up his own. The reason for this is more likely to have been attributable to economy than to availability of space at the cemetery.

After discussing this with Marta I agreed with her suggestion that the tomb had most probably belonged originally to an ancestor of Neferabet. This would have been more likely in view of the fact that the vacancies that were intermittently being created in the work force at the Place of Truth were normally filled up by the relatives of the outgoing workmen.

The first chamber of the tomb had been violated in the Ptolemaic period when it was used as a catacomb. A papyrus at the Louvre that was published by Revillout in 1880 informs us that this was the tomb of Abounofre.[490] This was an extremely interesting revelation, for as Marta observed, it gave us a possible indication as to the correct reading of the name of its owner. Was it 'Abetnefer' rather than 'Neferabet'? That 'nefer' should be 'nofer' is surmised from the modern Coptic equivalent where the word is still used, translating as 'good'. Thus 'Abou nofre' translated from the Coptic reads 'father good', or 'Good Father', even perhaps our 'Lord Creator'.[491]

After the Ptolemaic period, the Copts in all probability re-utilised the tomb as a habitation site, and this is highly suggested by the characteristic 'Coptic signatures' in the burn marks on the ceiling and walls of the first chamber and the two adjoining rooms. As a result of this, a large portion of the vault and the northern wall are charred and blackened to the point of rendering the reading of the texts and the study of the depictions an impossible task.

There is an unusual feature in the first chamber. This is a cavity fashioned into the ground; however this would not have been designated for a sarcophagus. Stone sarcophagi were only used for the elite members of the society and royalty.

The workmen at the Place of Truth would have considered themselves fortunate if they could afford a *cartonnage* coffin. This would have been placed upon a bier, rather than in a cavity dug into the earth. Furthermore a cavity of vat proportions for the royal sarcophagus to be deposited there only came into fashion in the late Ramessid period. Neferabet was far too early. It would seem more likely that the vat was drilled into the tomb's floor by the later users, either the Ptolemaic or the Coptic folk occupying the tomb. Even more so, if the tomb was known as the catacomb of Abounofre, the dating of the vat would seem to point towards this period.

There was a sort of platform or mastaba at the back of this first chamber, at its northern side. This was probably an altar where the relatives of the deceased left their offerings at the time of the funeral and at appointed festivals for the memory of the dead. Yet the original function of this mastaba was that of covering and hiding the shaft that gave access to the funerary chamber proper in the second hall beyond.

As a general rule, the surviving relatives and friends of the deceased, Neferabet, are represented upon the walls of the tomb in the act of making offerings to the gods. The deities with protective functions of the dead tend to be more concentrated in the arched vault above. Deceased individuals other than Neferabet are the intermediaries between the two entities and they occupy both areas of the chamber.

According to the Vandiers, the aspect of Neferabet's tomb had a decorative arrangement that was very agreeable to the eye, particularly with its divisions into picture scenes, and the choice of the subjects depicted as yellow figures on a white background and emphasized with red and black. Yet whilst the style was too lax, and despite the great ability of the artist, one perceived a free and popular style and a work that seemed to have been a bit hurried.

In the first chamber above all, the individuals in the procession of family members are of a careless draughtsmanship and the figures are truly plain. The bodily proportions are not elegant and the sketches of the feet and hands are non-existent, whilst the gestures are awkward and without any suppleness.

However, it seems that the artist intended to make a greater effort for the second chamber; the individuals on the plinth, all much resembling those in the first chamber, are of a draughtsmanship that is steadier and the faces significantly less plain.

Another point made by the Vandiers was that the hieroglyphs designed in black inside the yellow bands betray a sureness of hand and an exceptional skill. One instinctively felt convinced that the scribe painted them from the tip of his paintbrush without any hesitation on his part and even without any draft preparation.

The vault of the first chamber

The decoration upon the vault is divided up into eight vignettes. There are four on either side, and these are separated from one another by a band of hieroglyphs. Right in the middle of the vault, and along its axis, a long band of inscriptions separates the vignettes of the western vault from those on the East. This hieroglyphic strip reads

Courtesy of the French Institute of Archaeology in Cairo

Figure 61. The first underground chamber of Neferabet's tomb.

351

"A royal offering to Osiris, Lord of the West, King of Eternity, sovereign of the other world, the very great …[492] *justified; his son Neferrenpet, justified.'*

On the western section of the vault one can just barely make out a seated Osiris turned round towards the centre of the scene. Behind him a large winged serpent extends his wings as if to protect Osiris. The hieroglyphs identify it as Meretseger, the serpent goddess, to whom Neferabet had dedicated the stele that we had seen at the *Muzeo Egizio* in Turin. This was once again favouring the identity of the snake on Neferabet's statue as Meretseger rather than another deity.

Upon the arch on the side of the door, situated above Neferabet and his wife, Anubis is lying upon a *naos*, with a sash around the neck and the flail on his back. This god was the guardian of the necropolis and was very frequently found guarding the doors or the corridors of burial vaults.

The eight vignettes of the vault are decorated with larger individuals and correspondingly large hieroglyphic signs that are painted in red. Half of these individuals represent the four spirits, the sons of Horus and protectors of the canopic jars. They alternate with the four gods who are coming over to ensure the protection of the deceased.

At eye level, as one enters the first chamber there are horizontally disposed hieroglyphs towards the left side; these relate to Neferabet's deceased father. To the right a band of horizontal inscriptions separate the vignettes on the two sides of the vault from the plinth. The hieroglyphs relate to Neferabet himself, recently deceased. Neferabet's son, Neferrenpet, also deceased, assumes the position at the very top of his father's vault.

To the right there appears the painting of a couple seated on two chairs with leonine legs, in front of a table of offerings, upon which is placed a few long and round loaves and poorly defined vegetables. In front of them stands their eldest surviving son, who is making the offerings and presenting them with a type of vase with blue decoration

Figure 62. From left to right, Taese, Neferabet and
their son Nedjemger.

such as one sees amongst the fragments of the finds at Deir el Medina. This vase was utilised for the pouring of libations that purified the offerings. (Fig. 62)

According to the text the two seated persons are "the śdm-ꜥš in the Place of Truth, Neferabet, justified", and his wife, "the lady Taese, justified." The individual who stands in front of them is their son Nedjemger.

Nedjemger must have held a special place in Neferabet's heart. Translated the hieroglyphs that are disposed in vertical columns at the bottom run thus,

"the śdm-ꜥš in the Place of Truth, Neferabet, true of voice [justified]; the lady Taese true of voice. His son, in the place of his heart, Neb (This Neb translates as Lord or Master just as Nebet translates as Lady or Mistress) Nedjemger."

Justified in the judgement of Osiris, the deceased Neferabet holds in his right hand a small piece of fabric that falls on to his knees and he brings his left hand forward on to the offering table.

He wears a curly wig that ends in wavy locks. These are traced in black lines that frame the outline of his face. Neferabet is clothed in a long transparent robe that reaches down to his ankles. A necklace that is referred to by Vandier as a *wśh* and a few bracelets on the wrists and the arms are summarily represented by the artist through a number of wide black strokes.

Neferabet's wife Taese wears a long transparent tunic, a necklace, a few bracelets on the wrists and a wig that is fashioned in the same manner as that of her husband, though it is longer. It actually falls down to the waist and is strapped to the head by a band tied at the back. From the head band a lotus bud hangs down onto the forehead.

Although not included in their drawing of it, the Vandiers mention a 'cone, that was customary at the time, was placed at the top of the head' of Taese. On looking at that part of the vignette where Taese is supposed to have the

354

cone on her wig, this feature seems to be absent from Vandier's copy of it and so it appears that the 'cone' might most likely have been an artefact in the wall upon which it was painted.

Several Egyptologists of today dispute the hypothesis that the cone contained animal fat imbued with perfume. For when it melted it would have ruined the wig; at the time wigs were expensive items of fashion that were meant to last for many years. It is far more probable that the cones represented some other form of fashion accessory that is as yet not understood by Egyptology.

The young Nedjemger wears the same kind of wig as that of his father. He also has the big necklace and the bracelets, but he is simply dressed in a short kilt that is worn at the loins and fixed at the front by a knot.

A procession of the family members of the deceased is represented on the eastern wall. These close relatives are seen bearing their offerings and moving forward towards Hathor the cow that is coming out of the mountain of the West. She wears the solar disc in between her horns, and is thus symbolising the setting sun. Around her neck she wears the *menat* necklace that is an attribute of Hathor. Behind her is a small seated Anubis who is holding the *ankh*. (Fig. 63)

Ten males followed by eight females make up the defilé of family members. Nedjemger is there once again. He wears a tunic and the men are dressed up in the same sort of garment. The first two individuals have their hands elevated to the level of their face, in a gesture of veneration. The others have their left arm in a flexed position with the hand lifted to the level of the face. Their right arm falls by the side and carries either a vine branch with its grapes and leaves, or else a bundle of flowers between two lettuces.

The majority of the family members carry an object that is difficult to identify. This is in the shape of a sac containing small grains of two alternating types of texture. These could have been representing the small cachets made of fabric that used to be deposited near the coffin and which contained seeds of different species. In the Afterlife the deceased was believed to work in the Fields of Reeds. The seeds were left there to be handy so that he could start planting them just as soon as he entered the Underworld. This passage was of course subject to his having first successfully passed through the judgement of Osiris.

All of the women are holding an ovoid flask in their right hand. According to Vandier, this would have contained the sacred oil. However oil was an expensive commodity in ancient Egypt and the containers were quite large and would have held a large quantity of oil. This expensive possession was unaffordable to a workman. It is far more likely that these flasks simply carried water for purification.

The cortege is advancing towards a table of offerings that is covered over with the usual mat of reeds upon which the food offerings are placed. A few lines of vertical text above each individual indicate his or her name and sometimes his or her relationship to the deceased.

Figure 63. Defile of Neferabet's family members approaching Hathor on the eastern wall of the first chamber.

Justified or true of voice

When it comes to the next group of hieroglyphic blocks, a number of the individuals named are labelled literally as 'true of voice' whereas others are not.

As Marta explained however, the basic phrase 'true of voice'[493] is normally rendered as 'justified', and implied that the individual was deceased, had successfully gone through the judgement of Osiris and entered the Afterlife. Those who did not bear the title of 'justified' were still alive at the time of Neferabet's burial.' The *justified* rendering is the one that we have used henceforth in preference to '*true of voice*'.

The hieroglyphs mention a significant number of family members and friends. In translation they run thus.

"*Done for the śḏm-'š in the Place of Truth, Neferabet justified. His father*[494], *the charmer [of scorpions]*[495], *Amenmose. His brother, the guardian Amenemopet*[496]. *His son, Neferrenpet. His son, Ramose. His son Nedjemger justified. His son, his much loved Meron, justified. His brother 'Anhotep, his brother the painter Ipuy*[497].

"*His companion Djadja, justified after the great god. His brother Houi justified, his brother Meryma'a, his sister*[498] *the lady Taese justified, well and in peace, his mother Tenthay, justified. His sister Isisnofret, his daughter Henttou, his daughter Mahi, justified, his daughter Hetepi, justified, his daughter Moutemope, his daughter Isisnofret, justified*".

Two of Neferabet favourite sons and three daughters had predeceased him. Was this due to the higher mortality rate prevailing at the time, or was it due to Neferabet surviving to a ripe old age?[499] Most likely it was a combination of both.

The hieroglyphs on the eastern wall are dedicated to some deities of the ancient Egyptian pantheon, and included the goddess Meretseger. She was evidently an enduring favourite with Neferabet from having been instrumental in his recovery from blindness.

Still in the first chamber, another procession of relatives is portrayed on the western wall. This is made up of seven men and five women who are dressed in the same fashion. However the objects that they carry are different from the ones that are to be seen in the hands of the individuals on the eastern wall. One of the men holds a long floral shaft upon his shoulder; three of the women carry, apart from the bottles, a small basket that they hold up in their left hand and which contains three small conical pieces of bread. The last female holds a shaft of vine in her lowered hand. The defilé advances towards a falcon, behind which the hieroglyphic signs indicate that it is Horakhti, symbol of the rising sun. Placed upon the ground in front of him is a large basket in the form of a lotus flower; this contains flowers and vegetables.

The hieroglyphs describing this scene are slightly different from those on the opposite wall. They are dedicated to Neferabet's father.

"Done for the śdm-ꜥś in the Place of Truth, Neferrenpet. His son the śdm-ꜥś in the Place of Truth Neferabet, his son, his beloved 'Anhotep, his brother the painter Rehotep (this is usually rendered as 'Rahotep' by modern Egyptologists) *justified, his brother the painter Maaninakhtouf justified, his brother the painter Ipuy, the painter Pashed, justified, his mother the lady Mahi justified, the lady Taese, the lady Tentamente justified, the lady Taysennofret, the lady Toere justified"*.

There was therefore an Ipuy who was Neferabet's uncle, a brother of his father Neferrenpet, and a second Ipuy who was Neferabet's own brother. Besides his father, several of Neferabet's paternal uncles including Ipuy were painters and are named in this inscription.

The burial chamber proper

The second underground chamber had not been entered during the Ptolemaic and Coptic periods, and there are no evident signs of charring anywhere. The colours here have been admirably preserved. This is the burial chamber proper. It is vaulted in a low arch and measures 6.25 by 3 metres with a height of 2.60 metres. The eastern and western walls of this chamber are each furnished with eight scenes that are framed by vertical registers.

The general layout of this chamber follows more or less that of the first. Once again the vault is covered over with a column of hieroglyphs that run from right to left, from North to South. Translated they run so.

"An offering that the king gives to Osiris, Lord [of the West], the good Being, the King of the Living, to Hathor who resides in the Necropolis, to Anubis who is at the head of the divine pavilion, who is on his mountain, the Lord of the Necropolis, so that they give the glory in the sky, the power on earth and justification in the other world, for the ka of śdm-'š of the Lord of the Two Lands, Neferabet, justified".

There are eight vignettes upon the vault. There are no inscriptions in the first vignette, but eight blocks of inscriptions are to be found in the second. These translate into the:

"Words spoken by Re-Horakhti –: I come, I rest myself upon the table of offerings from the place where he resides who has done justice, [that is] the Amentit of the mysteries, who hides away all the dead bodies, and all that they have that is repulsive and evil, for the ka of the Osiris, the śdm-'š in the Place of Truth, Neferabet, justified".

The third vignette contains the cartouches of Amenhotep I, but there are no accompanying inscriptions. The inclusion of the pharaoh's cartouche is not of much help for dating purposes because, together with his mother, Amenhotep I is acknowledged as the founder of the Place of

Truth at the start of 18th dynasty. The couple had even been deified by the workmen of the village.

The fourth vignette has five smaller panels of hieroglyphs enclosed within it, and these include the significant mention of Neferabet's attainment of a ripe old age.

"Words spoken by Osiris, sovereign of the Ennead of the gods, the great god who resides in the necropolis, in order that he may give a good burial, after his old age, for the ka of the Osiris Neferabet, justified, his father Neferrenpet".

The texts in the five small panels relate respectively to the following expressions.

1. *"The One venerated, the master of Eternity, Neferrenpet; the lady Mahi justified".*

2. *"The One venerated next to Osiris, the śdm-'š in the Place of Truth, Neferabet".*

3. *"Words spoken by Hapi: Oh Osiris, the śdm-'š of the master of the Two Lands, Neferabet, justified, I come next to you, for eternity, so that your body may repose in its place."*

4. *"Words spoken by Anubis, who is at the head of the divine pavilion, great god, master of the sky and the earth, the justification in the other world, for the ka of the Osiris Neferabet, justified".*

5. Words spoken, *"to me belongs the South where you repose, oh Osiris, the śdm-'š in the Place of Truth to the West of Thebes, Neferabet, justified; his sister the lady Taese".*

In the very last line, the lady Taese, Neferabet's wife, is once again referred to as his 'sister'. This is in accordance with the prevailing convention at that time and place.

The western vault of the second chamber

Moving to the western vault, Neferabet is depicted with the hieroglyphs of his name in front of him, whereas behind him they speak of "[Nefer]*abet, justified next to the great god*".

The panel of 'baptism' follows. Above the picture scene are the hieroglyphs for "*words spoken by the master of Hermopolis, 'I give you the water at the place of the river'*".

Above the god Thoth are the hieroglyphs that refer to him and "Thoth, [possessor] *of divine words*". In front of Horus "*Horus, son of Isis*," below the *water "the water that issues out of Elephantine*," and in front of Neferabet "*the Osiris Neferabet*".

There are three blocks of hieroglyphs above Osiris that simply state "*Osiris, Lord of the West, great god*", and another three columns around Nut, "*words spoken by Nut the great, mistress of the sky, sovereign of all the gods, so that she gives me from the water at the place of the river, the Osiris Neferabet*".

"*The Osiris, the śdm-'š in the Place of Truth, Neferrenpet, justified*".

"[Words spoken] *by the one venerated before Osiris,' the śdm-'š in the Place of Truth, Neferabet, justified*'".

Words spoken by Duamutef: 'Oh the Osiris, the śdm-'š in the Place of Truth, Neferabet, justified, I come next to you for all eternity; may your heart be at peace with the subject of its protection'."

Words spoken by Anubis, who is in ..., the great god of the necropolis, for the ka of the Osiris, the śdm-'š in the Place of Truth, Neferrenpet, justified; his sister the lady Mahi, justified".

"*Words spoken by Qebehsenuef, 'Oh, the Osiris, the śdm-'š in the Place of Truth, that lies to the West of Thebes, Neferabet, justified; his sister the lady Taese, justified next to [the great god]*".

Between the vault and the plinth a long text runs so. Once again there is a reference to Neferabet's attainment of a ripe old age.

"An offering that the King makes to Ptah, to Thoth, to Horus, to Re, to Hathor, to Isis the Great, divine lady, mistress of the sky, sovereign of the Two Lands, to Rennenut[500] of all the world, from the ka of whom one lives, so that they would give a worthy burial, in accordance with his old age, in the great Amentit of Thebes, Necropolis of the justified, to the ka of the śḏm-ꜥš in the Place of Truth to the West of Thebes, Neferabet, justified according to the masters of justice: his father, the śḏm-ꜥš in the Place of Truth, Neferrenpet, justified; his mother the lady Mahi, justified; his sister [wife] the lady Taese, justified; his brother Houi ...".

This text behind Osiris makes mention once again of Neferabet's old age as entitling him to a 'worthy burial', and provides important documentary evidence that supports further the earlier hypothesis of Neferabet's longevity and the extreme likelihood that he was the same Neferabet mentioned on BM EA 5634 from year 46 of Rameses II. Our Neferabet most probably lived long enough to see his brother Ipuy's elevation to the office of foreman around regnal year 10 or 11 of Rameses III.

Since Amennakht, son of Ipuy was elevated to the office of the village scribe in year 16 of Rameses III, and since this was five years after his father's death, we presume Ipuy's appointment to foremanship took place around year 10 or 11 of Rameses III. Ipuy died in the office within a couple of years of his appointment.

On the eastern wall Osiris stands in front of a table of offerings[501]. He is providing a beautiful coffin to Neferabet[502]. In the vignette the latter is shown in a *cartonnage* coffin[503].

Next to be represented is the deified king Amenhotep I, who is making the offering for the deceased, the *ḥtp-dī-nśwt* formula; he was the founder and protector of the śdm-ꜥš workmen. Then comes Horus appeasing the apprehension that the deceased might have had at the moment of his entry into the West of the mysteries; and finally Amen and Hathor who protect the deceased at the moment of his entry into the Underworld.

The clue to the youngest individual down the generations in the 'Neferabet line' appears below line 6, for here are to be found the hieroglyphs for "[the daughter] *of his son Meritre*"504. This is the name of the little girl who is to be found placed between the legs of the third individual, Nedjemger, and most probably is his daughter.

Upon the eastern wall is Anubis, with a jackal head, the guardian of the dead. He is attired similarly to the canopic spirits. Orientated towards the South, he assumes the stance of walking, with the left foot in front. He holds the *ankh* in his right hand and the sceptre in his left.

A group of individuals are directed towards him. The individuals are twelve in all, four per picture. The first is a man wearing a skirt up to the middle of his leg. This skirt is draped and knotted at the waist. We next have successively a woman, a man and then another woman. The women are dressed up in a long pleated robe that only leaves the feet showing. The man would probably have been dressed up similarly to Neferabet: between his legs a young girl is standing, probably his daughter who is also dressed in a long pleated robe; she is raising both her arms and hands in a gesture of adoration.

In the second picture, two men and two women follow one other in the same manner as we have seen in the first scene. The shirt of the men is similar to that of Neferabet, though there is no fringed piece and it falls down on to the skirt. The women have a long pleated and transparent tunic that permits a view of the body through the coverings; they bear large short sleeves, and the edge of their garments is ornate with a fringe. They have long curly wigs that fall down to the waist, and these are retained by a headband that is ornate on the front with an open lotus flower that falls down on the front. They wear the large necklace or *wsh* in three rows, and their ears are decorated with [ear] rings. The first man and the last woman in the procession have their two hands elevated in a gesture of veneration; the other two individuals raise their left arm and keep an object in their right hand: the woman holds a vase and the man a flower.

The third and fourth scene each represent a man followed by three females. The costumes and postures are similar to those in the preceding scenes.

These vignettes upon the tomb walls are all representing defiles of the various members of Neferabet's large family. They mainly comprised scenes of his sons and daughters coming to the tomb with regular offerings, or so Neferabet would have wished them to do for him; he thus had them pictured in that act of veneration for eternity.

The western wall

After his entry into the Amentit[505] the deceased is assimilated to the sun that goes through its different phases and then comes out of the obscure depths of the night to appear in the morning in the Eastern sky to start again on its daily course.

In the upper register the deceased is depicted kneeling in front of Re-Horakhti bearing the solar disk encircled by a serpent on his head. Behind Neferabet is a sycamore tree with sinuous branches that bear figs. From its branches an arm comes out holding a libations vase out of which flows the water that falls on Neferabet. This arm is undoubtedly that of the goddess Hathor who is hidden inside the sycamore tree or assimilated into it.

Picture scene eight

Here the deceased stands in front of the doors of heaven. These doors are the one that the deceased was obliged to go through in the morning in order to leave the *douat* after his purification. He is basically being assimilated to the sun that will also go through its transformation at the end of its nightly course.[506]

The Northern wall

In the large curved picture of the northern wall the scene is divided up into two sections. In the upper one, a large goddess Nephthys is depicted.

Inside the angles of the arch, at the tip of each of the wings of the goddess, there is a standing person. To the East is Neferrenpet, the father of Neferabet, in a gesture of veneration; to the West is Neferabet himself who, with one hand beneath the wings of the goddess, gives the impression that he wants to support her.

The lower part of the wall is only decorated at a height of 0.8 metres from the ground. One sees two anthropoid coffins, undoubtedly those of Neferabet and of his wife. They are placed side by side and one sees only the upper contour of the second: this is the coffin of Neferabet since the mask bears the recurved beard.

The heads and hairdos are painted just like the *cartonnage* that usually cover the face of the mummy. The hairstyle is striped and reaches down to the middle of the chest.

Figure 64. The northern wall of the second chamber, the burial chamber proper.

The southern wall

On the western side, one sees Nephthys kneeling; she is depicted in profile, her body slightly inclined towards the ground, and her arms are extended forward.

There are nine blocks of hieroglyphs on the eastern wall of the second chamber and on the picture scene of the southern wall; these are dedicated to six of Neferabet's children who pre-deceased him, namely:

"His son Neferrenpet justified; his daughter Hentta, his son Ramose, justified, his daughter Tenthay, justified, his daughter Isisnofret, justified; his daughter Hentone, justified".

The sequence here may be significant, for it is - son, daughter, son, daughter, daughter and daughter. The daughter Hentta has been inserted between two sons; this may be an indication of the birth sequence of Neferabet's offspring.[507]

It is probably the elder children who are mentioned here; the following paragraph mentions his younger offspring, where the son Meron is not designated as justified. Yet this must have been an oversight on the part of the painter, for in the first chamber of the tomb, on the eastern wall of the plinth, where one of the processions of Neferabet's relatives is depicted, he is designated as his 'his son, his much loved Meron, justified'.[508] Another option that is more likely was that the second chamber was decorated before the first, whilst Meron was still alive.

There are six names for the four individuals who are represented, two males and two females. Nine blocks of hieroglyphs mention "his son Meron, his daughter Hetepi justified, his daughter Moutemope, justified, his daughter Mahi justified, his son Lot, justified". Once again we have a relevant sequence of – son, daughter, daughter, daughter and son.

The temptation to propose a sequence at this point for Neferabet and Taese's offspring had to be resisted, for it

367

would not take into account those who had survived their parents. And significantly, it did not account for their deceased son, who is designated as justified in the first chamber of the tomb, on the eastern wall of the plinth, just before Meron, in the procession of Neferabet's relatives. Nedjemger is also mentioned on the eastern wall of the plinth in the second chamber, and yet not designated as justified.

And so it seems that both these sons of Neferabet, Meron and Nedjemger, were mentioned as justified in the first chamber but not in the second. This might have been intentional, for an oversight in both instances could hardly be coincidental, and tends to confirm that the second chamber was decorated before the first. We had still not sorted out Nedjemger's place in the family.

After the mention of his children, a remembrance is made of his brothers and sisters. There are six blocks of hieroglyphs giving five names for the four individuals represented, one male and three females, "*his brother 'Anhotep, justified, his sister Tentamente, justified, his sister Taysennofret, justified, [his] sister ....*"

Neferabet next relates to Osiris and the hieroglyphs that follow are identifying three names that represent the four individuals depicted in the scene, one male and three females. "*Words spoken by the One venerated next to Osiris, the śḏm-ˁš in the Place of Truth, Neferabet, justified*".

On the arch to the North stands Nephthys, extending her wings and practically taking up all the space of the scene. To her right, that is towards the West, is Neferabet, and behind him two columns of text, "*the śḏm-ˁš in the Place of Truth, Neferabet*". To the left of the goddess, that is towards the East, was Neferrenpet, and behind him a block of text, "*His father Neferrenpet, justified*". Above the wings of Nephthys were eleven blocks of text, "*words spoken by Nephthys, mistress of the sky, sovereign of all the gods, to give the bread, the breeze and the water to the Osiris, the śḏm-ꜥš in the Place of Truth, Neferabet".*

The name of our Neferabet was rendered in no less than twenty three different hieroglyphic assemblages, and these various forms had also been outlined for us by the Vandiers in a tabular form. And similarly for the name of Neferrenpet a much smaller number of orthographic forms were found in these funerary texts, amounting merely to three in total.

There was no mention at all in Vandiers' text of the statuette that ended up in Malta.

Credits for the photography:

1. The *Brandenburgisches Akademie der Wissenschaften,* Berlin (BBAW)
2. The *Äegyptisches Museum,* Berlin
3. Heritage Malta
4. The Museum of Archaeology in Valletta, Malta
5. The Museum of Archaeology in Gozo
6. The Department of Egypt and Sudan in the British Museum
7. The *Museo Egizio* in Turin
8. The Supreme Council of Antiquities, Cairo.
9. The Museum of Egyptian Antiquities of Cairo
10. The French Institute of Archaeology in Cairo
11. The Museum of Ancient Egyptian Art in Luxor
12. The Museo del Papiro, Syracuse.
13. John Baldacchino
14. Frank Camilleri
15. Vincent Farrugia
16. Captain Charles Zammit
17. The present authors

Endnotes

1 Published by Proprint, Malta, in 1997. This publication furnished the evidence for the presence of man on the Maltese islands well before the traditionally accepted date of 5,300 BCE.

2 I had even included a 1931 photograph of the statuette in a publication of mine (*Malta: Echoes of Plato's Island. The Prehistoric Society of Malta*, 2000: 29, Fig. 19).

3 Alicia Meza, *Journal of the American Research Centre in Egypt* 2003 XL: 103-112.

4 *The Times of Malta* of the 10th November 2003, 'Letters to the Editor'.

5 'Neferabet' also sometimes transcribed as 'Neferabu'. We shall use the former version of the name except in quotations.

6 Henceforth referred to as the 'Place of Truth' in the context of New Kingdom Egypt, and 'Deir el Medina' otherwise.

7 *The Malta Independent*, in the 'News Section'.

8 Biographical notes of the Baron de Tott are included below.

9 Translated from the Latin as 'Propagation of the Faith'.

10 The Thebaid is an old term referring to the environs of Thebes. The statuette was allegedly found by an anonymous individual in the Thebaid and subsequently donated to the anonymous monk who subsequently (and allegedly) donated it to de Tott.

11 See below for details of these artefacts.

12 This wig was traditionally in the later Ramessid fashion, and was typical of the 19th and 20th dynasties. It was also to be seen in *ushabti*'s of the period, such as the one that is to be found in the Egyptian museum at Bologna, item 15, from the *Collezione Palagi*.

13 Henceforth referred to as a *pedestal* from its forming a base for the smaller figures, and to distinguish it from the *base* of the entire assemblage upon which the *pedestal support* (or *stand*) and the dedicatee stood. The pedestal measured 13.97 cm in height. The earlier measurements were in feet and inches and being are quoted as such below.

14 The term Ra-Horakhti is being used here instead of Re-Harakhti. Ra instead of Re, and Hor instead of Har, Hor as in the Greek Horus.

15 The identification of these three deities is discussed below.

16 The first edition of Sonnini's volume was published in French in 1798; translations into English were published in 1799 and 1800.

17 See the two artefacts at the Museum of Egyptian Antiquities in Cairo as JE 37186 [CG 42163], and the other in the Luxor Museum of Ancient Egyptian Art, already hinted at above. The dedicatee on the first of these

was Ramesses-Nakht, high priest of Amun, and the other was Qenu, the head of the storehouse of Amun. Both triad statuettes derived from Thebes, and had similar deities being represented, namely Khons, Amen-Re and Mut. In the same way, despite their resemblance, at that stage, Sonnini's engraving was not necessarily representing the Maltese statuette.

18 Antonio Annetto Caruana was a member of the first Committee of Management of the Museum of Malta alongside other key figures of Maltese archaeology, Fr. Emanuel Magri, Napoleon Tagliaferro and Sir Themistocles Zammit.

19 The first of our joint publications was an article that was published in *Ancient Egypt* in April 2006 under the title of 'Did the ancient Egyptians ever reach Malta?' Then Marta first-authored another under the title of 'The Royal Wives of Akhmim', and our third article that related to 'Serapis before and after the Ptolemies' appeared in the October 2008 issue. 'Minoan and Mycenaean depictions in Ancient Egypt' was published this year. All four articles were published in *Ancient Egypt*.

20 Cesare Vassallo *A Guide to the Museum*. Malta Government Printing Office 1872: 10-11.

21 See below for Sonnini's description of his sojourn in Malta and Egypt together with the Baron de Tott.

22 At the time in question it was believed that all the early antiquities on the islands were the work of the Phoenicians. This was partly due to what the Greek historian Diodorus Siculus had stated about the Phoenicians having been the first colonizers of the Maltese islands. This statement was assumed to mean that there had been no previous settlers on the islands.

23 Both photographs were scanned at a resolution of 1200 dots per inch for later enlargement and comparison.

24 Albert Mayr, *Die vorgeschichtlichen Denkmaler von Malta*. Verlag der k. Akademie, München 1901: 79-80 fn 2; 1908 [English translation, *The Prehistoric Remains of Malta*, Private publication].

25 Günther Hölbl. *Aegyptisches Kulturgut auf den Inseln Malta und Gozo in Phönikischer und Punischer Zeit*. Verlag der Österreichischen Akademie der Wissenschaften, Vienna 1989:168. See below.

26 Morris Bierbrier. *The Tomb Builders of the Pharaohs*. [British Museum Publications 1982] The American University in Cairo Press 2003: 125-6. Bierbrier merely glossed over the credentials of both Sonnini and De Tott, ending up by grossly inflating both of them, transforming the French naval officer Charles Sonnini into a naturalist, and the 'spy' for the French Government, the Baron Francois de Tott, into a diplomat on a mission.

27 Quoting from the above-cited 'Shedding New Light on the Egyptian Statue of Neferabet' panel at the exhibition, "Due to [the statuette] not having been on display since [1903], assumptions were made that the statue had actually disappeared from the Museum. While in fact research was being conducted that was to yield the rewarding results about the statue's owner, his social status and his family".

28 Mayr 1901: 79.

29 Themistocles Zammit, *Guide to the Valletta Museum*. Government Printing Office, Malta 1919: 44; *Guide to the Valletta Museum*. Empire Press: Valletta 1931: 12. See below for further elaboration.

30 This palace was situated opposite St John's Cathedral in Valletta.

31 Margaret A. Murray 'Egyptian finds in Malta', in *Ancient Egypt*, June 1928, pp. 45-51.

32 Themistocles Zammit, 1931: 42. Figure facing p. 32.

33 "An Egyptian statuette in Malta", *Journal of Egyptian Archaeology* December 1949, vol. 35: 132-4.

34 *Ibid.* p. 133, 134. Moss was aware of Sonnini's account, see below.

35 David H. Trump, *The Archaeological Collections of the National Museum*. Extract from the Malta Year Book, printed by Giov. Muscat & Co Ltd, Malta 1959; *National Museum of Malta- Archaeological Section*. National Museum of Malta Guides, printed by Richard Madley, London 1959.

36 Anton Mifsud & Simon Mifsud, *Dossier Malta - Evidence for the Magdalenian*. Proprint, Malta 1997; Anton Mifsud & Charles Savona-Ventura (eds.), *Facets of Maltese Prehistory*. The Prehistoric Society of Malta 1999.

37 In old age it is *recent* memory that suffers at the same time that the earlier memories remain.

38 *Personal communication,* Charles Zammit to Anton Mifsud, 8th August 2005. I went to visit him and his wife at the community home in Msida when he provided me with this information. He passed away the following year.

39 The 1800 edition by Sonnini was the one displayed at the exhibition.

40 Moss 1949: 132-134.

41 These households consisted of small two roomed houses that would hardly qualify as residences in the modern sense of the word.

42 John Romer, *Ancient Lives – The Story of the Pharaohs' Tomb Makers* [1984] Phoenix 2003: 103-5.

43 The list of the tombs of the painters and other craftsmen were the following -

1 - Sennedjem, craftsman under Rameses II and Seti I
2 - Khabekhnet
3 - Pashedu (also tomb 326)

4   - Ken (also tomb 337)
5   - Neferabet
6   - Nebnefer or Neferhotep
7   - Ramose (also tombs 212 and 250)
8   - Kha, architect of Amenhotep II
9   - Amenmose
10 - Kasa or Penbuy
210 - Raweben
211 - Paneb
212 - Ramose (also tombs 7 and 250
213 - Penamun
214 - Khawi
215 - Amenemopet (also tomb 265)
216 – Neferhotep
217 - Ipuy, sculptor under Rameses II
218 - Amenakhte and Iymway
219 - NebenMa'at
220 - Khaemteri
250 - Ramose (also tombs 7 and 212)
265 - Amenemopet (also tomb 215)
266 - Amenakhte
267 - Hay
268 - Nebnakhte (family tomb)
290 - Irinufer
291 - Nakhtmin or Nu
292 - Pashedu
298 - Baki or Wennefer
299 - Inherkau (also tomb 359)
321 - Khaemopet
322 - Penshenabu
323 - Pashedu
325 - Simen
326 - Pashedu (also tomb 3)
327 - Turobay
328 - Hay
329 - Mose and Ipuy
330 - Karo
335 - Nakhtamun
336 - Neferrenpet
337 - Eskhons or Ken
338 - May
339 - Huy or Pashedu
340 - Amenemhat (also tomb 354)

354 - Amenemhat (also tomb 340)
355 - Amenpahapy
356 - Amonemuia
357 - Tutihermaktuf
359 - Inherkau, under Rameses III and IV (also tomb 299)
360 - Kaha
361 - Huy

44 Moss 1949: 133; Hobson 1987: 118-9.
45 Christine Hobson. *The World of the Pharaohs*, Thames and Hudson [1987] 2000: 116. She is also known by her married second name, el-Mahdy.
46 Bierbrier [1982] 2003: 121, 122.
47 Miriam Lichtheim, *Ancient Egyptian Literature – A Book of Readings*, Volume II: the New Kingdom, University of California Press, Berkeley, Los Angeles, London 1976: 104.
48 Hobson 2000: 116.
49 Hobson 1987: 116.
50 This was found by Gaston Maspero on the 6th of February 1886. See Christine Hobson 1987: 118.
51 Moss 1949: 134.
52 Jacques Vandier, *La tombe de Nefer-abou*. L'Istitut Francais d'Archeologie Orientale, Cairo 1935: 1-3. See also below.
53 However I could not spot any mummy from amongst the vast number exhibited that could be identified with that of Neferabet.
54 See the publication by the Baron Francoise de Tott. On his mission to Tunis *en route* back to France he merely passed by Malta, then put in at Pantelleria and finally anchored and landed on Tunis. The strict quarantine regulations that then prevailed would have obliged the baron to spend a few weeks in quarantine on Malta if he as much as landed on its shores.
55 Charles Sonnini, *Travels in Upper and Lower Egypt*, John Stockdale, London, 1799: 68.
56 Charles Sonnini, *Voyages dans la haute et basse Egypte* 1798, Vol III: 77-9.
57 Sonnini 1799: 299 et seq.
58 Translated as 'Propagation of the Faith'.
59 Sonnini 1798, Vol III: 133-5.
60 Alberto Siliotti *(ed.) Belzoni's Travels, Narrative of the operations and recent Discoveries in Egypt and Nubia by Giovanni Belzoni*. The British Museum Press 2001: 8.
61 Sonnini 1798, Vol III: 131.
62 See below.
63 Meza 2003: 104.

64 Bierbrier [1982] 2003: 126.

65 Made available to me through my French son-in-law Guillaume.

66 Giovanni Vincenzo Antonio Ganganelli [born 1705], later on in life performing the duties of Roman Pontiff between 1769 and 1774 as Clement XIV.

67 Sonnini 1798, *passim*.

68 The quarantine period was literally meant to be 'forty' days.

69 Petra Bianchi and Peter Serracino Inglott (eds) *Encounters in Malta*, Encounter Books, Malta, 2000: 209, 212.

70 R. E. Martin (ed) *Malta – the Stamps and Postal History*. The Malta Study Circle. Robson Lowe Ltd, London 1980: 49.

71 François de Tott. *Mémoires du Baron de Tott, sur les turcs et les tartares*. Parts i-iv in two volumes. Amsterdam 1784.

72 Ibid., vol iv:2 : From Sicily the baron sailed in the frigate the Atalanta 'to Malta, where I acquitted myself of a commission I was charged with to the Grand Master, and we proceeded to the Isle of Candy [Crete], at which I began my inspection'.

73 See volume iv: 16-18.

74 The French *toucher à* is an indirect transitive verb that in this context can be translated into 'reach' or 'approach'. See B. T. Atkins *et al* (eds) *Collins-Robert French Concise Dictionary* (2nd ed) HarperCollins Publishers & Dictionnaires Le Robert 1993: 434.

75 At one time Lampedusa was being considered by the British as an alternative naval military base to Malta, but it was then considered to be 'an excellent appendage to Malta but a bad substitute'.

76 De Tott's volume II: 153 of Part IV. [Page 365 of the 'Google' publication]; quatrieme partie 1784: 184 in the original French version.

77 The *Manuel de Marins ou Explication des Termes de Marin*, by M. Bourde published at L'Oriente by Julien Le Jeune, 1773:245, the contemporary analogy cited for 'toucher à une Isle' is *pour y faire del'eau en passant* (to take in water whilst passing by it).

78 De Non, *Travels in Sicily and Malta*, translated from the French, Paternoster Row, London, 1789: 257-259; 287; 305-7.

79 See below for her identification.

80 See above.

81 Annetto A. Caruana, *The Royal Public Library in Malta*. Malta Government Printing Office 1898: 7. The archives were already rotting away in 1809, but the move to the building designated for them, the Bibliotheca, took another three years to materialize.

82 See his *Notizbuch* entry for the 14th of September 1842, figures 20 and 21.

83 Our italics – this statement supports our hypothesis that Sonnini simply *supervised* the drawings that were being carried out by the

baron, who would not have been required to do this if the statuette was in his possession.

84 The Inquisition was still very active in Malta at the time and would have confiscated the statuette had they been aware of it; they would then have submitted a copy of its inscriptions to their superiors abroad.

85 It is well known that Egyptian hieroglyphs had not been deciphered until 1822.

86 In their publications, several scholars in Malta highlighted the archaeological artefacts that had suffered under the Knights of St John; these included Count Abela Ciantar (1772) and Onorato Bres amongst others.

87 A. A. Caruana, *Report of the Phoenician and Roman Antiquities in the Group of the Islands of Malta*, Government Printing Office, Malta 1882: 45, 88, 126; 1898: 14.

88 Jean Quintin d'Autun. *The Earliest Description of Malta (Lyons 1536).* Translation and Notes by Horatio C. R. Vella. Interprint Ltd, Malta 1980: 17.

89 Abela and de Soldanis eventually published the respective histories of Malta and Gozo. De Soldanis was the first librarian to be appointed at the Malta Library, see below.

90 In the absence of a specific discipline responsible for the interpretation of these artefacts, individuals were free to offer their own versions and discuss the various hypotheses that were brought forward.

91 See David Trump, *Malta – an Archaeological Guide*, Faber and Faber Limited, London 1972: 109 on the statue of Hercules.

92 He was also responsible for Gozo's first history book.

93 W. K. R. Bedford, *Malta and the Knights Hospitallers,* Sheley and Co. Ltd, London 1894: 69-70. See also Caruana 1898: 7 for the state of the archives in 1809.

94 Caruana 1898: 7-8.

95 See also above for the museums in Valletta housing the archaeological artefacts.

96 Anthony Bonanno, 'The Archaeology of Gozo from Prehistory to Arab Times', pp. 11-45; 36-37 and figs. 43-46, in Charles Cini (ed.) *Gozo, Roots of an Island.* Said International Ltd, 1990.

97 Francesco Mocchetti, *Viaggio della Sicilia e di Malta, negli anni 1793 e 1794.* In *Opere.* Tom V. 1817: 270 fn 1.

98 Margaret A. Murray, 'Egyptian objects found in Malta', *Ancient Egypt.* June 1928, p. 45 *et seq.*

99 William Tallack, *Malta under the Phoenicians, Knights and English.* A. W. Bennett, London 1861: 135. Tallack saw the statuette in the Library Museum in Malta, and declared that it was 'formed of *Maltese* stone [his italics]. See also Caruana 1882: 45.

[100] Canon Giovanni Pietro Francesco Agius De Soldanis, *Gozo – Ancient and Modern, Religious and Profane* [1712-1770], Media Centre Publications 1999: 87.

[101] *Ibid*: 92.

[102] *Ibid*: 97.

[103] *Ibid*: 91.

[104] It was normally the Inquisitor's task to subject the person under charge to torture, and there was a designated area in the Inquisitor's Palace in Birgu for this procedure, yet the document that described the incident assigns the task of torture in this case to the Grandmaster. The fact that the Grandmaster was responsible for it suggests motivation other than a moral one.See *RML*, The Bibliotheca, Valletta, *Mss* 155, fol. 225-6 by the Baron de Stadel, 1737.

[105] Françoise Emanuel Guignard, Comte de Saint-Priest, *Malte par un voyageur François* 1791.

[106] Mocchetti, 1817: 277-8.

[107] Mocchetti 1817: 273-4.

[108] Caruana 1898: 14

[109] Sonnini visited Gozo in 1777 (Travels 1799: 66, 71, 72, 73) in order to compare the geological stratifications of the two main islands.

[110] Published by Sheley and Co. Ltd in London. Photographs and a description of the Egyptian and bronze statuettes that were found on Malta appear respectively on pages 13 and 72.

[111] Caruana 1882: 32.

[112] The Governor and Commander-in-Chief between 1836 and 1843 was Major General Sir Henry F. Bouverie.

[113] This cataloguing of the archives had already been promised by the Knight of the Order, de Boisgelin, at the turn of the 18th century, but it had not yet seen the light of day.

[114] Cesare Vassallo was born in 1800, and died on 1st March 1882 He studied Latin, Italian and jurisprudence and graduated in Law. But he did not practice at the bar, taking up teaching instead and dedicating his spare time to the musical arts. He also composed music along both 'sacred and profane' themes, and until 1838 was still publishing these music compositions of his that were referred to as the 'Ode.' (Robert Mifsud Bonnici – *Dizzjunarju Bio-bibliografiku Nazzjonali*. Dept of Information, Malta 1960: 509).

It was at this time that the British Governor in Malta appointed Cesare Vassallo chief librarian and compiler of all the literary works in the Public Library. His name is engraved on the marble slab on the way up to the main hall of the Bibliotheca in Saint Anne Square, Valletta. His publications in archaeology include the '*Monumenti antichi ...*' in 1851 and 1876, and the '*Guide...*' in 1871 and 1872. He also has a publication relating to the discovery of a statue in Grand Harbour that was discovered in 1865.

He is mentioned in *Pronostiku Malti* 1960: 62-63, *L'Arte* 1865, III: 72: 6, *Muzicisti* by Robert Mifsud Bonnici 142-3, the *Portofoglio Maltese* of the 4th June 1862, and the *Corriere Mercantile Maltese* carried his obituary on the 2nd March 1882 (Act of Death 671/1882).

[115] Caruana 1898: 8.

[116] The Knights of St John were expelled by the French in 1798, and then a state of siege prevailed until 1800. The British took over the administration of the islands initially as a Protectorate, but subsequently as a colony, in 1815. The setting up of the Maltese representatives to the new government was a very turbulent process.

[117] His first publication was out in 1851, with a second edition in 1876.

[118] Vassallo was involved in this process at the time that Carl Lepsius visited the Bibliotheca in September 1842.

[119] Caruana 1898: 13. Vassallo had free access to these documents during his long tenure of the librarianship at the Bibliotheca. He is therefore an exceptionally valuable and reliable source for their contents, particularly as they included events linked with archaeological discoveries, such as the discovery of the golden calf in 1729, and, one can justifiably presume, the discovery of other artefacts such as the Egyptian statuette with the triad. He was thus in a position that enabled him to specifically attribute the date of 1713 to its find, and its context to Gozo.

[120] Caruana 1898: 13.

[121] See below, in his *Notizbuch* 1 and 2.

[122] In his publications, see below, Vassallo mentions Lepsius's visit to the Maltese antiquities and his study of the statuette. In his *Notizbuch*, see below, Lepsius mentions his visit to the Bibliotheca and the antiquities there. He assigned the context to an archaeological find if this was available. He was thus able to give us a correct context of presently controversial find spots, e.g., for the bilingual inscription, known popularly as the *cippus*. Lepsius assigned it to the temple of Hercules at Marsaxlokk, thus putting to rest the recent hypothesis that this context for the cippus first appeared later on with Gesenius.

[123] Tallack 1861: 61, 135, 139.

[124] Bedford 1894: 70-2.

[125] See David Trump. *Malta Prehistory and Temples*, Midsea Books Ltd, Malta 2002: 7.

[126] This period extended between 1530 and 1798.

[127] Caruana 1898; 8. Dr Cesare Vassallo passed away on the 1st of March of 1882.

[128] 9th of November 2003.

[129] The fact that it could have more likely originated from the ruins of a temple was not mentioned in my article because of word number restriction.

[130] These references were those by the German Egyptologist Carl Lepsius in 1842, the British tourist William Tallack in 1861, and *four* publications by the first archivist of the Maltese library and antiquities under British rule, Dr Cesare Vassallo in 1851, 1871, 1872 and 1876.

[131] Their doctorates were respectively in Law, Theology and Medicine.

[132] A. A. Caruana, *Frammento Critico della Storia Fenicio-Cartaginese*, 1899: 97, 149, 164. Seventeen years earlier, in 1882, the censorship status in Malta was still so stiff that, although 'acquainted with the circumstances of its discovery and of its eventual migration to Malta,' the same author was not able to disclose the discovery context of the inscription (see Caruana 1882: 40). The owner of the artefact was Lord Gerald Strickland, and he assigned the origin of the inscription to the Ggantija temple in Gozo. He did this during his speech to the Legislative Assembly on the 26th of November 1923, in connection with the opening of the new museum of archaeology; quoted in Onor. Edwin P. Vassallo, *Strickland*. The Progress Press, Malta 1932: 41.

[133] The interpretation of the engraved text on the copy is also different from that on the original, and the former version is the one that is constantly quoted in the literature.

[134] See above.

[135] Hölbl 1989.

[136] *Ibid*, 168.

[137] *JARCE* XL (2003) pp. 103-112.

[138] *Ibid*, 2003: 104, fn 8.

[139] *Ibid*, 2003: 104.

[140] *Ibid*, 2003: 103, fn 2, 1.

[141] Karl Theodor Zauzich, *Discovering Egyptian Hieroglyphs*, translated from German by Ann Macy Roth. Thames & Hudson 1992: 11.

[142] Once we are tackling the name with the 'aAbt' hieroglyph, it was useful to mention a very similar name that however belonged to a female. There is a slab stele that bears the name of Princess Nefertiabet, and she was possibly a daughter of the pharaoh Khufu of the 4th dynasty. This artefact is in the Louvre collection under catalogue number E15591. It had originated from the tomb of the princess at Giza, G1225.

As the 't' after 'nefer' seems to suggest, hers may be the female version of the male name Neferabet. That is 'nefer' for a man and 'neferti' for a woman. The 'abet' ending seems to be identical to both names. However in the male version we have 'aAbet'. In the princess's name, the NFR.ti is followed by 'abet' glyph that looks like the so-called Isis Knot (amulet) on a standard pole, with a 't' (bread) glyph underneath. [See Aidan Dodson and Dyan Hilton, *The Complete Royal Families of Ancient Egypt,* Thames & Hudson 2004: 54.]

[143] Meza 2003: 107.

[144] With the baron deceased, there was nobody who could confirm or refute Sonnini's statements.

[145] See below.

[146] See above.

[147] Martin 1980, 47-54; A. Mifsud: Some Aspects of the Lazaretto Isolation Hospital in Malta, in 'La Storia della Medicina come Ponte Culturale nel Bacino del Mediterraneo'. *Atti del Convegno Internazionale di Studi, Malta,* 19-20 October 2001: 61-8.

[148] See Bierbrier's map on page 66-7.

[149] See below.

[150] See above re the private museum of the Marquis Barbaro.

[151] Sonnini 1799: 57-8.

[152] Richard Colt Hoare, *Recollections abroad: Journal of Tours on the Continent between 1785 and 1791.* Private Publication 1817: quoted in Bianchi and Serracino Inglott 2000: 194-7.

[153] Sonnini 1799: 67.

[154] Bertel Thorvaldsen, *Malta 1796-1797: Thorvaldsen's Visit.* Malta & Copenhagen, 1996: 59-60.

[155] *Ancient and Modern Malta,* in 3 volumes, published by G & J Robinson, Paternoster Row in London. 1804: 3-8; 8; 10; 16; 40.

[156] *Malta Antica Illustrata .* Rome: Stamperia de Romanis

[157] Andrew Bigelow, Travels *in Malta and Sicily.* Carter, Bondee and Babcock, Boston. 1831:199.

[158] His notes are held at the Bodleian Institute in Oxford. Later Egyptologists like Margaret Murray from University College, London published these steles.

[159] George Percy Badger, *Description of Malta and Gozo,* M. Weiss, Malta 1838: 184-7.

[160] Whether all of these artefacts were found in Malta or else some had merely been deposited or abandoned on the islands by returning travellers is a moot point.

[161] "14 Sept 1842 - Kleine männliche Statue in weißem feinem Kalkstein in Malta vor c. 40 Jahren gefunden, c. 1 ½ Fuß hoch. S. die Skizze der Figur, mit den Göttern Ra und Ma vor sich *Not.B. I. p. 172* vgl. *Notz. Buch II. p. 16*" – Notizbuch of Carl Lepsius. [14th September 1842 – statue in white limestone discovered in Malta more than before forty years ago, approximately one and a half feet in height. See the drawing of the figures, with the deities Ra and Ma in the Notebook B I p. 172, and Notebook II p. 16].

[162] Lepsius, *Notizbuch* 14th September 1842.

[163] Bierbrier was the first to doubt the Gozo 1713 provenance. The earlier scholars and Egyptologists of the likes of Rosalind Ross and Bertha Porter supported the context furnished by the Maltese directors of antiquities – Cesare Vassallo, A. A. Caruana and Themistocles Zammit - and ignored Sonnini's alleged context.

[164] One of the individuals involved in the 1729 discovery of the golden calf in Gozo was subjected to torture that led to his death.

[165] Tallack 1861: 135.

[166] Eduard Naville, Walter Wreszinski and Hermann Grapow published it in Leipzig in 1913.

[167] Mayr 1901: 79; T. Zammit 1919: 44; 1931: 12.

[168] 'Neferabu' is the obsolete and old hieroglyphic transcription. Egyptologists from the 1980s have read his name as Neferabu but 20 years ahead the correct rendition of the name appears to be Neferabet.

[169] Modern day 'Deir el-Medina'.

[170] Mayr 1901: 79; Zammit 1919: 44; 1931: 12.

[171] The building was the Xara Palace in Valletta, in front of St John's Co-Cathedral.

[172] Already alluded to, see above.

[173] Volume 35: pp. 132-4.

[174] Ross 1949: 133; Vandier 1935: 69. See below for the elucidation of these dates.

[175] See below for Jacques Vandier and for the statuette of Penchenabu.

[176] Moss 1949: 134.

[177] *Ibid*, 133.

[178] Geraldine Pinch, *Magic in Ancient Egypt*. British Museum Press 1994: 54.

[179] *Ostrakon* Petrie 3, Length: 9.1 cm, width 12.5 cm. Translation in Andrea G. McDowell, p. 54-55.

[180] Ipuy and Amenemopet are considered to have been the same individual by Romer 2003: 106, but they are represented as two separate individuals in Neferabet's tomb.

[181] The name 'I' as quoted by Vandier could not be found elsewhere.

[182] It was common to have more than one child with the same name. They were distinguished by nicknames.

[183] The letter 't' is the female ending, similar to the Maltese 'mar-et'. Thus Nefer is male and Neferet is female. But Nofret is just as good, as in modern Coptic the word 'nofer' is used for 'good'.

[184] Or Meritre.

[185] Ernesto Schiaparelli was one of Italy's leading Egyptologists. He was born on the 12th of July 1856 and died on the 14th of February 1928 in Turin. Trained in Paris by Gaston Maspero, between 1881 and 1893 he directed the *Sezione Egizia del Museo Archeologico di Firenze*,

subsequently moving to Turin for the *Museo Egizio* in 1894. In 1903 he inaugurated the activities of the *Missione archeologica italiana* in Egypt. In 1907 he was *Soprintendente alle Antichità del Piemonte (e Valle d'Aosta) e Liguria*, and from 1909 became also involved in the teaching of Egyptology at the *Ateneo Torinese*.

[186] Leonard H. Lesko (ed.) *Pharaoh's Workers – The Villagers of Deir el Medina*, Cornell University Press, Ithaca and London 1994: 7.

[187] Wallis Budge. *A Guide to the Egyptian Collections*, 153.

[188] See below – Bruyère was in charge of the French excavations at Deir el Medina in the 1920s and 1930s.

[189] *Tablets and other monuments from the collection of the Earl of Belmore, now deposited in the British Museum*, plate VII.

[190] *Receuil de travaux*, II, p. 111 et seq.

[191] *Sitzungberichte der Königlich Preussischen Akademie der Wissenschaften* 1911: 1100-1102.

[192] *Journal of Egyptian Archaeology*, 1916 Vol. III, pp. 88-9.

[193] See below.

[194] There was another Ipuy during the early years of Rameses II, see Stele Turin 50052.

[195] Prahotep was a draughtsman at the Place of Truth, see below.

[196] Vandier 1935: 51.

[197] This stele is discussed further below pp. [128, 129]. The 'Skylight Stele' is so termed because it would have been placed in a niche in the centre of the tomb chapel pyramid, and would thus have produced the resemblance to a skylight.

[198] E. 13993.

[199] Wilkinson Mms – V. 126, The Griffith Institute, Oxford. In 1815 Henry Salt was appointed British Consul-General in Alexandria. He started collecting antiquities for sale to the British Museum, procuring the services of Giovanni d'Athanasi and Giovanni Belzoni towards this end, and acquiring a number of important monuments from Thebes in this manner. There were at least two artefacts from Neferabet's repertoire that he got hold of, the BM stele 693 (305) and this fragment mentioned by Moss.

[200] *Ibid*, fig 1, p. 134.

[201] The Italian equivalent of Poseidon was Nettuno, or Neptune.

[202] See above.

[203] See Hobson 118-9.

[204] See below for Meretseger's representations at the museum in Turin.

[205] Catalogue number 3032.

[206] Possibly 'Penchenabet' when making the corollary with Neferabu / Neferabet.

[207] Eleni Vassilika, *Treasures from the Museo Egizio*. Allemandi & C. Yurin, London, Venice, New York 2006: 44.

[208] Lise Manniche, *L-Art Ègyptien*, Flammarion, Tout l'Art Histoire 1994: 236.

[209] Manniche 1994: 235.

[210] His wooden statue is now displayed at the Berlin Museum. Standing 33 cms in height, Amenemopet is represented sitting together with his wife, wearing a double wig and skirt stylistically similar to those of Neferabet in the standard canon of the Ramessid period. The couple sit on separate chairs, both carved in the style of that of the nobility. The wife Hathor may have held either a mirror or more likely a sistrum as a baton of her priestly office. The backrest of Amenemopet's chair is engraved with hieroglyphs that were dedicated to Amen-Re.

[211] Lichtheim 1976: 104, 107.

[212] *Ibid.* 107-108.

[213] Bierbrier [1982] 2003: 97-98.

[214] See above.

[215] Horemheb, originally a general in the service of three successive pharaohs before becoming the last pharaoh of the 18th dynasty. His pre-royal tomb is at Saqqara; his pharaonic tomb is in the VOK, KV57.

[216] She published the memoirs of her Egyptian adventures in Milan in 1848, as the 'Memorie sull'Egitto e specialmente sui costume delle donne orientali e gli harem.'

[217] See text and photographs above.

[218] Henceforth referred to as the *DES*.

[219] Lichtheim 1976, pp. 109 ff.

[220] It later on turned out that there were even more spellings of Neferabet's name, see below.

[221] See below. As it turned out later on in the investigation, it was the 'Neferabet' version that occurred three times on the statuette in question.

[222] The subject of the Bighi steles is treated in another publication that is forthcoming.

[223] Bierbrier's treatment of 'Neferabu' is to be found in his *Tomb Builders of the Pharaohs*, 1982: 54, 97-8, 125, *38,40, 71* and *86-7*. The year should really read 46 rather than 40, see below.

[224] Bierbrier was not specifying whether there was just one or more 'Neferabu's at Deir el-Medina.

[225] As already indicated above, 'Neferabu' was the other name that Neferabet was known as in the earlier literature.

[226] Romer 2003: 106 ff.

[227] There were other near contemporary Egyptians with the same name as Neferabet during the 19/20th dynasty. For instance, one of these was

the son of Khay - Troop Commander of Traders and Goldwashers - and his wife Tawerethetepi, and he was mentioned in his parents' tomb at Saqqara, where he was actually quoted as Neferabu. Saqqara was a long way off from Thebes, so this Neferabet could not be considered as one of our Neferabet's. Yet there could still be a Neferabet whose record has not survived.

[228] Ipuy died 5 years before his son Amennakht was appointed scribe, in year 16 of Rameses III. So Ipuy must have died in year 11 of Rameses III. See Romer 2003: 106.

[229] A photograph of this stele is shown on page 57 of Morris Bierbrier, *Tomb Builders of the Pharaohs*.

[230] See above.

[231] The man is not dressed up as a priest as he does not have shaven head and nor has a white sash across the breast.

[232] For 'Theban Tomb'.

[233] We became acquainted with this second Neferrenpet from the web site by Jane Akshar, who posted her notes from a lecture that she attended in Luxor. (http://luxor-news.blogspot.com/). The lecture was delivered on the 6th of January 2009 by the excavator of TT147, Dr B Ockinga from the MacQuarrie University.

[234] Megaera Lorenz, 'Women and Their Employment', pp. 100 *et seq.*, in (E. Teeter and J. H. Johnson eds.) *The life of Meresamun*, The Oriental Institute Museum Publication no.26, 2009.

[235] The name Neferrenpet was also found in other 19th dynasty tombs, such as by Dr Carl H. Leser, though not at Deir el-Medina but at El Khokha.

[236] Vandier 1935: 72.

[237] Marta made it easy for me to confirm this date, 'the small hills correspond to decades, and the vertical lines represent single years'. There were four small hills and six vertical lines.

[238] Casa Editrice Bonechi, *Art and History of Egypt*, 2000: 88.

[239] *Recueil de travaux*, II: 112.

[240] The present authors have not examined the Belmore stele and cannot comment upon its authenticity.

[241] Hawkings, *Tablets and other Monuments from the collection of the Earl of Belmore, now deposited in the British Museum*, London 1843, pl. VII.

[242] The Skylight Stele is also discussed elsewhere.

[243] See below.

[244] The same argument applies to the context of the statuette of Neferabet holding the triad.

[245] *Proceedings of the Society of Biblical Archaeology*, 1886: 225.

[246] Mentioned elsewhere in text in relation to the *Muzeo Egizio* in Turin.

247 Jacques Vandier was an eminent French Egyptologist who married Jeanne Abbadie d'Arrant in 1934. She was an artist devoted to archaeology and Egyptology and had even spent a year of training at Cairo's Museum of Antiquities where she developed her artistic talent through the reproduction of several Egyptian inscriptions and drawings from the tombs and *ostraca* that were preserved there.

248 M. Bernard Bruyère compiled a list of artefacts obtainable from outside the tomb of Neferabet, and this is included below.

249 On her own steam, Jeanne Vandier then published the tomb chapel of Kha and Merit in 1936/37. Her artistic talents were also utilised in the publication of two volumes of *ostraca* found at Deir el-Medina. Besides their practice drawings, these *ostraca* also bore the informal sketches of the royal artisans that reflected their observations upon the life and people of the village.

The Vandiers were back in Paris in 1939 and in anticipation of the war, Mme. Vandier helped her former teacher Charles Boreux evacuate the treasures of the Louvre's Egyptian Department to a number of chateaus that were selected for their protective capabilities. All the objects survived the war and were able to be reinstalled under her husband's supervision in 1946, when he advanced to the post of Conservator.

250 See below.

251 Mark Lehner. *The Complete Pyramids*, Thames & Hudson 1997: 192.

252 Manniche 1994: 250.

253 Casa Editrice Bonechi, *Art and History of Egypt* 2000: 122.

254 Mark Lehner. *The Complete Pyramids*, Thames & Hudson 1997: 192.

255 Bernard Bruyère, *Les fouilles de Deir el Medineh (1934-1935), Deuxieme partie: la necropole de l'est*, Cairo 1937. Vol.15 of 'Fouilles de l'Institut Francais du Caire'.

256 *Ibid*, p.145.

257 Carol Andrews, *Egyptian Mummies*. British Museum Press 1998: 67.

258 Rosanna Pirelli. The Monument of Amenemimet pp. 877-8, in *Proceedings of the Seventh International Congress of Egyptologists*, Cambridge 3-9 September 1995. Published by Uitgeverij Peeters in Leuven, 1998.

259 Barbara S. Lesko, 'Rank, Roles and Rights', pp. 15-39, in Lesko 1994: 23.

260 Bierbrier [1982] 2003: 53-54; see also BM 5634.

261 Romer 2003: 33.

262 The tomb of Neferabet is dealt with in more detail in the Appendix.

263 For 'Amen in the Barque'.

264 Vandier & Vandier d'Abbadie 1935: 5.

265 In his *Rapport de 1926*, page 86, Bernard Bruyère considered the chapel as a *spéos*, the Greek equivalent of a 'grotto'.
266 Bernard Bruyere, *Rapport de fouilles de Deir el Medineh de 1929*, p. 82, fig. 38.
267 See Vandier 1935 and below.
268 See Vandier 1935 and below.
269 Bierbrier [1982] 2003: 40; see also Lesko in Lesko 1994: 25.
270 Vandier 1935: 29, 39, 41.
271 Bierbrier [1982] 2003: 98.
272 Neferabet had to be a young lad at the time of *ostrakon* BM 5623 if he survived up to the reign of Rameses III.
273 A quart was a measure in the pre-metric system, and was roughly the equivalent of 0.93 litres.
274 Pascal Vernus, *Affairs and Scandals in Ancient Egypt*, Cornell University Press, Ithaca and London 2003. Translated from the French by David Lorton 2003: 53-54.
275 This situation was in contrast with the somewhat cramped housing conditions during the time of Rameses III when the workmen's complement rose sharply to 120 accommodation sites.
276 Lesko in Lesko 1994: 21.
277 Well known compiler of ancient Egyptian texts and inscriptions.
278 1976: 107; 109.
279 See above.
280 Romer [1984]: 2003: 40-1, 135.
281 Bierbrier [1982] 2003: 50.
282 Vandier 1935: 33, 35.
283 Lichtheim 1976: 106.
284 Bierbrier 2003: 97.
285 Romer 2003: 105.
286 *Ibid*. 2003: 103, 104, 105.
287 See Meza 2003: 109-111.
288 Meza 2003: 110.
289 Catalogue number 104.
290 Mark Collier and Bill Manley, *How to read Egyptian Hieroglyphs*, University of California Press, Berkeley and Los Angeles 1998: 101.
291 Florence D. Friedman, 'Aspects of Domestic Life and Religion', pp 95-117, in Lesko 1994: 96.
292 Lesko in Lesko 1994: 33.
293 See Romer 2003: map 3. The Valley of the Queens was known as the Place of Beauty, whilst that of the Kings was known as the Great Place. The pharaoh at the time of Neferabet was Rameses the Great.
294 Bierbrier [1982] 2003: 52; Lesko in Lesko 1994: 22; Romer 2003: 48.
295 Romer 2003: 36 *et seq*.

296 Romer 2003: 36. The names inscribed on the seats were those of the foreman Neferhotep and the scribe Kenherkhopshef.

297 Bierbrier [1982] 2003: 39. Wood-cutters are also mentioned by Bierbrier. We have chosen to omit this in view of the dearth of wood in ancient Egypt.

298 Lesko in Lesko 1994: 25.

299 The Medjay were established in the fortress up the path from the Valley of the Kings towards Deir el Medina. See below.

300 Lesko in Lesko 1994: 18.

301*Ibid.*: 19.

302 *Ibid.*.

303 Romer 2003: 34.

304 Bierbrier [1982] 2003: 36-7.

305 According to *ostrakon* CGC 25237 *verso*, Paneb was a member of the gang of workmen since at least year 66 of Rameses II, as cited in Vernus ('Paneb' in III) 2003: 71.

306 Bierbrier [1982] 2003: 29. Neferhotep the Younger adopted the notorious Paneb as a child and raised him up as his own son.

307 Vernus 2003, III: 70-86.

308 Bierbrier [1982] 2003: 29, 31. According to Vernus 2003: III, 71, Paneb gave five servants of Neferhotep to the vizier Pareeheb and thus bribed him to take over the post of foreman.

309 *The British Museum*, Papyrus Salt 124, recto 1, 1-4.

310 We could not confirm whether this individual was the same Amennakht who was Neferabet's nephew.

311*The British Museum*, Papyrus Salt 124, recto 1, 18.

312 *Ibid*, recto 14; *Ostrakon* Gardiner 167, verso 3-6; Papyrus Amherst-Leopold II, 3, 3-4; Papyrus British Museum 10054, recto 1, 11.

313 Vernus 2003, III: 68.

314 Turin Strike Papyrus recto 4, 1-4, 16a.

315 Vernus 2003, III *passim*.

316 Romer 2003: 92.

317 Bierbrier [1982] 2003: 32.

318 Bierbrier [1982] 2003: 33.

319 Romer 2003: 34 *et seq.*

320 Romer 2003: 32 *et seq.*

321 Romer 2003: 32.

322 Bierbrier [1982] 2003: 32.

323 Vandier 1935: 31, 40.

324 Bierbrier [1982] 2003: 33-5.

325 Bierbrier [1982] 2003 gives the name of the draughtsman as *Parahotpe*, an obsolete reading, today spelt as *hotep*. Romer (2003: 33) gives the name as *Prahotep*.

326 Bierbrier [1982] 2003: 33-5.
327 Romer 2003: 15.
328 See Romer 2003: 17-18.
329 See *La Collezione Egiziana del Museo Archeologico Nazionale di Napoli*, Ministero per i beni culturali e ambientali. Arte Tipografica, Napoli, 1989: 36, being biographical information from a statue dedicated to Hathor found in temple of Tuthmosis III at Deir el Bahri [J141] at the Luxor Museum.
330 Lesko in Lesko 1994: 18.
331 This was equivalent in the modern calendar to between the 26th May and the 24th June.
332 Romer 2003: 48-9; Bierbrier [1982] 2003: 97.
333 Kent R. Weeks. *The Illustrated Guide to Luxor*, The American University in Cairo Press 2005: 284.
334 Bierbrier [1982] 2003: 52. There was also a first tomb for Rameses III that had also to be abandoned for the same reason.
335 Romer 2003: 25, 43.
336 Romer 2003: 137-8.
337 Weeks 2005: 284.
338 Bierbrier [1982] 2003: 52-3.
339 Bierbrier [1982] 2003: 54; Romer 2003: 29-30.
340 Weeks 2005: 286.
341 Romer 2003: 40.
342 The names of 52 sons are documented in N. Reeves & R. H. Wilkinson. *The Complete Valley of the Kings*, Thames & Hudson 1996: 144.
343 We quoted the spelling of 'Banenre' from Aidan Dodson and Dyan Hilton, *The Complete Royal Families of Ancient Egypt*, 2004: 291.
344 Romer 2003: 40.
345 Weeks 2005: 288. The right angled plan had been abandoned in the reign of Akhenaten who wanted a straight axis for the sun rays of the Aten to penetrate inside the tomb.
346 Romer 2003: 43.
347 The tomb was practically complete when Merenptah died.
348 The 'blunder' hypothesis is not universally accepted by all Egyptologists.
349 Weeks 2005: 288 *et seq.*; John Romer, *Valley of the Kings*, Phoenix Press 2005: 47.
350 Romer 2005: 312.
351 Romer 2003: 38-39 describes the incident in some detail.
352 See pp. 18, 21, 22 in Steve Cross, 'The Re-sealing of KV42' in *Ancient Egypt* 10 (2) Oct Nov 2009, pp. 16-22.
353 See above.

354 Horus in the Barque.

355 Bierbrier [1982] 2003: 53-4.

356 Bierbrier [1982] 2003: 50.

357 2003: 52.

358 Bierbrier [1982] 2003: 50.

359 See for example, Joan Haslip, *Lady Hester Stanhope: A Biography*. Frederick A Stokes Company, NY. 1934: 125.

360 Richard Parkinson. *The Painted Tomb of Nebamun*, The British Museum Press 2008: 50.

361 The ophthalmologist or *swnw irty* [see Nunn (endnote below this) 1997: 198], would not normally have been available at the Place of Truth.

362 John F. Nunn, *Ancient Egyptian Medicine*. British Museum Press 1997: 147. Malachite in ancient Egyptian was known as *shesmet*. The green eye paint derived from it was known as *wadju*. Malachite inhibits the growth of some bacteria and it was used in ancient Egypt to treat eye infections.

363 *Ibid.*, 105

364 See Gunn, B., 'The Religion of the Poor in Ancient Egypt'. *JEA* III, 1916.

365 We have not been able to identify this particular Neferrenpet.

366 David Smith 106.

367 *Egyptologist's Electronic Forum*, EEF Library on Line. 'Blindness in Ancient Egypt' 2004. Huy was the viceroy of Nubia under Tutankhamen, and on the ceiling of his tomb in Thebes the N46b determinative appears in text that translates into 'may thy sight be clear in the way of darkness.' However it is clear from the context of this text that the darkness being referred to here is the Afterlife. A stele of Huy that was discovered in the Karnak cachette does not include the N46b determinative, and yet is translated into 'I see the daytime darkness thou has made.'

368 Manniche 1994: 170, 235, 246, 247, 258, 368. On pp. 229-237 she deals with the statuary of the Ramessid period.

369 See Galán, J.M., *Seeing Darkness*. CdE 74, pp. 18–30, 1999, and Manniche, L., *Symbolic Blindness*, CdE 53/105, 1978: 13-21.

370 Gunn 1916: 81-94.

371 Bierbrier [1982] 2003: 98.

372 *PubMed* - indexed for MEDLINE - PMID: 1635443. Katedry i Zakładu Fizjologii AM we Wrocławiu.

373 2003: 103-5.

374 Bierbrier [1982] 2003: 45.

375 Bierbrier [1982] 2003: 45.

376 Romer 2003: 19.

377 It seems that at any one time there was only one scribe at the Place of Truth, and this was the Scribe of the Tomb; and there were only two foremen, one for the Left gang and another for the Right.

378 See Romer 2003: map 3.

379 There is some discussion about the length of leave during the work cycle at the Great Place. According to Lesko in Lesko [1994: 22] this was *officially* meant to be one day off per ten, and that the extensions to two or even three days off were local arrangements. Other scholars like Bierbrier [2003: 52] and Romer [2003: 48] simply propose a regular arrangement of eight days of work and two of rest. Each Egyptian month had 3 'week periods' of 10 days each. The monthly rations most probably also depended on the 30 days per month. The workmen would have probably received them on the last weekend.

380 Romer 2003: 48.

381 The name was not uncommon amongst the workmen at the Place of Truth. Another Amenemopet was a scribe in the early years of Rameses II, too early for him to have been the same individual as Neferabet's younger brother. TT265 was his tomb and TT215 his chapel. See David G. Smith *Deep Solar Eclipses in Ancient Egypt* 2007: 19.

382 Vandier 1935: 29. Ipuy and Amenemopet were two separate individuals, both brothers of Neferabet.

383 Bierbrier [1982] 2003: 36. Ipuy and his brother Amenemopet were occasionally assumed to be one and the same person, such as by Romer 2003: 106.

384 Romer 2003: 106.

385 Vandier 1935: 29.

386 Bierbrier [1982] 2003: 38.

387 Leonard H. Lesko, 'Literature, Literacy and Literati', pp. 131-144, in Lesko 1994: 137.

388 Respectively the Valley of the Kings and the Valley of the Queens; rather than the 'Place of Beauty' the latter should strictly read 'The Place of Beauties', derived from *Ta Set Neferu*.

389 Romer 2003: 106; Bierbrier [1982] 2003: 35, 36.

390 Weeks 2005: 284.

391 Romer 2003: 106; Bierbrier [1982] 2003: 35, 36.

392 Bierbrier [1982] 2003: 27.

393 See Vernus, II. *passim*.

394 Neferabet's grandfather Amenmose was also buried in the cemetery of the Place of Truth, though this was in TT9 rather than in Neferabet's TT5.

395 See Vandier 1935 and above for the genealogy.

396 Friedman in Lesko 1994: 96.

397 Vandier 1935: 30.

398 Vandier 1935: 30.

399 Vandier 1935: 29, 39, 40.

400 Andrews 1998: 16 *et seq.*

401 Lesko 1994: 90, 93.

402 Manniche 1994: 236.

403 Still untraced at the time of publication.

404 Alicia Meza, 'Ancient Egypt in Malta: an ancestor bust from the Delta and other objects', vol. III pp. 307-314, in Zahi Hawass & Lyla Pinch Brock (eds.), *Egyptology at the Dawn of the Twenty-first Century*. Proceedings of the Eighth International Congress of Egyptologists, Cairo 2000 in 3 vols. The American University in Cairo Press 2003.

405 Reeves & Wilkinson 1996: 172; D. Rohl, *The Test of Time*, Century 1995: 23, 92.

406 Nigel and Helen Strudwick, *Thebes in Egypt*. Cornell University Press, Ithaca, New York 1999: 210.

407 *Egyptian Antiquities*, vol I. The British Museum. London: Charles Knight, Pall Mall East 1832: 235.

408 Lichtheim 1976: 104.

409 Gunn 1916: 81-94.

410 Lichtheim 1976: 104-5.

411 Arles Museum, Berlin. Cat. No.20377.

412 Lichtheim 1976: 105-7.

413 Vandier & Vandier d'Abbadie 1935: 4.

414 The date was proposed early on in the 20th century by the Maltese director of Museums, Sir Themistocles Zammit, and has been accepted and in use from that time.

415 At Thebes there were Amen, Mut and their (moon god) son, Khonsu; at Memphis, Ptah, Sekhmet and Nefertem; at Edfu it was Horus, Hathor and Harsomtus (Horus the Younger) and at Elephantine, Khnum, Anukis, and their daughter Satis.

416 Sonnini 1799: 336.

417 Vassallo [1851] 1872: 10-11.

418 Tallack 1861: 135.

419 Caruana 1882: 32.

420 Caruana 1882: 32.

421 Themistocles Zammit, *Guide to the Valletta Museum*. Empire Press, Valletta, 1931: 42.

422 1949: 132.

423 See above.

424 Respectively from left to right as seen from the front.

425 Toby Wilkinson, *Lives of the ancient Egyptians*. Thames & Hudson 2007: 267-8.

426 A limestone statuette I had seen at the Louvre, N 4196, belonged to Setau, the director of the storehouse of Amen at Karnak. It was 36.5 cm height and was dedicated to 'Nekhbet, the white of Nekhen' depicted as a giant serpent. This was unusual, for Nekhet was more commonly depicted as a vulture.

427 E 16378, preserved at the Louvre.

428 See above.

429 Earl L. Ertman, 'Under the Disk and Crescent', *KMT* vol 20 (1) 2009: 39.

430 The goddess was first considered by the present authors to be Mut because of her title on the back pillar of Neferabet's statuette, 'Lady of Isheru', the sacred lake at Karnak. See Moss 1949: 133.

431 Meza 2003: 109-111.

432 Arielle Kozloff, 'What the workmanship in Ramose's Tomb (TT55) tells us about its history', *KMT* xx (1) 2009: 44, 45.

433 Or *Waset* in ancient Egyptian.

434 See also Toby Wilkinson, *Dictionary of Ancient Egypt*. Thames & Hudson 2008: 141.

435 The base of the statuette carries invocations to both Re-Horakhti and Ma'at, corresponding to their reliefs on Neferabet's shoulders.

436 The term is not related to the eye of Horus, the *wadjet*, the magical eye that was fashioned by Isis for Horus when the latter's eye was gouged out by Seth during combat. The *wadjet* eye was used in ancient Egypt as an amulet for protection and healing. In European witchcraft a stylized eye was also used for protection; the eyes drawn on Mediterranean boats, including the Maltese ones, are also used for protection, though they are incorrectly termed the 'Eye of Osiris'.

437 The Valley of the Kings is dominated by a hillock in the form of a natural pyramid. This was known as the 'Lady of the Peak' and was the domain of the snake-goddess Meretseger, also known as the 'Silent One', or 'She who loves silence.' She was venerated in particular by the workmen of the necropolis, and represented as a snake goddess, a *uraeus* with a female head, and sometimes as a scorpion with a woman's head.

438 See pp 128 and 133, Neferabet's steles to Meretseger, BM 742 and E.13993.

439 From the Egyptian word *Meret*, 'she loves'.

440 2003: 106 ff.

441 *JEA* December 1949, vol. 35: 132-4.

442 This was available in one of the editions of Caruana 1882.

443 On this same proper left side of the base of the statuette, most of the hieroglyphs have been damaged beyond recognition. *Heritage Malta* solved this problem by inserting Sonnini's hieroglyphs instead.

444 A part of the dedicatee's skirt had also sustained injury, but no repair work was ever done here.

445 Meza 2003, see above.

446 Carl Lepsius provided a partial rendering of the hieroglyphs in his journal, and a complete and accurate one through his casts.

447 From the photographs supplied to her from Malta and from the notes of Dr Iversen who examined the statuette before her.

448 The pilaster or the pillar supporting the platform; the pilaster and platform made up the 'stand'.

449 Rosalind Moss had translated the name of Neferabet's brother as 'Anhotpe, very similarly to what Allen had done later on and she had also commented on the same problematic glyphs with a '[sic]' note. Moss had read the hieroglyphs in 1949 in the same way as Allen did. In fact it seemed to me that the entire text transliterated by Moss in 1949 had been adopted by Allen and Meza in 2003. 'Hotpe' is the old reading of 'hotep'.

450 Moss 1949: 133.

451 The 'eye' sign reads 'ir'. The 'water' sign with waves reads 'n'. A straight horizontal line reads 'ta', as in the title 'tawy', (lord) of the two lands.

452 The apostrophe before the A is there from transliteration but it does not fit after 'hotep' where it gives the impression that it is representing inverted commas.

453 Although it says 'rear' in the 'Times' article, Egyptologists prefer the term 'back' pillar instead.

454 The sign is composed of two triangles lying on their side one directly above the other and these triangles are sandwiched between a 'feather' sign on one side and a 'club' sign on the other.

455 See Fig. 51 and below for its discussion after obtaining its cast.

456 This is the right epithet for Ma'at rather than the previously cited one as a goddess of Thebes; she had no association with Thebes.

457 Some clarification of these Egyptian deities is useful at this stage. Saker or Sokar in Egyptian myth was a mummified falcon-headed god of the Underworld who was eventually identified with Osiris; Horakhti, or Hor-m-akhet, was the name given to the falcon headed Horus on the horizon. The association of Re-Horakhti with Ma'at is seen in other artefacts, such as the Late Period painted wooden *ushabti* box of a priest of Amen Ptahhotep, who is depicted on the side of the box in an act of veneration of these two deities. This artefact is preserved at the Birmingham Museum.

458 The vowels do not really count here, as the ancient Egyptian script was consonantal; vowels were not written or incised, and they are arbitrarily added on and inserted by modern Egyptologists.

459 The second edition was published twenty five years later in 1876.

460 Or 16.5 and 13.97 cm respectively. The measurements at the time were in inches and feet, and these have been maintained in the text.

461 These readings tallied comfortably with the laser readings that I obtained with the laser.

462 The original measurements were in inches, as taken by Dr Cesare Vassallo in the 1850s.

463 The smallest unit that was used at the time of Vassallo in British Malta was the eighth of an inch.

464 The so-called 'variance' is basically the difference between the manual fixation of the points and those reckoned by laser precision technology.

465 Other measurements taken included the length of back strip 28.4 cm, length of wig 8.4 cm, width of back strip 3.1 cm, width of the dedicatee's shoulders 13.4 cm, Face 5.5 by 5.5 cm. the entire pedestal, pilaster and base together measure 20.5 cm in height, and that is equivalent to just under eight inches.

466 Meza 2003: 105.

467 "un pied et plus" [more than a foot] in length. [1798, vol. ii: 389].

468 Lepsius was specific for the width of the pedestal at 3½ inches; he gave a very rough estimate of the height of the statuette, "c. ..." [circa a foot and a half] for the entire statue with its base, which today actually measures a foot and a third.

469 See pp. 36-37 and figs. 43-46 in Anthony Bonanno, 'The Archaeology of Gozo from Prehistory to Arab Times', pp. 11-45, in Charles Cini (ed.) *Gozo, Roots of an Island* Said International Ltd, 1990.

470 His original notes read thus, "Kleine männliche Statue in weißem feinem Kalkstein in Malta vor c. 40 Jahren gefunden, c. 1 1/2 Fuß hoch. S. die Skizze der Figur, mit den Göttern Ra und Ma vor sich Not.B. I F. p. 172 vgl. Notizbuch II. p. 16. – Bibl. in Malta. 1. Rückeninschrift. – 2. Basis unter derselben. – 3. Basis links daneben. – 4. Inschrift am Fuße des Altars unter dem linken Arme. – 5. Basis der kleinen Figuren unter dem linken Arme. – 6. Vorderseite des Altars unter den kleinen Figuren. – 7. Vorderseite der Basis. – 8. Vorders. der Basis der kleinen Figuren. – 9. Basis unter dem rechten Fuße. – 10. Inschrift am Fuße des Altars unter dem rechten Arme. – 11. Basis der kleinen Figuren unter dem rechten Arme."

471 The terms 'Malta' and the 'Maltese Islands' are synonymous for all intents and purposes.

472 As already mentioned, all artefacts that were not Roman were viewed with suspicion by the ruling establishment in Malta during the time of the Knights. These were transferred abroad for intensive investigation and analysis quite frequently and they usually remained there. We know

of a few of these through documentation – the Greek Melitensis was later found in Italy, the gold foil hieroglyphs ended up in Palermo, the bilingual inscriptions were reburied perhaps because they were too heavy or conspicuous to move out of the country. Amongst the precious items lost are the so-called *Torremuzza* Punic inscriptions, the original statue of Hercules, the golden ingots and the golden calf, and the golden hoard of coins beneath the Cathedral after the earthquake of 1692.

473 This was the 'Melitensia Quinta', discovered in 1855 in the Ggantija temple in Gozo. It provided evidence for child sacrifice on the islands.

474 Already mentioned in some detail above.

475 Lepsius's *Notizbuch* I 12° 172-181; II 6, fol. I 2-3.

476 *Denkmaler aus Aegypten und Aethiopien* [J. C. Heinrichs's Buchhandlung], pp. 396 to 397.

477 Henceforth the *BBAW*.

478 Regine Schulz and Matthias Seidel (eds), *The Rise of the State to the Second Dynasty*, Könemann 1998.

479 He did manage to find the missing cast a few weeks later, and he sent me its scanned image by e-mail. In the meantime we used the image from his website, though this was of a lower resolution.

480 *Topographical Bibliography of ancient Egyptian Hieroglyphic texts, reliefs, and paintings. VII. Nubia, the deserts, and outside Egypt.* Clarendon press, Oxford 1951: 406.

481 *The Lost Tombs of Thebes*, Thames & Hudson, 2009: 241.

482 This 'two-in-one' cast was made up of two adjoining sides of the base, namely the back side and the proper left.

483 These were the Libyans to the West, the Nubians in the South and the Asiatic peoples on their eastern borders.

484 His heirs lost these holdings; Rameses II tried to reclaim Kadesh but did not succeed.

485 Moss 1949: 132.

486 These were Dr Cesare Vassallo and William Tallack, mentioned above.

487 See Lepsius's entries for September 1842 in his *Notizbuch*.

488 Vandier 1935.

489 According to the Vandiers, it is likely that the original tomb dated to the beginning of the 18th dynasty.

490 'Taricheutes et Choachytes', in *Zeitschrift für Äegyptisches Sprache, XVIII*, 1880: 114.

491 As in the Semitic languages like the Maltese where the phrase reads 'Missier Tajjeb', the adjective comes after the noun, unlike others like English, Slovak and other languages where the adjective precedes the noun.

[492] The three dots represent a lacuna due to missing text; the square bracketed text denotes the presumed text that is missing.

[493] See Zauzich 1992: 88.

[494] The ancient Egyptians did not have a 'grandfather' title but used the phrase 'father of my father' or simply 'father'. Since it is well attested that Neferabet's father was Neferrenpet, then Amenmose would have been the grandfather of Neferabet and designated simply in hieroglyphs as 'father'. Vandier translated him as such with 'grand' enclosed in parenthesis.

[495] See above for 'charmers of scorpions'. In Vandier's translation he bracketed 'of scorpions' as the presumed missing title.

[496] Amenemopet is here being mentioned separately from Ipuy, see note below this.

[497] Although Romer identifies Amenemopet with Ipuy, these were two separate individuals as attested in the hieroglyphs in this inscription.

[498] The title of 'sister' here means 'wife'. The present authors believe that this particular title may have carried a sort of hidden message, 'my half-sister' or 'my cousin'. If the wife was not Neferabet's sister, he could have referred to her as wife 'hmt', [the 'h' with a dot beneath it]. If he is referring to her as 'sister', he is most likely sending the message that he had married a woman from his clan, a relative. Since Taese's father was the village *swnw*, she is obviously not Neferabet's sister, but could have been his cousin.

[499] His old age is referred to below, in the inscriptions between the vault and the plinth of the second chamber.

[500] Renenutet, also Ernutet, and Renenet, meaning, *(she who) gives Ren*, with *Ren* being the Egyptian word for this *true name*. Renenutet was increasingly confused with Wadjet, Lower Egypt's powerful protector and another snake goddess represented as a cobra.

[501] He wears the traditional costume of Osiris mummified, that is, he is enveloped in his shroud out of which issue only his hands that hold the sceptre and the flagellum. He is covered with the *atef* and wears a large necklace that acts as a counterweight.

[502] There was a standard formula that said 'may he provide a good funeral to X'.

[503] Rather than a stone sarcophagus that would have not been affordable to Neferabet.

[504] Or Ra' meret.

[505] Amentit, also spelled Amunet, Amonet, Amaunet, Amentet, Imentet, Imentit, and Ament was a deity with a number of different characteristics during the long history of the pantheon of Ancient Egypt. When Amen was given a greater importance and his identity overlapped that of Atum, Amaunet, as the female aspect, became increasingly

identified with Iusaaset. Iusaaset was identified as the mother and grandmother of the deities. Through being identified as Iusaaset, Amunet was regarded as the mother of creation.

506 Nagel *BIFAO*, 1929, p. 11.

507There was probably insufficient space for her 'justified' epithet.

508 See above.

509 Index

Camilleri, Fr. Victor 98, 158.

Caruana, Annetto A. 36, 41, 42, 80, 90, 91, 92, 93, 95, 96, 97, 103, 105, 116, 249, 267, 273, 287, 331, 346, 374, 378, 379, 380, 381, 382, 384, 394, 395.

Catriona, 23, 24.

Cenni Storici, 92, 287, 290, 291.

Chapel, 4, 10, 86, 108, 119, 128, *132*, 144, 175, 177, 180, 182, 184, 185, 197, 199, 242, 243, 348, 385, 388, 393.

Chevalier, 9, 17, 18, *19*, 20, 38, 39, 47, 97, 345.

Ciantar, Count Abela Giovann Antonio, 87, 377.

Colt Hoare, Sir Richard, 110, 383.

Constantinople, 64, 68, 70, 71, 72, 106, 107.

Copper, 189, 206, 211, 231, 235.

De Boisgelin, Louis, 111, 380.

De Non, 71, 72, 378.

De Rohan, Emmanuel, 64, 76, 88, 110.

De Soldanis, Pietru Agius,81, 82, 85, 86, 377, 378.

De Stadel, Fra Ferdinand Ernest, 86.

De Tencin, Bali Ludovicus Guerin, 82.

De Tott, the Baron Françoise, 3, 30, 34, 43, 61, 62, 63, 64, 68, 69, 70, 71, 76, 77, 79, 88, 105, 106, 110, 111, 371, 372, 375, 376.

Depasquale, Suzannah, 99.

DES, [Department of Egypt and Sudan],.11, 160, 161, *162*, 233, 372.

Foreman, 116, 130, 140, 169, 170, 197, 198, 199, 200, 201, 202, 204, 231, 260, 362, 388.

Gabinetto della Antichita, 82.

Ggantija, 97, 297, 343, 380, 396.

Ghajnsielem, 87.

Gouder, Tancred 50, 97.

Grand Harbour, 10, 66, 67, 71, 80. 84, 112, 167, 298, 303, 345, 381.

Grandmaster, 61, 68, 76, 83, 84, 86, 87, 88, 107, 110, 111, 380.

Great Place,[Valley of the Kings] 5, 167, 187, 188, 199, 203, 204, 205, 206, 207, 208, 209, 210, 215, 216, 217, 219, 220, 224, 225, 237, 239, 242, 390, 393.

Grenfell, Lord Francis Wallace, 10,99, 100, *101, 102,* 340.

Grunert, Stefan, 12, 299, 306, 307, 310, 311, *314*, 317, 319.

Gunn, B, 129, 191, 234, 242, 392, 393, 394.

Hathor, 13, 56, 185, 199, 214, 242, 356, *357,* 360, 363, 364, 365, 386, 391, 394,

Hawass, Zahi, 36, 196, 219, , 302, 303, 316, 344, 392.

Hercules, statue of, 9, 44, *45,* 81, 85, 110, 111, 117, 379, 381, 397.

Hölbl, Günther, 42, 98, 372.

Nebre, 148,191, 242.
Neferabet, 4, 5, 9, 10, 11, 12, 13, 23, 24, 26, 27, 28, 36, 50, 53, 54, 55, 56, 57, 60, 61, 63, 93, 99, 101, 106, 107, 108, 109, 112, 113, 120, 121, 122, 123, 127, 128, 130, 131, 132, 133, 134, 135, 136, 138, 139, 140, 143, 145, 146, 147, 148, 149, 154, 156, 158, 164, 165, 166, 167, 168, 169, 170, 171, 172, 174, 175, 176, 177, 178, 179, 180, 181, 182, 183, 184, 185, 186, 188, 189, 190, 191, 192, 193, 194, 195, 196, 197, 199, 200, 202, 203, 204, 205, 206, 214, 216, 217, 220, 222, 223, 224, 225, 227, 228, 229, 230, 231, 234, 238, 239, 240, 241, 242, 243, 244, 245, 246, 247, 251, 252, 257, 259, 260, 261, 262, 264, 265, 269, 270, 271, 272, 286, 287, 293, 294, 295, 297, 298, 327, 328, 329, 330, 331, 332, 338, 340, 353, 354, 356, 359, 361, 362, 363, 364, 365, 366, 367, 368, 369, 371, 372, 373, 374, 375, 376, 377, 378, 379, 381, 383, 384, 385, 388.
Neferrenpet, 4, 26, 28, 53, *54*, 104, 126, 127, 128, 129, 130, 131, 133, 171, 172, 173, 185, 187, 191, 196, 197, 199, 217, 233, 237, 275, 283, 284, 341, 348, 353, 358, 359, 361, 362, 363, 366, 368, 369, 370, 376, 387, 398.
Nefertanpet, 5, 116, 171, 248, 283, 326.
Nephthys, 185, 252, 366, 368, 369.
Notizbuch, 10, 112, *114, 115*, 300, 301, 304, 305, 308, 309, 316, 378, 381, 383, 397, 398.
Officials, 4, 9, *35*, 41, 144, 182, 194, 196, 197, 198, 202, 229, 232, 249.
Osiris, 199, 248, 249, 251, 252, 353, 355, 357, 358, 360, 361, 362, 363, 369, 370.
Paneb, 183, 199, 200, 201, 231, 347, 374, 388.
Panhesy, 250.
Peak of the West, 4, 11, 128, 144, 151, *152*, 153, 225.
Penchenabu, 10, 118, 143, 144, *145*, 158, 251, 330, 382, 385.
Phoenicians, 18, 98, 99, 298, 310, 339, 343, 344, 374, 379.
Physician of the village, [*swnw*], 124, 169, 187, 188, 210, 226, 229, 230, 283, 339, 390, 397
Pigments, 189, 229, 234.
Place of Beauty, [Valley of the Queens], 203, 390, 393.
Place of Truth, [Deir el Medina], 4, 5, 23, 52, 53, 108, 116, 118, 123, 124, 127, 128, 131, 133, 134, 135, 142, 143, 144, 147, 149, 151, 159, 167, 169, 175, 179, 181, 182, 183, 185, 188, 189, 191, 192, 193, 194, 196, 197, 199, 201, 204, 205, 206, 207, 208, 209, 211, 220, 227, 228, 230, 232, 233, 237, 238, 239, 241, 242, 243, 252, 261, 318, 346, 349, 350, 355, 358, 359, 360, 361, 362, 363, 369, 370, 373, 385, 389, 392, 393.
Porter, Bertha 63, 118, 119, 312, 314, 382.
Priest, [anonymous in Cairo], 3, 34, 60, 61, 63, 70, 72, 77, 79, 105, 106, 315.
Propaganda Fide, 30, 61, 62, 77, 79, 105, 106, 315.

Ptah, 10, 11, *109*, 129, 147, 151, 153, 160, 161, *162*, 163, *164*, 165, *166*, 171, 177, 199, 231, 233, 255, 340, 341, 363, 394.

Quarantine, 9, 10, 61, 64, *65*, 66, *67*, 68, 70, 71, 72, 106, 143, 377, 378.

Rameses II, 5, 11, 169, 170, 171, 173, 174, 176, 187, 191, 197, 199, 204, 207, 209, 210, 212, 213, 214, 215, 216, 217, 218, 219, 220, 221, 224, 225, 236, 239, 251, *257*, 262, 339, 363, 385, 390, 393, 398.

Rameses III, 169, 171, 187, 191, 197, 210, 236, 239, 241, 261, 262, 363, 387, 389, 391.

Ramesses-Nakht, *35*, 249, 250, 259, 260, 372.

Ramose, 54, 126, 129, 195, 196,208, 251, 357, 367, 375, 394.

Re-Horakhti, 28, 34, 251, *253*, 254, 283, 359, 364, 394, 395,

Reid, Governor General William, 112.

Romans, 297, 338, 342, 343, 344.

Romer, John, 53, 123, 168, 170, 188, 190, 191, 197, 223, 234, 236, 260, 374, 383, 385, 386, 388, 389, 390, 391, 392, 398.

Salt, Henry, [British Consul General in Alexandria], 58, 128, 175, 383, 388.

Schiaparelli, Ernesto 10, 59, 127, 140, *141*, 175, 177, 242, 382.

Scicluna, Hannibal, 47.

Scribe, 4, 10, 125, *125*, 142, 144, 166, 172, 183, 189, 193, 195, 197, 198, 199, 200, 201, 202, 203, 204, 205, 212, 217, 220, 226, 230, 231, 232, 236, 242, 250, 251, 339, 350, 362, 385, 388, 391.

Seidlmayer, Stephan, 300, 303, 304, 305, 306.

Senedjem, 140, 316, 317.

Sonnini, Charles 3, 9, 10, 12, 30, *31*. 34, 37, 40, 42, 43, 47, 50, *51*, 55, 56, 58, 59, 60, 61, 62, 63, 64, 68, 69, 70, 73, 74, *75*, 76, 77, 78, 79, 88, 97, 103, 105, 108, 110, 117, 118, 168, 247, 248, 272, 273, 274, 275, *279*, 280, 296, 314, 323, 324, 326, 334, 372, 373, 374, 376, 377, 379, 382, 383, 393, 394.

Spencer, Neal, 159, 160, 164, 170.

St Agatha, 98, 157, 309.

Strike action, 5, 142, 232, 233, 388.

Strudwick, Nigel, 159, 392.

Taese, 13, 124, 126, 133, 187, 188, 195, 196, 198, 317, *353*, 354, 357, 358, 360, 361, 362, 367, 397.

Tallack, William, 84, 94, 103, 113, 248, 286, 377, 379, 380, 382, 392, 396.

The Malta Independent, 24, 90, 371.

Thorvaldsen, Bertel, 66, 111, 381.

Thoth, 184, 232, 233, 251, 361, 362.

Times of Malta, 3, 21, 36, 96, 100, 285, 371.

Tunis, 70, 72, 375.